Scottish Property Law

Scottish Property Law

Second edition

Tom Guthrie

Published by

Tottel Publishing Ltd   Tottel Publishing Ltd
Maxwelton House   9-10 St Andrew Square
41-43 Boltro Road   Edinburgh
Haywards Heath   EH2 2AF
West Sussex
RH16 1BJ

ISBN 978-1-84592-057-9
© Tottel Publishing Ltd 2005
Reprinted 2006, 2007, 2008, 2009 & 2011

British Library Cataloguing-in-Publication Data
A catalogue record for this book is available from the British Library

Typeset by The Partnership Publishing Solutions Ltd
Printed and bound in Great Britain by
Thomson Litho Ltd, East Kilbride, Glasgow

Preface

Since the first edition of this book was published the law relating to heritable property in Scotland has been rewritten to a considerable extent. Gone is the feudal system and the law relating to real burdens has been significantly altered, though not always in the clearest of terms. Because many of these changes were coming into force as this edition was being written the explanation given of some of them is necessarily speculative pending litigation to offer further clarification and guidance on the correct interpretation of the legislation. In recognition of this new regime no attempt has been made to give a full explanation of the law prior to 28th November 2004, the date on which most of the changes came into force. Also included, as before, is an explanation of the main principles of conveyancing as they apply to heritable property.

As well as providing updated coverage of the law relating to heritable property the coverage of the book has been extended to include all aspects of property law in Scotland. Some of this coverage is necessarily brief, but I hope it deals with the main points in each area.

As with the first edition, the book is primarily directed at students undertaking a law degree, but it should also be useful for students studying property law as part of other degree programmes, and, as with the first edition, I would hope that it would be found useful by practitioners and others.

Angus McAllister was not involved in the preparation of this edition, his focus is now much more specifically on Landlord and Tenant law. I am grateful to him for his offer to look at the draft of this edition, though force of circumstances prevented my being able to take advantage of this offer, and for involving me in the first edition, as well as for the advice he offered during the production of that edition.

Most importantly thanks are due to Frances, Veronica, Edward and Madeleine for their support and for tolerating my lengthy disappearances.

I have attempted to state the law as at 10th December 2004, but have anticipated some changes which are due to come into force in the course of 2005.

Finally, for those who are still puzzled after reading the section of chapter 7 on copyright, the difference is, or at least was, Bing sings and Walt disnae (I am indebted to Angus for enlightening me on this point).

Tom Guthrie
January 2005

List of abbreviations

Bell G J Bell *Principles of the Law of Scotland* (10th ed, 1899)

Cusine & Rennie D J Cusine & R Rennie *Missives* (2nd ed, 1999)

Erskine J Erskine *An Institute of the Law of Scotland* (8th ed, 1871)

Gordon W M Gordon *Scottish Land Law* (2nd ed, 1999)

Gretton & Reid G Gretton & K Reid *Conveyancing* (2nd ed, 1999)

Halliday J M Halliday *Conveyancing Law and Practice in Scotland* (2nd ed by I J S Talman), Vols I (1996) and II (1997)

McDonald D Brand, A Steven & S Wortley *Professor McDonald's Conveyancing Manual* (7th ed, 2004)

Sinclair J H Sinclair *Handbook of Conveyancing Practice in Scotland* (4th ed, 2002)

Stair Viscount Stair *The Institutions of the Law of Scotland* (5th ed, 1832)

Contents

Table of statutes

Numbers on the right-hand side are to paragraph numbers. Those paragraph numbers in **bold** indicate where an Act is set out in part or in full.

Table of statutory instruments

Table of cases

A

C

D

E

H

I

L

M

N

O

P

S

T

U

V

W

Y

Z

CHAPTER I

Nature and classification
of property

MEANINGS OF PROPERTY

1.1 The term 'property' is used in two broad senses

Legal relationship to an object

1.2 This is concerned with our legal rights over an object, for example, ownership of a car and how the law describes the legal rights of the owner in respect of the car. Sometimes this legal relationship is characterised as involving a collection or bundle of legal rights. In this context the most extensive relationship is that involved in ownership of property and the term property is sometimes used as equivalent to ownership. An example of this is Erskine's definition of property as being 'the right of using and disposing of an object as our own'[1]. As well as ownership there will be consideration of other, subsidiary, property rights, for example those of a possessor and those of a tenant.

[1] Erskine *Institute* II, 1, 1.

Subject/object of property rights

1.3 The second sense of property describes the object or subject which is owned or possessed. These objects/subjects are classified in various ways:

(a)   as heritable or moveable;
(b)   as corporeal or incorporeal;
(c)   as fungible or non-fungible.

These classifications, which will be considered in more detail shortly, are important for a variety of purposes, for example, succession (what happens to property after the owner's death), obtaining and transferring property rights, and creating security rights over property.

1.4   Before going on to look in more detail at these classifications it is worth noting a number of points about the nature of property rights:

1   Different people can have different rights in the same property. For example, both owner and renter have interests in a rented television, and both landlord and tenant of a rented flat have property interests in the flat.

2   Different people can have different ownership interests in heritable property. Thus, it is common for one person to own a piece of land but another to own the minerals lying under the piece of land.

3   In some cases a number of people may together enjoy a property right, for example, joint tenants and joint or common owners. Joint and common ownership will be considered more fully in CHAPTER 2.

4   Rights in property can be classified as *iura in re propria*, that is, rights in property owned by the person having the right; and *iura in re aliena*, that is, rights in property which is owned by someone else. The former category encompasses all the rights which go with owner-ship of property, for example, the right to make free use of it, to alter it, to sell it, or even to destroy it. The second category includes the right which a tenant has in the property he or she rents and the rights of someone holding a security over property. In general rights in the second category are more restricted than those in the first.

HERITABLE AND MOVEABLE PROPERTY

1.5   This is one of the two major classifications of property. All property in the sense identified in para **1.3** above is either heritable or moveable. The distinction between the two categories is rooted in the law of succession. Historically heritage was the property which descended to the heir, with the remainder of the property, the moveables, going to the executor for distribution to the remaining survivors of the deceased. Following the passing of the Succession (Scotland) Act 1964 this distinction is of far less importance than it was. It is now only important in the context of the legal rights which the surviving spouse and children have a legal entitlement to claim, even in the case of attempts to disinherit them. These rights can only be claimed from the moveable estate of the deceased.

1.6 The most important category of heritable property is land and the buildings erected on land together with the rights associated with these. In addition, at common law, heritable property also includes rights having a tract of future time, for example annuities and pensions, and titles of honour.

1.7 Although at common law everything else is moveable (since whatever is not heritable is moveable), statute has changed the classification of some items. For example, shares in companies and partnerships are moveable, even though the company or partnership owns heritable property[1]. In addition heritable securities are deemed to be moveable in the succession of the creditor except as far as legal rights and the tax authorities are concerned[2]. It should be noted that this provision only applies to the *creditor* and only applies to *succession*. For all other purposes, including the debtor's succession, heritable securities are regarded as heritable property.

[1]   Companies Act 1985, s 182(1)(a); Partnership Act 1890, s 22.
[2]   Titles to Land Consolidation (Scotland) Act 1868, s 117.

1.8 Property can fall into one of the categories, heritable or moveable, for a number of reasons. According to Bell[1], property may be heritable or moveable:
1   by its nature as being immoveable, like lands or houses; or as moveable, like furniture or cattle; or
2   by connection or accession to some subject which has by its nature the character of moveable or immoveable; or
3   by destination of the owner, either in connection with something else, or in regard to succession.

[1]   Bell para 1470.

Heritable/moveable by nature

1.9 This is quite straightforward. Land and the buildings attached to land are heritable. In addition things attached to and growing on land are heritable, as are the other items noted above as having been added to this category by common law[1]. Everything else, including those items noted as being altered by statute, is moveable. In general not too much difficulty is caused in deciding whether by its nature something is heritable or moveable. The problems arise when there is a question as to movement between the categories caused by accession or destination.

1   Subject to what is said below about crops at PARA **5.33**.

Heritable/moveable by accession/connection

1.10   This has two aspects. The first of these relates to the attachment or connection of moveable to heritable property, for example, when a carpet is fitted in a house, where machinery is bolted to the floor of a factory, or where building materials are converted into a house attached to the land. In these cases the question will arise as to whether or not the moveable items have become heritable through their attachment to heritage. This question, which is of considerable importance, will be considered more fully in CHAPTER 5.

1.11   The reverse process is equally important, though it tends to give rise to fewer problems. Examples would be the demolition of a house producing (scrap) building materials, the quarrying and carrying away of stone, and the cutting down and selling of Christmas trees. In all of these cases property which was originally heritable has been converted by separation or disannexation into moveable property.

Heritable/moveable by destination/conversion[1]

1.12   This process is relevant only in the context of succession and involves the conversion of heritable property into moveable and *vice versa* based on the intention of the deceased.

1   H Hiram *The Scots Law of Succession*, paras 3.55–3.59.

1.13   The intention of the deceased may be derived from the circumstances surrounding the property. For example, in *Reid's Executors v Reid*[1] the subject at issue was dung and whether it was heritable or moveable in the succession of a farm tenant. The Inner House was of the view that[2]:

'It became heritable *destinatione* – that is, by destination of the deceased tenant, because he was under an obligation to apply every ounce of the manure to his farm. He must be presumed to have intended to apply it to the benefit of his farm, because he was under an obligation to do so[3]. Accordingly, although the dung is moveable *sua natura*, it became heritable by being dedicated to the land, as much as the parts of a building which are brought to the ground for the purposes of being added to the building, but are not yet added.'

In other cases the deceased's intention may be derived from his or her express statements. For example, there may be instructions to trustees to buy heritage with moveable estate or to sell heritage and distribute payments to beneficiaries. These instructions effectively convert the property, in the succession, from moveable to heritable and *vice versa*. In these cases reconversion is possible, where, for example, a beneficiary elects to take heritable property rather than having it sold and receiving a cash payment.

[1]   (1890) 23 R 519; see *Johnston v Dobie* (1783) Mor 5443 for another example.
[2]   *Reid's Executors v Reid* (1890) 23 R 519 at 522–523, per Lord President (Inglis).
[3]   Under a local custom.

1.14   Finally, the nature of property on succession, and thus who is entitled to benefit from it, may be altered by an uncompleted agreement to buy or sell heritable property. An example of this is *Ramsay v Ramsay*[1]. The deceased had purchased heritable property at auction, but the price had not been paid at the time of his death. There was a dispute between the heir and the executors as to what should happen about it. It was held that the executors were bound to pay the price out of the moveable estate, but that on payment the property was heritable and so went to the heir. In other words the agreement to purchase had effected a conversion of the property from moveable to heritable in the succession of the deceased[2].

[1]   (1887) 15 R 25.
[2]   See *Chiesley v Chiesley* (1704) Mor 5531 for the case of sale by the deceased.

Nature of ownership rights

1.15   Until November 2004 there was a significant difference in the nature of ownership held over heritable and moveable property. In the case of moveable property a person who owned an item of moveable property was, leaving aside cases of joint ownership[1], the outright owner of that item and there was no one else with an ownership interest in it. In contrast, there were normally two people with an ownership interest in the same piece of land. The reason for this was the feudal system of landholding introduced into Scotland in the eleventh and twelfth centuries.

[1]   See CHAPTER 2.

1.16   The system was based on a fundamental claim by the Crown to the ownership of all land. On this basis the Crown made grants of land to individuals, originally in return for the individuals providing military service. When this grant of land was made the Crown became a feudal superior and the individual to whom the grant was made became a feudal vassal. The vassal owed a duty of loyalty to the Crown, and the system of land holding was linked to a political and economic system in which, at least in the initial form of the feudal system, the Crown also had certain obligations towards the vassal. Anyone who held land from the Crown (A) could in turn make a grant of this land (or part of it) to a third party (B). B then become A's vassal with A being B's superior. This process (known as subinfeudation) could be repeated many times with the result that the feudal system could be likened to a pyramid with the Crown at the top and the ultimate vassal at the bottom.

1.17   It is important to note that the feudal system is a system of land tenure rather than a system of land ownership. The vassal holds the land from the Crown (or another superior) and the latter retains rights in the land, essentially the right to recover the land if the consideration in respect of which the grant was made is not forthcoming. The vassal is not therefore the outright owner of the land, in the sense that an individual is the outright owner of an item of moveable property, and there is a continuing relationship between the superior and the vassal.

1.18   It should be clear that the consequence of this is that there were in fact two interests in the same piece of land. That of the superior is described as the *dominium directum* and that of the vassal is the *dominium utile*.

1.19   Although the feudal system dates from the eleventh and twelfth centuries it had continuing importance into the twenty-first century. The process of creating new feudal estates and transferring land by subinfeudation rather than outright sale was widely used by volume house builders. The reason being that it was easier for a superior to enforce restrictions in the use of land than it is for mere disponers. This system of landownership was abolished in November 2004, with the result that, as with moveable property, the owner of land will now have outright ownership[1].

1   Abolition of Feudal Tenure (Scotland) Act 2000.

Conclusion

1.20   As we have already noted, the importance of the distinction between heritable and moveable property for the purposes of succession is now limited; so too is the importance of conversion/destination.

1.21   Although this distinction is of less importance for succession it is still of great importance in other areas. Whether or not property is heritable or moveable is of great significance in the context of acquisition and transfer of property, grants of security over property, and the types of diligence that are available to a creditor.

1.22   Finally, as already seen in the context of connection/disconnection, the same property may be treated as either heritable or moveable according to circumstances. For example, kitchen units in their packaged form are moveable, but once they have been attached to a kitchen to form a fitted kitchen they are heritable. A further instance of this is the goodwill attaching to a business. Depending on the circumstances this may be regarded as either moveable or as heritable. It is likely to be considered the former if the goodwill arises from the personality of the person running the business, whereas if the goodwill results or derives from the premises themselves it will be regarded as heritable. In *Muirhead's Trustees v Muirhead*[1] the goodwill attaching to public houses was held to be heritable as it derived from the character of the premises themselves rather than the attributes or bonhomie of the landlord.

1   (1905) 7 F 496.

CORPOREAL AND INCORPOREAL PROPERTY

1.23   The distinction here is based on whether or nor the property has a physical existence: corporeal property can be seen and touched; incorporeal property cannot. Incorporeal property exists solely in the form of legal rights. Examples are rights to take legal action (for example, following personal injury), rights in security over land, titles of honour, debts, intellectual property rights, and shares in companies. In some cases there will be a written document setting out or stating the existence of such rights: a share certificate is one such example. These documents are, however, simply evidence of the existence of incorporeal property rights; they are not the incorporeal property itself.

FUNGIBLE AND NON-FUNGIBLE PROPERTY

1.24 Fungibles are goods which can be replaced by others of the same type, that is, they are property which has no unique individual value. Erskine[1] describes fungibles as being goods 'which may be estimated generically by weight, number or measure', and gives as examples grain and coin; another example would be cans of Tennents Lager. Non-fungibles, in contrast, are items which have a particular value which is unique and individual. Erskine gives as examples pictures (presumably originals), horses and jewels.

[1] Erskine III, i, 18.

1.25 The distinction is largely of historical importance. At one time it was of some importance in connection with a form of loan of property called *mutuum*, described as follows in the *Stair Memorial Encyclopaedia*[1]:

> '*Mutuum* is a loan for consumption in which the borrower is bound to return not the same thing, but the same quantity of that kind and quality (that is, an equivalent) at the end of the period of loan.'

The main outstanding example of this is loan of money, where it is not necessary to return precisely the same money as was originally lent.

[1] *Stair Memorial Encyclopaedia* vol 13, 1705.

CHAPTER 2

Basic concepts in property law

REAL AND PERSONAL RIGHTS

2.1 The term 'real' is used in a variety of ways in the law of property. Sometimes, for example, it is used as referring to rights and duties relating to heritable property, as in 'real burdens'. The most important sense of real, however, is in the context of real rights and the distinction between these real rights and rights which are merely personal.

2.2 A real right (or *ius in re*) is a right in a piece of property, that is, the legal relationship is between the individual and the property. It is a right which can be enforced against the world at large, that is against anyone who challenges your proprietory interest. Your rights against the challenger derive from your real right in property. The owner of property generally has a real right and can protect his/her ownership against challenge by anybody. However, it is not only the owner of property who can have a real right, for example, in most cases the tenant of land or premises will also have a real right in his/her property interest.

2.3 In contrast, a personal right (or *ius ad rem*) is simply a right of action against another person. A personal right results from the creation of an obligation owed by one person (in this context sometimes referred to as the debtor) to another (in this context, the creditor). The obligation may be created by agreement, as in contract, or by the operation of law, as in delict. In the property context, the debtor has a personal obligation to transfer property to the creditor in the obligation, and the creditor has a personal right against the debtor which can be enforced by legal action. A personal right, then, in contrast to a real right is available only against the other party to the obligation. It is a right to take action against an individual and not a direct right in property. The right in property conferred by a personal right is an indirect one, arising from the right of action to enforce delivery; as Erskine explains it[1],

> '... the creditor in a personal right or obligation has only a *ius ad rem*, or a right of action against the debtor or his representatives, by which they may be compelled to fulfil that obligation, but without any right in the subject which the debtor has agreed to transfer to him.'

[1]   Erskine, III, i, 2.

2.4   In some cases it is necessary to perform some specific act in order to obtain a real right. For example, in order to obtain a real right to heritable property your title must be registered in the Land Register[1]; in order to obtain a real right in an insurance policy assigned to you the assignation must be intimated to the insurance company[2].

[1]   See CHAPTER **18**.
[2]   See CHAPTER **6**.

2.5   The importance of the distinction between real and personal rights should be obvious. An example might illustrate it. Frank has agreed to buy a television from Greg and it is agreed that he will become the owner of the TV (thereby obtaining a real right in it) when he pays the price on 11 November. On 4 November Greg sells the television to Barry who pays there and then, becoming owner and thereby acquiring a real right in the television. Frank, at the time of the sale to Barry, has only a personal right as far as the TV is concerned, Barry has a real right which prevails over this. Frank's only remedy is to sue Greg for compensation for breach of contract, in other words Frank is left with a personal right against Greg. Changing the facts slightly gives a completely different answer. Frank owns a television which he rents to Greg. Greg sells it to Barry. Because Frank, as owner, had a real right in the TV he is able to recover it from Barry, rather than simply seeking compensation.

OWNERSHIP AND LESSER INTERESTS

Ownership

2.6   As we have already noted the most extensive property interest which can be held in a particular item of property is ownership. This was defined by Erskine as: 'the right of using and disposing of a subject as our own, except in so far as we are restrained by law or paction'[1]. The right of ownership, therefore, gives the owner the right to do whatever he/she wants with his/her property except as far as there are restrictions imposed on him/her by law or by agreement.

[1]   Erskine, II, i, 1.

2.7   The restrictions on ownership can take a variety of forms. They can be imposed by statute: for example the planning system and the requirement to obtain a licence for a shotgun or television. They can be imposed by common law: for example the law of nuisance which prevents you from making use of your property in such a way that it interferes with neighbours' enjoyment of their property. Or they may be imposed by agreement: for example the title conditions which normally affect residential properties. Restrictions by agreement mainly affect heritable property, and are principally in the form of real burdens. These may restrict the uses that can be made of property, impose conditions about maintenance, and restrict the additions or alterations that can be made to the property[1].

[1]   See CHAPTER 14.

2.8   The owner of property can retain ownership while parting with some of the rights which make up ownership. The most common case is where the owner parts with the actual use and enjoyment of the property, eg, where the owner of a house lets it out, or where the owner of a television rents it out. These cases can also be seen as instances where the absolute right of the owner in the property is restricted by agreement.

Possession

2.9   The term 'possession' is used, rather loosely, in a variety of ways and with a variety of meanings. For example, it is common to speak of a tenant as being in possession of rented premises. There is, however, a quite specific meaning of possession in the context of property and it is with this sense that we are concerned. It involves two elements. Firstly, a mental element, the intention to possess an object and make use of it *as owner*. Secondly, a physical element, actual control direct or indirect, over the object involved. This dual element is emphasised by Erskine[1]:

> '... possession when made use of in its strict sense, is defined as the detention of a subject, with an animus or design in the detainer of holding it as his own property. It is made up partly of fact and partly of right. The fact consists in the detention of the subject which the possessor has in his custody. The right consists in the view with which he holds it: he holds it in his own name as his own property.'

[1]   Erskine, II, i, 20. See also Stair II, i, 17.

2.10   The control element required of possession may be direct, as where the subject is in the hands of the intending possessor, or indirect, where it is in the hands of someone else, eg a tenant or employee, and that other person holds the subject on behalf of the intending possessor. The former case is described as natural possession and the latter as civil possession.

2.11   Possession of property has significance in the context both of heritable and moveable property. In the case of heritable property, possession over a period of time can mature into ownership[1]. In the case of moveables, a presumption of ownership arises from possession.

[1]   See CHAPTER 3.

2.12   Finally, it is worth making explicit a point which has already been adverted to: that possession is a lesser right than ownership with the consequence that an owner can always recover property from a possessor[1].

[1]   Though in the case of rented accommodation the owner's rights may be limited (see CHAPTER 12).

Custody

2.13   Custody is a lesser right again than possession. It describes the situation where an individual has a limited right of control or use of property, but no intention to possess it as owner. The extent of use and control is more limited than that exercised by a possessor (who, after all, intends to own the property). Examples of custody are cases where property is deposited for safekeeping and cases where an employee has control over property belonging to his/her employer.

2.14 An illustration of this latter case is *Barnton Hotel Co Ltd v Cook*[1]. Here the defender had been the company secretary to the pursuers, who sought return of the company books. The defender refused to return these on the grounds that he had not been paid and that he had a right of retention in respect of the books allowing him to keep them until he was paid. This was rejected by the sheriff (whose views were affirmed by the Inner House) on the grounds that Cook's 'possession was for behoof of the company'[2]. He was therefore a mere custodier of the books and as such did not have possession sufficient to give rise to a right of retention.

[1]   (1899) 1 F 1190.
[2]   At 1192.

2.15 The further implication of the status of custody as a lesser right is that it confers only restricted rights on the custodier and is inconsistent with having the full use and enjoyment of the property[1].

[1]   *Sim v Grant* (1862) 24 D 1033.

COMMON PROPERTY; JOINT PROPERTY; COMMON INTEREST[1]

Common property[2]

2.16 Common property describes the situation where an item of property is owned by a number of individuals, with each of these individuals having a *pro indiviso* share in the common property. An example would be a group of people getting together to buy a racehorse. The racehorse would then be the common property, and each of the contributors would be a co-proprietor having a share in it. The horse could then be said to be in common ownership. In common property each co-owner has a share in the ownership of the property, not a right to a particular part of the property. Common ownership has a number of consequences, detailed below.

[1]   For a judicially approved definition of joint and common property see Gloag and Henderson *Introduction to the Law of Scotland* (11th edn, 40.35), approved of in *Magistrates of Banff v Ruthin Castle Ltd* 1944 SC 36 at 68.
[2]   *Stair Memorial Encyclopaedia*, vol 18, 22–33.

Power of sale

2.17   Each co-proprietor can dispose of his/her share in the property without reference to the other owners. On the death of a co-proprietor his/her share goes to his/her heirs.

Management

2.18   Each co-owner is entitled to a say in the management of the property. In effect this amounts to a right of veto making the consent of all co-proprietors necessary before anything can be done with or to the property. The only exception to this right of veto is the case of essential or necessary repairs or reconstruction or where the effect of any work or change to the common property is *de minimis* (ie very minor)[1]. Here the work can be done without first obtaining the agreement of all co-proprietors[2]. Each co-proprietor has the right to seek interdict to prevent interference by co-proprietors with his/her management rights which are contrary to his/her interests. An example of this is *Bailey's Exrs v Upper Crathies Fishing Ltd*[3]. The pursuer and defender were co-proprietors of salmon fishings on the River Dee; the defenders wished to introduce a time-share scheme for fishing which the pursuers viewed as prejudicial to their interests in the management of the common property. The pursuers sought and obtained an interdict preventing the defenders from proceeding with the scheme.

[1]   See *Rafique v Amin* 1997 SLT 1385.
[2]   *Deans v Woolfson* 1922 SC 221.
[3]   1987 SLT 405.

Division and sale

2.19   Each co-proprietor has the right to seek division of the common property. This would involve the property being divided up into smaller properties each of which would then be distributed to a co-proprietor who would then be sole proprietor of that smaller property. If division of the property is impractical or where it would significantly affect the value of the property[1], the co-proprietor has the right to have the property sold and the proceeds distributed amongst the co-owners. There is conflicting authority on whether the court can order sale to one of the co-owners[2].

[1]   *Stair Memorial Encyclopaedia*, vol 18, 33.

¹   *Stair Memorial Encyclopaedia*, vol 18, 33; *Gray v Kerner* 1996 SCLR 331; *Ploetner v Ploetner* 1997 SCLR 998.

2.20   This right of division and sale is said to be absolute. This point was made in *Morrison v Kirk*¹ where Lord Salveson said²:

'Unless a *pro indiviso* proprietor has barred himself by contract from resort to an action of division and sale he has an absolute right at common law to insist on such an action.'

This formulation was quoted with approval in *Upper Crathies Fishings Ltd v Barclay*³. This case followed on from the case discussed above of *Bailey's Exrs v Upper Crathies Fishing Ltd*⁴, and involved an action for division and sale. The defenders attempted to defend the action on the equitable grounds that the pursuers had acted in bad faith: they had never intended to join in the management of the common property; they were only interested in commercial exploitation of the property which could not happen during common ownership; and, finally, they had infringed the defenders' rights in the management of the common property. The court decided that these defences were irrelevant, the right to division and sale was absolute, and

'[i]t does not appear to me that the right of a co-proprietor to free himself from his association with another co-proprietor is qualified by equitable considerations'⁵.

The case was remitted to a man of skill for advice on whether it was practicable to divide the property.

¹   1912 SC 44.
²   At 47.
³   1989 SCLR 560.
⁴   1987 SLT 405.
⁵   1989 SCLR 560 at 561.

2.21   The contract barring division and sale must relate specifically to this right and will not be implied. This means that a co-owner is not barred from raising an action for division and sale after agreeing to buy the other co-owner's share, even if he has then raised an action for implement of that agreement¹.

¹   *Bush v Bush* 2000 SLT (Sh Ct) 22; *Wilson v Harvey* 2004 SCLR 313.

2.22   One possible difficulty with the absolute right of division and sale is the situation in tenement properties where either at common law, as in the case of stairs, or by agreement, eg, as regards the *solum* or roof, owners of the flats are common owners of parts of the building. There is authority for two views on this question. According to Halliday[1]:

> 'Almost certainly the right may not be exercised where it subsists in property which is necessarily ancillary to the ownership of more valuable property which is not being disposed of along with it, as in the case of common property in the roof, walls or stairs of flatted property in a tenement owned in connection with a flat therein, although it is highly improbable that any proprietor would seek to do so or that any person would buy it if he did.'

[1]   Halliday, 33-41.

2.23   On the other hand in *McLean v City of Glasgow District Council*[1], which concerned compensation for a tenement which had been compulsorily purchased, it was suggested that '... the position is clear, Mr McLean is a *pro indiviso* proprietor of the site of the former tenement and he could at his own hand have pursued an action of division and sale [of the common parts of the building]'[2]. This case should, perhaps, be treated with caution for two reasons. In the first place, as we have noted it concerned the assessment of compensation on compulsory purchase. Secondly, the building had, by the time of the case, been demolished. For these reasons, then, the Lands Tribunal was not faced with a case where division and sale would be likely to go ahead, only with the possible abstract existence of the right which would augment the compensation payable. Halliday's view is now supported by judicial authority[3].

[1]   1987 SLT (Lands Tr) 2.
[2]   At 4L.
[3]   *Michael v Carruthers* 1997 SCLR 1005; *Rafique v Amin* 1997 SLT 1385.

2.24   There is a further, statutory, restriction on division and sale. This is found in s 19 of the Matrimonial Homes (Family Protection) (Scotland) Act 1981. This applies to actions of division and sale involving a matrimonial home owned in common by husband and wife. In such cases the court may decide not to grant decree if it considers that it would not be fair and reasonable in all the circumstances to do so. In deciding whether it is fair and reasonable the court is specifically directed to the following matters: the conduct of the spouses, the respective needs and family resources of the spouses, the needs of any child of the family, the extent to which the matrimonial home is used for business, trade or professional purposes by one of the spouses, and whether the spouse bringing the action has offered to provide suitable alternative accommodation for the other spouse[1]. Other aspects of the 1981 Act and of matrimonial property are considered in CHAPTER 18.

[1]   On this last point see *Hall v Hall* 1987 SLT (Sh Ct) 15.

Joint property[1]

2.25   Although there is some confusion in judicial decisions about the precise differences between joint and common property, joint property is best regarded as an unusual example or instance of common property.

[1]   *Stair Memorial Encyclopaedia*, vol 18, 34–36.

2.26   Joint property occurs in the situation where a person acquires a right in property by virtue of his/her membership of a particular group. Examples include a body of trustees or a club. In such cases the property is owned jointly by all the members of the group, eg, all the members of the club. There is therefore, as in common property, an item or items of property which is/are owned by more than one person. Unlike common property, in the case of joint property the co-proprietors acquire rights in the joint property only by virtue of their membership of a particular group or body which exists independently of the property.

2.27   There are two other important differences between common and joint property. In joint property the shares of the joint proprietors cannot be sold separately or bequeathed on death. Instead, on the death or departure of the joint proprietor his share accresces to the remaining joint proprietors. Secondly, there is generally no right of division and sale in respect of joint property. Unlike common property, where the relationship between the parties derives from the ownership of the property and the only way out of the relationship in some cases will be division and sale, in joint property the relationship derives from membership of an organisation and it can be simply severed by leaving the organisation.

2.28   In the case of joint property the terms of the deeds, eg a constitution, regulating the body will generally provide for management of the property. In *Murray v Johnstone*[1] it was held, however, that the agreement of all joint proprietors was necessary before joint property was given away.

[1]   (1896) 23 R 981.

Common interest[1]

2.29   Common interest is sometimes confused with common property, but the two are quite distinct. In the case of common property there is some property owned in common between those enjoying rights of common property. In common interest the situation is completely different. Common interest arises where there are *separate* properties *separately* owned, but which are close enough together so that what one person does on his/her property can adversely affect others on their property. Thus common interest arises between neighbouring proprietors and between riparian proprietors (ie the owners of land on the banks of a river). In common interest there is no property owned in common between those having a mutual common interest and which forms the foundation of that common interest. Common interest is therefore not based on shared ownership of property, but on separate ownership of adjacent or propinquitous properties. The common law relating to common interest explained here no longer applies to tenement properties, having been replaced by a statutory scheme[2].

[1]   *Stair Memorial Encyclopaedia*, vol 18, 354–374.
[2]   Tenements (Scotland) Act 2004, ss 7-10; see CHAPTER 11.

2.30   Common interest has two aspects.

Negative

2.31   A proprietor can prevent something adverse to the common interest, ie something which interferes with his legitimate interests as a property owner. An example is *Donald & Sons v Esslemont & Macintosh Ltd*[1] where the pursuers owned property fronting onto a main street in Aberdeen. The defenders owned property on either side of this street above ground level, which they proposed to join by way of a bridge across the street. The pursuers sought interdict to prevent this, one of the grounds being common interest. Interdict was granted on the grounds that the bridge would infringe the frontagers common interest '... not merely in the superficial area of the street, but in the space above it as a means of its illumination'[2].

[1]   1923 SC 122.
[2]   Per Lord President (Inglis) at 134.

2.32 Before an action based on common interest can succeed, the interference alleged must be substantial rather than trivial. This is illustrated in *McCallum v Gunn*[1]. The pursuer was seeking an interdict to prevent the defender from permitting one of their employees to leave a bicycle propped up against the wall of the common passage. On appeal to the sheriff the case was held to be one of common interest, but, since the obstruction of the passageway was not substantial, interdict was refused.

[1]   1955 SLT (Sh Ct) 85.

Positive

2.33 This imposes a positive, enforceable duty to repair and maintain property. Most of the case law in this area is concerned with tenement properties and, as we have noted, the common law of common interest no longer applies in the case of tenement properties. It is likely that the positive aspect of common interest has limited application outside tenement properties[1]. Where an action based on common interest is raised in anticipation of some failure to maintain which will affect that common interest, all that must be established is that there will be a substantial impact on the proprietor raising the action.

[1]   Gordon, 15-49.

2.34 In contrast, where the action is raised retrospectively, claiming compensation for damage caused by a failure in this positive duty, it is now clear (on the authority of the Inner House) that the proprietor whose failure led to the loss will only be liable if it can be established that the failure was negligent[1]. In some cases the actions of the proprietor may be such as to give rise to a presumption of negligence on their part[2].

[1]   *Thomson v St Cuthbert's Co-operative Association Ltd* 1959 SLT 54.
[2]   *Kennedy v Glenbelle* 1996 SCLR 411.

2.35 Finally, the importance of the distinction between common interest and common property, as well as some aspects of the law of common interest, can be seen in *Thom v Hetherington*[1]. The dispute concerned a boundary wall which was owned from the centre line to either side respectively by the pursuer and defender who were neighbours. The defender constructed a fence adjacent to the wall which the pursuer suspected had caused damage to the wall. In essence his case was: that sections of the concrete foundation of the wall had been cut away to receive fence posts resulting in a weakening of the foundation, damage to the wall, and destabilisation of the wall; and that because the fence posts were bonded by concrete to the wall the wind loading on the wall was increased making repair and maintenance more difficult and expensive. The pursuer was unsuccessful; the wall was not common property and the only basis for his claim was common interest which could only succeed if he could establish a measurable or significant interference with his interests. This he could not do. Note that if the wall had been common *property* he would have succeeded as he would have had a right of veto on any work affecting the wall which was not *de minimis*.

[1]   1988 SLT 724.

2.36   There are two other features of this case which are not legally relevant but which illustrate the complete breakdown in relations between parties which often underlies property disputes. Firstly the proof lasted 28 days. On the sixteenth day the Lord Ordinary suggested that the parties should try to reach a settlement and adjourned the case for negotiations to take place. After one and a half hours the parties were back ready to continue the action. (The Lord Ordinary also noted that the total value of wall and fence was about £2,000.) Secondly, the pursuer was away when the fence was erected. On inspecting it he noticed some pieces of concrete and concrete chippings near the posts. 'Some days later during the hours of darkness the pursuer entered the garden of no. 37 [the defender's property] and removed a plastic bag full of concrete chippings...'[1].

[1]   1988 SLT 724 at 726C–D.

Law of the tenement[1]

2.37   The area in which common property and common interest are found most often is in the context of tenemental or other flatted properties. Here an extensive common law developed, known as the law of the tenement, which regulated the ownership rights of the owners of the various flats, the areas in which there is common property, and the area of common interest. These rules provided, for example, that all owners have a common interest in the building as a whole and that the owner of a top flat also owns the roof and roof space above his/her flat[2]. The rules on ownership remain substantially unchanged, but common interest now has a statutory basis[3].

[1] See CHAPTER 11.
[2] See *Taylor v Dunlop* (1872) 11 M 25.
[1] Tenements (Scotland) Act 2004, ss 7-10.

PROTECTION/VINDICATION OF RIGHTS

Heritable property

2.38 The remedies available to the owner of heritable property will be considered in CHAPTER 9.

Corporeal moveables[1]

Restitution/vindication

2.39 These two terms are often used interchangeably, but, historically at least, are quite distinct. The latter, vindication, has now largely fallen from use. It is described by the Scottish Law Commission as essentially an action for declarator of ownership. They also note that by the end of the nineteenth century it seemed to be of little importance[1]. It has been suggested that one reason for vindication's fall from grace was that it was simply a declaratory order: there was no accompanying order from the court requiring that the property be handed back to the person entitled to it. In contrast, restitution is an action requiring the person having possession or custody of property to return it to its rightful owner, subject to the exception that where this cannot be done compensation may be payable.

[1] D L Carey Miller, *Corporeal Moveables in Scots Law*, ch 10; Scottish Law Commission Memorandum No 31, *Corporeal Moveables: Remedies*.

2.40 The right to seek restitution applies in any case where the owner of property has been deprived of possession in circumstances where he/she did not intend to part with ownership of the object. Most commonly this covers cases of theft. It also applies and is available against someone who has acquired the property in good faith, provided that they are not protected by one of the provisions considered below. This point cannot be stressed enough: someone acting in good faith who buys stolen property (or other property to which the seller has no title) does *not*, except in the very limited circumstances discussed below, obtain a good title to the property. Good faith on the part of a purchaser is therefore, unless one of these circumstances exists, no defence against the owner of the property seeking to recover possession.

2.41 Restitution is quite straightforward when the property is still in the hands of the third party against whom the action is brought. The situation is rather more complicated in two situations:

1 Where the person sued has parted with the property. Here it depends whether that person parted with the property in good faith, ie in ignorance of the fact that he/she had no legal right to the property, or in bad faith. In the former case the pursuer is only entitled to recompense, ie compensation in the amount of any profit made by that person as a result of the transfer on of the property. In the latter case the pursuer is entitled to compensation for the value of the property.

2 Where the person sued has consumed the property or converted it, either by manufacture or some form of mixing, into something else. Here the case law is rather confused, reflecting a lack of clarity in the law relating to original acquisition of property[1].

[1] See CHAPTER 4.

2.42 In *Faulds v Townsend*[1] the pursuer's horse was stolen and was later sold to the defender, who carried on a chemical business. The horse was brought to the defender's between 11pm and midnight, and was almost immediately slaughtered and boiled up for manure. The pursuer sued successfully for the value of the horse. The Lord Ordinary, whose judgment was approved of by the Inner House, appears to have proceeded on a delictual basis, involving a breach of a duty of care, rather than a consideration of the property consequences of the defender's actions. He said[2]:

'But such is the peculiar nature of the [defender's] business, and such the inducement and temptation which that business must present to the theft of horses, lame, infirm, or old, yet not meant by the owners for slaughter, or condemned by the police, that great

care and caution on the part of the [defender] is necessary, both in the purchase of horses and in the disposal of horses when purchased. Some peculiar responsibility, in respect both of purchase and disposal, must attend the conduct of such a business.'
In the circumstances of the case, including the fact that the horse was in too good a condition for this fate, and, indeed, such a good condition that the defender's servant ought to have been placed on his inquiry, the defender was held to have breached this duty.

¹   (1861) 23 D 437.
²   At 439.

2.43   In *Oliver & Boyd v The Marr Typefounding Co Ltd*¹, over one and a half tons of lead type was stolen from the pursuers' premises. It was bought, quite innocently, by the defenders and most was converted into new type. This was the common way of dealing with old type. The exception to this conversion process was the last batch purchased, which was found on the defenders' premises. The defenders argued that transformation of an article, as had happened here, should be treated in the same way as sale, so that they should only be liable for recompense. One obvious difficulty with this argument, as the Lord Ordinary pointed out, is that in cases of sale restitution of the original property is still possible; in this case it was not. In the end the defenders' argument was rejected and they were held liable to compensate the pursuers for the value of the type. As the extract from the judgment below indicates², this conclusion seems to have been arrived at on the basis of equitable distribution of loss, rather than on the application of any rules derived from the law of property:

'Here the shape of the article was changed so much, and its identity so completely lost, that it is impossible to say what has now become of the metal that was stolen: some of it may have been sold; some or all of it may still be among the defenders' stock in the form of new type. Most probably it remained in the defenders' possession for some time after the discovery of the theft: and certainly there is no-one else against whom the pursuers could proceed for its recovery. In such circumstances, I can see no greater hardship in the defenders having to account for the value of the metal which they themselves melted down and used, than in their having had to give up the metal which had not had time to reach the melting pot. And I fail to see why so accidental a distinction in fact should make any difference in legal result.'

¹   (1901) 9 SLT 170.
²   At 171.

2.44   Finally, in *International Banking Corporation v Ferguson, Shaw & Sons*¹, a quantity of oil belonging to the pursuers came into the hands of the defenders. The defenders then used the oil in the manufacture of a lard compound which they sold on to their customers. In this case the Inner House treated the case as one of *specificatio*², with the manufacturers becoming owners of the new compound, but being under a duty to compensate the pursuers for the value of the oil used.

¹   1910 SC 182.
²   See below PARAS **4.11-4.18**.

2.45   Both *Faulds* and *Oliver & Boyd* should probably be regarded as restricted to their own particular facts. This appears to have been the view of Lord Ardwall in *International Banking Corporation*, where he said of *Oliver & Boyd* that 'the circumstances ... were very special'¹. The last case at least offers an attempt to apply the rules of property to the situation which arose, although, as we shall see in CHAPTER **4**, these rules are by no means clear. Despite the different grounds for these decisions, the consequences were the same: the pursuer was entitled to compensation.

¹   1910 SC 182 at 193.

2.46   Finally, there is an important legal difference between restitution and compensation. The former is a real right, ie it is a right in property; the latter is a personal right, ie only a right to take action against the person obliged to compensate.

Unlawful occupation

2.47   Although there is no law of trespass in relation to moveable property, it is possible to seek an interdict to prevent continued unlawful occupation of such property. An example is *Phestos Shipping Co Ltd v Kurmiawan*¹, where the owners of a vessel, the *Bulk Trader*, sought interdict to prevent its continued occupation by a sacked crew. Interdict was refused at first instance, but allowed on appeal. Lord Dunpark expressed the view that: 'Scots law offers remedies for the unlawful occupation of property be it heritable or moveable, even where the occupation is not affecting the owner's pocket'[2].

1   1983 SLT 388; see also *Shell UK Ltd v McGillivray* 1991 SLT 667.
2   1983 SLT 388 at 391.

Spuilzie

2.48   This is a remedy for unlawful dispossession of moveable property, available to both owners and possessors. The Scottish Law Commission's Memorandum on *Corporeal Moveables: Remedies*[1] notes that: 'Prewar and immediately post-war Scottish works dealing with the law of reparation and moveable property either do not discuss spuilzie at all or considered the remedy to be obsolete'[2]. Walker, however, considers that it is still competent, and gives it lengthy treatment[3]. This treats it as partly based in the law of delict and partly as apparently identical with restitution as outlined above. Despite its apparent obsolescence, a number of recent cases have purported to be based on spuilzie[4].

1   Memorandum No 31 (1976).
2   At 17.
3   *Delict* (2nd edn, 1981), 1002–1011.
4   *Mackinnon v Avonside Homes* 1993 SCLR 976; see also *Harris v Abbey National plc* 1997 SCLR 359; *Gemmell v Bank of Scotland* 1998 SCLR 144.

2.49   It is not clear whether this remedy is available only to possessors or is also open to custodiers. Opposite views are expressed in the *Stair Memorial Encyclopaedia* vol 18 and in Walker on *Delict*. Taking the former first, the view expressed is that an action for delivery can only be raised by someone with a legal right in the property[1] and that possessory remedies, such as spuilzie, are only available to those in possession and that custodiers are specifically excepted[2]. Walker's view, by contrast, is that custodiers have a right to the remedy of spuilzie[3] and may therefore be entitled to normal and even violent profits lost because of dispossession[4].

1   *Stair Memorial Encyclopaedia*, vol 18, 158.
2   *Stair Memorial Encyclopaedia*, vol 18, 161–163.
3   *Delict* (2nd edn, 1981), 1003.
4   *Delict* (2nd edn, 1981), 1005.

Exceptions to the right of restitution

COMMON LAW

2.50   At common law a purchaser in good faith is protected where the original transfer is reducible, but has not been avoided at the time of the transfer to the *bona fide* purchaser. The main example of this would be where the original transaction was induced by fraudulent or other misrepresentation, but the property was transferred to a purchaser in good faith before the original seller had that sale set aside. An example of this is *McLeod v Kerr*[1]. Kerr sold a car to a man called Galloway who paid with a stolen cheque. Galloway in turn sold the car to Gibson. It was held that the initial contract of sale was voidable because, as Lord Guthrie explained: 'Galloway bought the car from Mr Kerr by fraudulent misrepresentation that he would pay the price by cheque, he well knowing that the cheque he gave was worthless, being stolen'[2]. Since the contract had not, however, been set aside by the time Gibson bought the car, he, as an innocent third party acting in good faith, acquired ownership of the car.

[1]   1965 SLT 358.
[2]   At 364.

2.51   It has also been suggested that in some circumstances the owner may be prevented from recovering his/her property through personal bar[1]. This might arise, for example, where the owner acted in such a way as to suggest concurrence with, or approval of, a sale by someone without title.

[1]   D L Carey Miller, *Corporeal Moveables in Scots Law*, para 10.19.

STATUTORY LAW
2.52
(i)   *Bankruptcy (Scotland) Act 1985*. This protects purchasers in good faith and for value against reduction of the sales to them on the grounds that the transaction involved, or the transfer to the seller involved a gratuitous alienation or fraudulent preference[1].
(ii) *Sale of Goods Act 1979*. This contains a number of protections for purchasers. There is a statutory version of personal bar, applying where 'the owner of the goods is by his conduct precluded from denying the seller's authority to sell'[2]. There is also a provision protecting a purchaser in good faith from a seller who has a voidable

title which has not been avoided at the time of the sale[3]. Buyers from sellers in possession, ie a seller who remains in possession of goods after their sale, are protected, provided that they are in good faith and purchase without notice of the previous sale[4]. Similarly, someone who buys from a purchaser in possession, ie a purchaser who has been given possession of goods before property in them has passed to him/her, is protected, again provided that he/she has acted in good faith and without notice of the original seller's continuing rights[5].

(iii) *Hire Purchase Act 1964.* This covers the situation where what the Act describes as a 'private purchaser', ie someone who is not buying in the course of business, buys a car which is the subject of a hire purchase or conditional sale agreement. Provided such a purchaser acts in good faith and without notice of the agreement he/she obtains a good title to the car[6]. The private purchaser is also protected if the car has been bought by a trade purchaser and then sold on[7].

[1] Sections 34, 36.
[2] Sale of Goods Act 1979, s 21(1).
[3] Sale of Goods Act 1979, s 23.
[4] Sale of Goods Act 1979, s 24. The relevance of this, as we will see in CHAPTER 4, is that, in terms of the 1979 Act, property (ownership) normally transfers to the buyer as soon as a contract for sale is made.
[5] Sale of Goods Act 1979, s 25(1).
[6] Hire Purchase Act 1964, s 27.
[7] Hire Purchase Act 1964, s 27(3).

RESTRICTIONS ON THE USE OF PROPERTY

2.53 As we have already seen, Erskine's definition of property noted that our rights in property could be restricted 'by law or paction'[1]. In other words, our rights to use property we own can be restricted through the operation of law, by statute or common law, or by our own agreement.

[1] Erskine, II, i, 1.

2.54 Examples of the former are the law of nuisance, which prevents interference with reasonable enjoyment of heritable property by restricting the uses neighbouring proprietors can make of their property[1]; common interest, discussed above; planning controls; building control, which requires that the permission of the relevant local authority is obtained before building works are carried out; and, road traffic legislation, which imposes limits on what can be done with a car and imposes certain requirements as to construction and maintenance.

1   Eg *Shanlin v Collins* 1973 SLT (Sh Ct) 21.

CHAPTER 3

Prescription

WHAT IS PRESCRIPTION?

3.1   Prescription is, in general, concerned with the acquisition and loss of legal rights through the passage of time. Positive prescription is concerned with the former: in other words rights are acquired with the passing of time. Negative prescription with the latter: in other words rights are lost with the passing of time. Prescription plays an important role in relation to acquisition of some rights over land, for example servitude rights[1] and even ownership[2]. Its importance in this last context, which will continue for some time, derived from the system of acquiring a real right in land which existed until April 2003. Until that date a transferor, for example a purchaser, obtained such a right by recording the deed transferring the property to him in the Register of Sasines. This involved a copy being made of that deed and kept in the Register. Once this was done the purchaser obtained a real right in the land and could be described as its owner. However, if the right of this new owner was challenged, for example, by someone who claimed to own all or part of the land, the purchaser could not simply point to the existence of his/her recorded title. Instead he/she had to go behind this and prove that the person who sold the property to him/her had a good title to do this, and that the person who sold it to them also had a good title, and so on, in principle back to the very first transfer of the property. Such a search is clearly difficult, if not impossible. The effect of prescription is that it provides a cut off point for this search. As we will see, possession for the requisite period based on a recorded title cures any defects in title and gives an unchallengeable right of ownership.

Because of this then, the purchaser's solicitor only had to look back at the first deed beyond this period and be satisfied with the validity of any transfers since then[3]. If these are all valid it could be assumed that the seller had a good, unchallengeable title and would pass this on to the purchaser, thereby allowing them to protect their ownership against any challenges.

1   See CHAPTER **13**.
2   For the history of and justifications for prescription see D Johnstone, *Prescription and Limitation*, ch 1.
3   See CHAPTER **18**.

3.2   Since April 2003 there is a new system of acquiring a real right involving registration of title in the Land Register. Once a title is registered it is guaranteed by a state indemnity and, broadly speaking, cannot be challenged[1]. Because of this, prescription is less important once a title has been registered. It will continue to be important, however, in three cases. First, in disputes about ownership of land where the title is still recorded in the Register of Sasines. Second, in transfers of property which result in registration of the property in the Land Register for the first time. Because of the state guarantee the Keeper of the Registers of Scotland will need to be satisfied that the seller has a good title to the property supported by possession for the period required by prescription and therefore that the title will not be open to challenge. Third, in some cases the title may be registered under exclusion of indemnity, meaning that it is not guaranteed. This exclusion can be removed if the land affected is possessed for the necessary prescriptive period.

1   See PARA **18.75**FF.

3.3   Here we will consider the operation of prescription where title is registered in the Register of Sasines. This will clearly also be relevant where property is being registered in the Land Register for the first time. We will then consider prescription where land is registered in the Land Register, followed by acquisition of other rights by prescription and negative prescription.

POSITIVE PRESCRIPTION IN THE REGISTER OF SASINES

3.4   Ownership rights in land can be acquired through possession. Normally the period of possession required is ten years[1], though the period is 20 years in the case of acquisition of salmon fishings or rights in the foreshore in a question with the Crown[2].

1   Prescription and Limitation (Scotland) Act 1973, s 1(1).
2   Prescription and Limitation (Scotland) Act 1973, s 1(4).

3.5   Three main requirements have to be fulfilled:

1   The possession must be based on a title recorded in the Register of Sasines[1]. This title must be irredeemable, ie confer a permanent right, and must be *ex facie* valid. This latter requirement means that there must be no patent defect: in other words, a defect which is obvious simply by looking at the deed itself, for example a missing signature. In addition the deed must not be forged, though it is not forgery for someone who does not have title to a piece of land to grant a deed in his/her own name transferring that land. Such a lack of title will, of course, not be obvious from looking at the deed and such a deed will therefore be *ex facie* valid.

2   The terms of the deed must be sufficient to cover the area of ground to which title is claimed by way of prescription[2]. For example, if the deed describes certain boundaries, no land lying outside those boundaries can be acquired by prescription, regardless of how long possession has lasted.

3   The possession must be for a period of ten years[3] and be open, peaceful and without judicial interruption. The requirement for openness means that the possession must be obvious so as to allow anyone else claiming title to the property to be aware of it and to challenge the possession, though it is not necessary that they are in fact aware of it. Judicial interruption requires a court action to be raised challenging the possession. The use of the word 'peaceably' suggests that the prescriptive period may also be interrupted by non-judicial means, if the person claiming the right is only able to remain in possession by means of force or violence.

1   In cases involving an unrecorded title the period of possession required is 20 years: Prescription and Limitation (Scotland) Act 1973, s 2.
2   *Suttie v Baird* 1992 SLT 133.
3   Subject to the longer periods set out in PARA **3.4** above.

3.6   The possession involved may be either natural possession (physical occupancy) or civil possession, where the person possessing does not occupy the property, but is represented by another who is the actual occupant; the most obvious example of this is the case of a tenant who has natural possession, but occupies on behalf of his landlord who has civil possession. In addition, the nature of the possession required will depend on the nature of the land and the extent to which possession and use of the land would be expected to occur[1]. In one case use of what was described as a piece of waste land for shooting was held to be enough to establish the required possession, though the absence of any assertion of adverse possession was also considered to be relevant[2]. On the other hand occasional hedge cutting, grass cutting and rubbish clearing was held not to be enough to establish prescriptive possession in the case of an urban gap site[3]. Finally, possession need not be in good faith, in other words, the possessor need not believe that he/she has a good title to the property occupied[4].

[1]   *Lock v Taylor* 1976 SLT 238.
[2]   *Hamilton v McIntosh Donald* 1994 SLT 793, per Lord Wylie at 805A–F, though Lord Justice Clerk Ross considered that dumping on part of the ground was also relevant possession; see R Rennie, 'Possession: Nine Tenths of the Law', 1994 SLT (News) 261.
[3]   *Stevenson-Hamilton's Exrs v McStay (No 2)* 2001 SLT 694.
[4]   *Duke of Buccleuch v Cunynghame* (1826) 5 S 53.

3.7   The effect of these rules is simply that possession for a period of ten years[1] on the basis of an *ex facie* valid, irredeemable title recorded in the Register of Sasines confers an unchallengeable real right to the property possessed. In other words, although prescription cannot cure patent defects in deeds, it can cure latent defects, such as the absence of title on the part of the person granting the disposition of the property. This is the case because the courts will not look behind the deed on which prescriptive possession is based[2]. One consequence is that ownership can be acquired following possession on the basis of an *a non domino* disposition, that is a disposition granted by someone having no title to the property purportedly transferred[3]. This means that it is possible for someone to settle on land to which he/she has no right having got an accomplice (with no more right than him/her to the property) to sign a disposition purporting to transfer ownership. If he/she recorded the disposition and possessed the land for ten years without challenge, he/she would become owner. In the vast majority of cases, of course, such a pioneering venture would be thwarted by the arrival of the real owner, long before the ten years was up.

[1]   Subject to the longer periods set out in PARA **3.4** above.
[2]   *Fraser v Lord Lovat* (1898) 35 R 603.
[3]   See, for example, *Hamilton v McIntosh Donald* 1994 SLT 793.

POSITIVE PRESCRIPTION IN THE LAND REGISTER

3.8 Because, as we noted above, the Land Register guarantees title, once a title is registered acquisition of an ownership interest by positive prescription is of little relevance, except in cases where indemnity has been excluded in respect of ownership of all or part of a piece of land[1]. Once possession for the prescriptive period has followed from the date of registration[2] an application can be made for the exclusion of indemnity to be removed. It is still possible to register a title based on an *a non domino* disposition in the Land Register, though indemnity will be excluded[3].

1   Prescription and Limitation (Scotland) Act 1973, s 1(1)(b).
2   Rather than the date when possession actually started, which might be before this: *M R S Hamilton Ltd v Baxter* 1998 SLT 1075.
3   *Registration of Title Practice Book*, 6.4.

ACQUISITION OF OTHER RIGHTS BY PRESCRIPTION

3.9 Other rights in land can be acquired by the operation of positive prescription. These include servitudes and public rights of way, both requiring a 20-year prescriptive period[1].

1   Prescription and Limitation (Scotland) Act 1973, s 3; see CHAPTER **13**.

NEGATIVE PRESCRIPTION

3.10 As we saw above, negative prescription is where rights and obligations are extinguished rather than created by the passage of time. It is extremely important in relation to contractual obligations and reparation claims, as it sets time limits within which such claims may be made. In relation to property law, it is much less important than positive prescription, but it has a few applications that should be briefly noted.

3.11 There are two types of negative prescription, the 20-year prescription and the 5-year prescription. In the property field, the 20-year negative prescription can operate to wipe out servitude rights, public rights of way, claims under the law of nuisance, and any other property rights that are not specifically declared to be imprescriptible[1]. The 5-year prescription applies, among other things, to the obligation to pay a periodic sum of money such as rent[2]. However, it should be clear what this implies; only those payments which are five years or more in arrears will be extinguished, and those falling due within the five-year period can still be legally claimed.

1   Prescription and Limitation (Scotland) Act 1973, s 8.
2   Prescription and Limitation (Scotland) Act 1973, s 6 and Sch 1.

IMPRESCRIPTIBLE RIGHTS AND OBLIGATIONS

3.12   Certain rights and obligations are not subject to the process of negative prescription, and will not be extinguished however much time has elapsed[1]. These include a real right of ownership in land (ie where there is a recorded or registered title) and the right of a lessee under a recorded lease. It also includes the right to take any steps necessary for making up or completing title to any interest in land. This would include, for example, someone who had a title deed but had not yet recorded it; it does not include someone who has merely completed Missives, as he has only a personal right under the law of contract. Such a right can be extinguished by the 20-year negative prescription[2].

1   Prescription and Limitation (Scotland) Act 1973, ss 7, 8 and Sch 3.
2   *Macdonald v Scott* 1981 SLT 128.

3.13   The suggestion that a right of ownership in land cannot prescribe may seem rather curious given what is said above about the possibility of someone with no title to land (A) obtaining title to it by possession based on a recorded or registered title. What is happening here is, however, not that the owner is losing title but that, as a result of prescription, A is acquiring a real right in the property. Once the prescriptive period has passed, the general consensus is that the owner's title will be extinguished and ownership conferred on A[1].

1   *Stair Memorial Encyclopaedia*, vol 18, 674; see the discussion in R Paisley, *Land Law*, 3.13.

CHAPTER 4

Corporeal moveable property

ORIGINAL ACQUISITION OF OWNERSHIP

4.1 In the context of acquisition of ownership of corporeal moveable property there is a distinction between original acquisition and derivative acquisition. Derivative acquisition describes the situation where the ownership of property is transferred by the previous owner. Original acquisition describes the acquisition of ownership of property which either has never been owned before (in legal terms a *res nullius*), or, less usually, the acquisition of property which has been owned before, but where the previous owner has lost his/her ownership interest. Examples of this latter category will be encountered in the context of *occupatio*. Where an entirely new thing is made from existing things, eg, the making of beer from its various ingredients, this is treated as a case of acquisition of property which has never been owned before.

4.2 There are four means of original acquisition to be considered: *occupatio*, accession, *specificatio*, and *commixtio/confusio*.

Occupatio[1]

4.3 *Occupatio* involves the taking of possession of some thing or property which is not owned with the intention of becoming its owner. The combination of the physical and mental element described here is enough to constitute ownership of the object in question. Things which are not owned, and are therefore open to acquisition through *occupatio*, are referred to as *res nullius*. The examples which are usually given of this are: wild animals, shells, pebbles on a beach, pearls, and fish, with the exception of certain fish described as Royal Fish, principally, sturgeon, dolphins, large whales and, possibly, salmon[1].

1   D L Carey Miller, *Corporeal Moveables in Scots Law*, ch 2; *Stair Memorial Encyclopaedia*, vol 18, 540–546.

4.4   Where wild animals are contained or confined in some way, for example, deer in a deer park or birds in an aviary, they become the property of the person confining them and anyone removing them is guilty of theft[1]. An illustration of this is *Anderson v Valentine*[2] where the accused were charged with the theft of a number of rainbow trout which had escaped from a reservoir stocked with them. They were found guilty on the basis that although fish were *res nullius* they lost that status once they were confined; and even if they escaped occasionally despite the precautions taken by the confiner, they were not immediately converted into *res nullius*[3]. The suggestion that the fish, on escaping, did not immediately become *res nullius* reflects the point, made by the Institutional writers, that animals escaping from confinement will still be owned by the confiner at least until the effort to recapture them has ceased (or can, because of the passage of time, be taken to have ceased): at that stage the animals can be regarded as having reverted to the wild[4]. *Anderson v Valentine* perhaps represents an extension of this doctrine in the particular circumstances of the case to allow continued ownership when escapes take place despite the proper precautions/efforts at confinement made by the owner.

1   Erskine, II, i, 10
2   1985 SCCR 89.
3   As was noted it would have been more difficult (if not impossible) to arrive at this conclusion if the case had involved an indiginous species, because of the difficulty of proving that the fish caught had escaped.
4   Stair, II, i, 10.

4.5   The degree of confinement required to retain ownership varies with the type of property concerned. In the case of pebbles and other inanimate, immobile objects they can, presumably, simply be retained in the owner's land. In the case of animals which are possessed of a homing instinct in that they will return home themselves, like homing pigeons, no real confinement is required, and ownership will continue as long as they keep coming back. Finally, in the case of animals which do not have a homing instinct some degree of confinement will be required to keep them within the owner's possession, in the form, for example, of fencing or caging.

4.6 A *res nullius* which has not been acquired by *occupatio* cannot be stolen. So that, for example, unconfined wild animals cannot be stolen[1]. Thus, without some effort at confinement, ownership of land does not confer ownership rights of any wildlife on that land. There is, therefore, a distinction between rights to game associated with the ownership of land (which are generally the right to take game), and the actual *ownership* of individual animals/birds/fish. It follows that if a poacher illegally takes game or fish, that game or fish becomes his/her property by *occupatio* at common law. There are, however, statutory provisions which provide for forfeiture of fish, deer and game on conviction for poaching[2].

[1]   *Wilson v Dykes* (1872) 10 M 444.
[2]   For example, Game (Scotland) Act 1772, s 3; Salmon and Freshwater Fisheries (Protection) (Scotland) Act 1951, s 19(1); Deer (Scotland) Act 1996, s 31.

4.7   Finally, domesticated animals remain the property of the owner even if lost, and are treated as lost property (considered below).

Accession[1]

4.8   Acquisition by accession takes place when one object/substance becomes attached to, is combined with, or produced by, another. The rules of accession will determine who is the owner of the first object after combination/attachment/production. Stated in abstract this is not very clear, but a look at some of the particular cases which are considered under the general heading of accession will perhaps make it clearer.

[1]   D L Carey Miller, *Corporeal Moveables in Scots Law*, ch 3; *Stair Memorial Encyclopaedia*, vol 18, 570–577.

4.9   Accession applies to the offspring of animals, they belong to the owner of the mother. In the case of heritable property *alluvio* is an example of accession. Here land is gradually added to by the operation of a river. The added land, by attachment, belongs to the owner of the existing land[1]. The same does not apply to cases of *avulsio*, where land is carried off by a flood and ends up attached to land belonging to a different owner. Here the original owner remains owner of the land carried away.

[1]   *Campbell v Brown* 18 Nov 1813 FC; *Stirling v Bartlett* 1992 SCLR 994.

4.10   When moveable property is attached to heritable property it generally becomes the property of the owner of the heritage. The rules which determine whether this happens are known as the law of fixtures[1]. Finally, accession covers what is known as industrial accession. This takes two main forms: *specificatio* and *commixtio/confusio*. It is to these that we now turn.

1   See CHAPTER 5.

Specificatio[1]

4.11 The rules of *specificatio* apply to determine property rights when something new is manufactured out of materials belonging in whole or in part to someone other than the manufacturer[2]. Before the rules of specification apply there must be some form of manufacture involving, or transformation of, the original materials. Something new must be created which is different in form and/or substance from the raw materials: it is not enough that something new is created merely by building components together into a whole, at least in a form where they can easily be separated again, for example, children's building bricks. In other words: 'It is of the essence of specificatio that the original article disappears'[3]. If there has been no such transformation there has, in reality, been no *specificatio*, and the materials continue to belong to their original owner(s).

1   D L Carey Miller, *Corporeal Moveables in Scots Law*, ch 4; *Stair Memorial Encyclopaedia*, vol 18, 559–563.
2   For an innovative attempt to extend the range of *specificatio* see *Kinloch Damph v Nordvik Salmon Farms Ltd & Ors*, (unreported), 30 June 1999 OH.
3   *North-West Securities Ltd v Barrhead Coachworks Ltd* 1976 SLT 99, per Lord McDonald at 101.

4.12   This last point is sometimes expressed as a rule of *specificatio*; for example Stair says that 'if the product can easily be reduced to the first matter, the owners of the matter remain the owners of the whole'[1]. The examples given are a metal cup and plate made from bullion; in both cases the final product can be melted down to give the original material. This rule was applied to the rather different circumstances presented in *McDonald v Provan (of Scotland Street) Ltd* [2]. Here a Mr Feldman had obtained two cars, one of which was stolen. He cut both cars in half and welded the front of one vehicle to the rear of the other. The resulting car was then sold to the defenders who in turn sold it to the pursuer. Some months later the car was taken away by the police on the grounds that it was stolen property. The pursuer then sued the defenders for breach of a statutory warranty that they had title to sell the car. The defenders argued that they did have a right to sell the car, the welding together of the car amounting to *specificatio* which conferred ownership on Mr Feldman. This argument was rejected for two reasons. First, it was said that *specificatio* did not apply in cases where there was bad faith on the part of the manufacturer, as here. Secondly the rule noted above was applied.

[1]   Stair, II, i, 41, presumably only if no materials belonging to the manufacturer were involved. See also Erskine, II, i, 16; Bell, 1298(1).

[2]   1960 SLT 231.

4.13   *Prima facie* at least if a vehicle can be constructed by welding together the front half of one vehicle and the rear half of another, it would appear to be equally practicable to cut them into two once more. If so, the defenders could not successfully contend that Mr Feldman created a new entity which wholly belonged to him as its maker[1].

[1]   1960 SLT 231 at 232, per Lord Clyde.

4.14   The question of the need for good faith will be returned to. The second point about the reducibility of the product to its components seems rather strained. According to Stair, the process of reduction must be easy; one can see that this might apply to the example he gives of melting down a product but it is less easy to see that cutting apart a car (and presumably reuniting it with its original other halves) is an easy process.

4.15   The real point about this supposed rule of specification is that in cases where the final product can be easily reconverted to the original materials it is doubtful that the sort of transformation required for specification to exist has taken place. It is difficult to say, in the words quoted earlier, that the original article has disappeared. This approach was adopted in *Zahnrad Fabrik Passau GmbH v Terex Ltd* [1]. The pursuers had sold the defenders some axles and transmissions, incorporating into the sale agreement a retention of title clause. When receivers were appointed to the defenders they raised an action for declarator that these items were their property and for delivery. By this time the items had been incorporated into finished and partly finished vehicles. Because of this the defenders claimed that they had acquired the property in the axles and transmissions by accession. Their argument was rejected. There had been no accession because the items could be removed from the vehicles without diminution of their efficiency. This suggests that where separation of materials/objects without diminution of efficiency[2] is possible there has been no accession, and so no *specificatio*.

1   1986 SLT 84.
2   Or, as the test was formulated in another case, without diminution in market value: *Wylie & Lochhead v Mitchell* (1870) 8 M 552.

4.16   There seems to be no reason why this principle should not apply to other cases where the final product can be easily returned to its original constituent(s). It may be objected that in the case of metal objects they no longer exist in the form of the raw materials and so cannot immediately be returned in that form. But the whole point of distinguishing these cases from the other rules of *specificatio* is that they can be *easily* returned to their original form, although this might require some work. In this sense they are in the same position as the axles and transmissions. These were no longer in their original form, but with a little work they could be detached from the vehicles, returned to their original form and then returned to their original owners. There are two rules which determine ownership of property produced by *specification*:

(a)   Any agreement between the parties will regulate the ownership of the manufactured property.

(b)   In the absence of agreement the final product will be owned by the manufacturer, subject to an obligation to compensate the owner of the raw materials for their value. This is illustrated in *International Banking Corporation v Ferguson, Shaw & Sons*[1] where a quantity of oil belonging to the pursuers was stolen and sold to the defenders, who bought it in ignorance of its provenance. The defenders used the oil to manufacture a lard compound which was sold on. The pursuers raised an action for delivery of the oil or, alternatively, compensation for its value. The Inner House treated the case as one of *specificatio*. In the words of Lord Dundas[2]: '... the defenders became the sole proprietors of the lard compound, and ... the pursuers have a good claim against them for the value of the oil'.

1   1910 SC 182.
2   At 194.

4.17   There are differing views on whether the specificator has to act in good faith to acquire ownership of the manufactured property. As we have seen, in *McDonald v Provan (of Scotland Street) Ltd*[1] it was suggested that the 'doctrine can only be invoked when there is complete *bona fides* on the part of the manufacturer'[2]. The reasons for making this statement were that the doctrine has an equitable basis[3] and Bell's comment that 'if the materials, as a separate existence, be destroyed in *bona fide*, the property is with the workman'[4]. Neither of the other Institutional writers mention the need for good faith on the part of the manufacturer[5]. It has subsequently been pointed out that *specificatio* is not an equitable doctrine and that the case cited in *McDonald* does not support that view[6]. The better view is probably that expressed by Miller that: '... the proprietary consequences of the making of a new thing follows (sic) regardless of the state of mind of the maker'[7].

[1]   1960 SLT 231.
[2]   Per Lord Clyde, at 232.
[3]   Based on certain comments in *Wylie & Lochhead v Mitchell* (1870) 8 M 552 at 558.
[4]   1298(1).
[5]   Stair, II, i, 41; Erskine, II, i, 16.
[6]   *North-West Securities Ltd. v Barrhead Coachworks Ltd* 1976 SLT 99, per Lord McDonald at 101.
[7]   D L Carey Miller, *Corporeal Moveables in Scots Law*, 4.04.

4.18   Finally, where the manufacture or process involves the attaching of a moveable item to heritable property the consequences will not be decided by reference to *specificatio*; rather the law of fixtures will prevail.

Commixtio/confusio[1]

4.19   Both of these involve the mixing together of properties belonging to more than one person. Strictly speaking *commixtio* is applied to the mixing together of solids, and *confusio* to the mixing together of liquids. The general rules as to ownership of mixtures, as stated by the Institutional writers[2], are:

1   Where things of the same type are mixed casually (ie without the prior agreement of the owners) and can be practically separated, ownership remains with the original owners of the various constituents of the mixture. The example given by Erskine is of the mixing of flocks of sheep; another example might be the mixing of two record collections.

2   Where things of the same kind are mixed casually and cannot be practically separated the resulting mixture is the common property of the owners of the ingredients in accordance with the extent of their

contribution to the mixture. Examples would be the mixing together of wine, or flour, or oil.

3   Where *commixtio/confusi* takes place by agreement of the owners of the ingredients, property in the final mixture will be common.

4   Finally, when the consequence of mixing is the production of something new and distinct from the original ingredients, the rules of *commixtio/confusio* are displaced by those of *specificatio*.

1   *Stair Memorial Encyclopaedia*, vol 18, 564; D L Carey Miller, *Corporeal Moveables in Scots Law*, ch 5.

2   Erskine, II, i, 17; Bell, 1298(2).

The general rule

4.20   Where the rules of *specificatio* and *commixtio/confusio* do not apply, there is a general equitable principle to be applied to cases of industrial accession. This is derived from *Wylie & Lochhead v Mitchell*[1]. Here there was a contract between the pursuers and a Robert Hutton for the construction of a hearse. Some of the materials and work were to be provided by the pursuers, being the bulk in value at £112. Hutton was to provide the remainder of the labour and materials, and specifically was to construct the basic body of the hearse; the value of his contribution was £95. Before work was completed, albeit very little remained to be done, Hutton was sequestrated. The remaining work was completed at the expense of the sequestrated estate and a dispute arose between the pursuers and the defender, the trustee in the sequestration, as to ownership of the finished hearse. The pursuers claimed that they were entitled to delivery on payment of the £95, the defender contended that the hearse belonged to the sequestrated estate. In the Inner House the case was not regarded as being one of *specificatio* since it did not involve 'the production of a new subject of property by art and industry, where the materials belong to one party, and the skilled labour is supplied by the other'[2]. Nor was it to be regarded as a case of *commixtio/confusio*. This left the court free from the authorities relevant to these areas and free to follow the general principal that

'the two or more persons who have each contributed to the production of a new subject, either materials, or skill and labour, or both, should hold it in common property, in such shares as correspond to the value of their several contributions'[3].

As the pursuers had already obtained delivery of the hearse pending the action all that remained was for them to pay the £95 to the defender. It has been pointed out this is an entirely fortuitous result of the reasoning applied by the court, deriving from the parties' prior agreement and delivery[4], since in the absence of agreement between the parties the remedy for a co-proprietor is to seek division and sale of the common property.

1   (1870) 8 M 552.
2   Per Lord President (Inglis), at 556.
3   Per Lord President (Inglis), at 558–559.
4   Scottish Law Commission Memorandum No 28, *Corporeal Moveables: Mixing, Union and Creation*, para 22.

Conclusion

4.21   The law in the area of industrial accession has been described as a Serbonian bog[1]. It is difficult to derive any clear statement of principles from the sparse judicial authorities.

1   By Lord Ardmillan in *Wylie & Lochhead v Mitchell* (1870) 8 M 552 at 561. This is a reference to Milton's name for Lake Serbonis in lower Egypt, a marshy tract (now dry) covered with shifting sand.

LOST OR ABANDONED PROPERTY[1]

4.22   Unlike *res nullius* and escaped wild animals, lost property does not become available for acquisition by anyone who finds it; rather – at least at common law – such property continues in the ownership of the prior owner, vesting in the Crown either temporarily or permanently where he/she does not come forward to claim the property. Abandoned property is in a slightly different position: on abandonment the owner loses ownership which then vests in the Crown[2]. Abandoned property is covered by the same statutory provisions as lost property.

1   *Stair Memorial Encyclopaedia*, vol 18, 547–554; D L Carey Miller, *Corporeal Moveables in Scots Law*, 2.07–2.08.
2   See *Stair Memorial Encyclopaedia*, vol 18, 568.

4.23   One consequence of this is that buried treasure belongs to the Crown, since the person who buried it is clearly in no position to claim it, and it will usually be impossible to identify anyone with a good claim over the property[1].

1   *Lord Advocate v Aberdeen University* 1967 SLT 361.

4.24 Another consequence is that appropriation of lost property by the finder amounts to theft[1], although there may be special circumstances where such appropriation does not amount to theft. An example is *Mackenzie v MacLean*[2] which involved damaged cans of lager which had fallen out of a lorry onto the roadway. The original owners of the lager had told the owner of a hotel to keep the undamaged cans and to dispose of the damaged ones. The accused were the employees delegated to carry out this task. As they did this, members of the public removed some of the damaged cans and insisted on making small payments to the accused, amounting to a total of £19. The employees were charged with theft. They were acquitted: the goods had been abandoned by their owners and technically belonged to the Crown. The sheriff concluded that[3]:

> 'In these circumstances and against a background of abandonment of ownership it seems to me that we are in a very narrow field of law where one is entitled to look at the question of whether there was any real wickedness on the part of the accused and particularly whether there was any intent to steal.'

The sheriff decided that there was no such intention.

1   *Lawson v Heatly* 1962 SLT 53.
2   1981 SLT (Sh Ct) 40.
3   At 40.

4.25 The area of lost and abandoned property is one which is now largely regulated by statute, with the main provisions being found in the Civic Government (Scotland) Act 1982, the Environmental Protection Act 1990, and the Dogs Act 1906.

Civic Government (Scotland) Act 1982

4.26 The finder of lost or abandoned property must report the finding and/or deliver the property to the police, to the owner of the property, to the person entitled to possession of the property, or to the owner of the land or premises on which the property is found, or to the representative of one of these. Where the report is made to the proprietor of land or premises he/she must in turn report to one of the first three people in the list[1]. There are some exceptions to this requirement, mainly where there are in place alternative arrangements for dealing with lost property, eg items found on Network Rail property.

[1]   Civic Government (Scotland) Act 1982, s 67.

4.27   Where the finding is reported to the police, they must make arrangements for the care and custody of the property and take reasonable steps to find the owner[1].

[1]   Civic Government (Scotland) Act 1982, s 68(2), (3).

4.28   If the owner of the property does not come forward within two months the police may offer the property to the finder, sell it, or otherwise dispose of it as appropriate[1]. Where the property cannot be kept conveniently or safely for two months it can be disposed of earlier[2]. Someone taking property disposed of by the police in good faith becomes the owner of the property, subject to the proviso that if they did not pay for it the original owner can reclaim it within one year of the disposal by the police[3]. Where the property has been sold the original owner may be entitled to compensation from the police if he/she claims within one year of the sale[4].

[1]   Civic Government (Scotland) Act 1982, s 68(4).
[2]   Civic Government (Scotland) Act 1982, s 68(5).
[3]   Civic Government (Scotland) Act 1982, s 71.
[4]   Civic Government (Scotland) Act 1982, s 72.

4.29   In the case of living creatures, other than dogs and livestock, the finder may be allowed to have custody of the animal. Where that happens the finder will become owner of the animal after two months if it remains unclaimed by the original owner[1]. As we will see shortly, separate legislative provision is made for dogs. Livestock are defined in the Act as being cattle, horses, asses, mules, hinnies, sheep, pigs, goats, poultry, deer not in the wild state and while in captivity, pheasants, partridge and grouse. Livestock presumably fall to be treated in the same way as inanimate property and can be disposed of by the police as appropriate.

[1]   Civic Government (Scotland) Act 1982, s 74.

Environmental Protection Act 1990

4.30   This imposes a duty on the finder of a dog to return it to its owner, take it to the police, or take it to the relevant official of the local authority[1]. Where the dog has been taken to the local authority the finder may, on complying with certain requirements, be allowed to keep the dog. If the finder wants to keep the dog he/she must do so for at least one month, and if he/she keeps the dog for two months without a claim being made by the original owner the finder will become the owner of the dog[2]. Where the finder does not wish to keep the dog it is to be treated in the same way as a stray dog[3].

[1]   Environmental Protection Act 1990, s 150(1).
[2]   Environmental Protection Act 1990, s 150(2)–(4).
[3]   Environmental Protection Act 1990, s 150(2)(b).

4.31   The Act empowers an authorised official of the local authority to seize stray dogs. Once seized they must be kept for seven days, after which they can be sold, given away or destroyed. A purchaser or donee of a dog becomes its owner. The seven-day period runs from the date of seizure, or if the dog has information about its owner, from the date on which the owner is notified of the seizure[1].

[1]   Environmental Protection Act 1990, s 149.

Dogs Act 1906

4.32   This contains similar provisions for stray dogs[1] and found dogs[2] to those in the Environmental Protection Act 1990. The difference is that the provisions relate to the police rather than local authorities.

[1]   Dogs Act 1906, s 3.
[2]   Dogs Act 1906, s 4.

TRANSFER OF OWNERSHIP[1]

4.33   At common law three requirements must be fulfilled to successfully effect a transfer of corporeal moveable property.

[1]   D L Carey Miller, *Corporeal Moveables in Scots Law*, chs 8 and 9; *Stair Memorial Encyclopaedia*, vol 18, 619–639.

Title and capacity

4.34 The transferor must have both title and capacity. The former requires that he/she has a sufficient legal interest in the property to be able to confer ownership on the transferor. The transferee of property can obtain no better title to the property than that held by the transferor[1]. Effectively this means that to be able to transfer ownership of property the transferor must be the owner of the property as, for example, a purchaser cannot acquire ownership from a seller unless the seller has the legal right of ownership to transfer to the purchaser.

1   The phrase *'nemo dat quod non habet'* is often used in this context, indicating that no transferor of property can pass on a title better than the one he has.

4.35 The second branch of this requirement refers to contractual capacity. A party entering any contract (not just relating to property), or signing a legal document, must have contractual capacity. This means in the case of a person that he must be under no legal disability (eg from age[1] or mental disorder[2]); in relation to companies or trustees it means that they are acting within the scope of the powers conferred upon them.

1   Age of Legal Capacity (Scotland) Act 1991.
2   See Adults with Incapacity (Scotland) Act 2000.

4.36 The powers of a company are set out in its Memorandum of Association which is lodged in the Register of Companies when the company is formed. The Memorandum sets out the purposes of the company and the powers that it has to act, eg to buy and sell property. Dealings not authorised by the Memorandum are referred to as *ultra vires* transactions (ie beyond their powers) and, historically, such obligations were unenforceable against the company, even though the person dealing with the company had done so in good faith. This situation was modified in 1973, and the current situation is that dealings with companies are not open to challenge on the ground that they are outwith the powers conferred in the Memorandum. This means that a third party is now able to enforce an agreement with a company even if that agreement is not authorised by the company's Memorandum of Association[1]. Similarly, third parties dealing with a company in good faith are protected even where the directors of the company exceed their powers[2], and there is no requirement upon persons transacting with companies to enquire as to the capacity of the company or its directors[3].

1   Companies Act 1985, s 35.

²   Companies Act 1985, s 35A.
³   Companies Act 1985, s 35B.

4.37   The powers of trustees will normally also be limited by the terms of the trust which they administer; however, in terms of the Trusts (Scotland) Act 1961[1] a person acting in good faith who purchases property from trustees obtains a title to the property which cannot be challenged on the ground that the trustees exceeded their powers in selling it.

[1]   S 2.

Intention to pass ownership

4.38   The transferor must intend to transfer ownership to the transferee, and not merely some lesser right, such as possession or custody.

Delivery

4.39   At common law delivery of the property was necessary to complete the transfer of ownership. This delivery could take one of three forms.

Actual delivery

4.40   Here there is either actual handing over of the property to be transferred or the transfer of control over the property. An example of the latter is the handing over of keys to a locked storage area where the goods have been placed[1].

[1]   *Liquidator of West Lothian Oil Co v Mair* (1892) 20 R 64.

Constructive delivery

4.41   This arises in situations where the goods or property being transferred are in the hands of a third party, for example, in a warehouse or store. The transfer is effected by notifying the person who has the goods in his/her hands of the change of ownership; thereafter he/she will hold the goods on behalf of the transferee rather than the transferor. For notice to a third party to effect constructive delivery two requirements must be fulfilled.

4.42   The first of these is that the custodier must be independent of the transferor and transferee. In *Anderson v McCall*[1] a company sent an order to the manager of a grain store for delivery of wheat which was being kept there by the defenders. The grain store was operated by the company and managed by one of their employees. The order was held not to have effected delivery to the defenders, the goods were effectively still on the company's premises and were still in their hands through the agency of their servant.

[1]   (1866) 4 M 765.

4.43   The second requirement is that the goods to be transferred must be identified or ascertained in some way within the warehouse or store, so that these identified goods will be held on behalf of the transferee rather than the transferor. In *Hayman & Sons v McLintock*[1], a firm which was subsequently sequestrated, transferred by means of several delivery notes a quantity of flour to Moorhead, Watson & Co. They claimed that the effect of these notes was to transfer property in the flour to them. At first instance the claim was rejected because for transfer to operate the goods had to be specific in the sense that they are capable of identification either as one total undivided quantity stored in a particular place, or at least as a specific quantity forming part of an identifiable whole. Here, in contrast, the flour was stored in a haphazard fashion, and delivery notes were issued regardless of whether there was enough flour in store to meet them, with the intention that they would be met out of any of the transferor's flour which might come into the hands of the custodier.

[1]   1907 SC 936; the decision was affirmed on appeal; see the comments of Lord McLaren at 952–953.

Symbolical delivery

4.44   In symbolical delivery transfer is effected by delivery of a symbol of the property being transferred. The example usually given is of bills of lading; these are regarded as symbols of the cargo to which they relate and delivery of a bill of lading is equivalent to actual delivery of the cargo it represents.

The continuing significance of delivery

4.45   Statutory intervention in the form of the Sale of Goods Act 1979 has dramatically reduced the importance of delivery as a requirement for transfer of ownership. The result is that the above considerations will only be relevant to those cases, primarily barter and gift, which are not covered by the Act. The major innovation of the sale of goods legislation, which is repeated in the 1979 Act, is to make it possible for ownership to transfer without delivery.

4.46   A detailed consideration of the rules set out in the 1979 Act is beyond the scope of this text. The basic rule, however, is that property in (ie ownership of) goods passes at the time intended by the parties[1]. This is supplemented by a number of rules setting out a series of presumptions as to what is to happen where the parties make no express provision about time of transfer, when their provisions are unclear, and when the goods sold have still to be manufactured or identified. The most important of these is Rule 1 which provides that in contracts for the sale of a specific item or specific ascertained goods property passes immediately on conclusion of the contract, regardless of delivery.

[1]   Sale of Goods Act 1979, s 17.

RETENTION OF TITLE

4.47   Both at common law and under the terms of the Sale of Goods Act 1979 it is possible for a seller to retain title to (ie ownership of) property notwithstanding delivery. A common law example is *Murdoch & Co Ltd v Greig*[1] where the pursuers sold a harmonium to a Mrs Taylor. The sale was subject to a suspensive condition that property in the harmonium would not pass to her until full payment was made. Mrs Taylor disappeared after paying one instalment and her furniture was sold at auction, with Greig buying the harmonium. The pursuers sought delivery of the harmonium on the grounds that Mrs Taylor had no title to it and therefore no title could pass through her to Greig. They were successful.

[1]   (1889) 16 R 396.

4.48   More recently, and in part as a form of security, suppliers of goods have inserted conditions into their contracts to the effect that they retain ownership of the goods until payment in full has been made. There was some doubt about the validity of such terms until the House of Lords' decision in *Armour v Thyssen Edelstahlwerke AG*[1]. Here the term was to the effect that: 'All goods delivered by us remain our property ... until all debts owed to us ... are settled ... Debts owed to companies, being members of our combine, are deemed to be such debts.' This was held to be a perfectly valid exercise of the right conferred by s 19(1) of the Sale of Goods Act 1979. This section allows a seller to 'reserve the right of disposal of the goods until certain conditions are fulfilled'; this reservation has the effect that 'the property in the goods does not pass to the buyer until the conditions imposed by the seller are fulfilled'.

[1]   1990 SLT 891.

POSSESSION AS AN INDICATOR OF OWNERSHIP

4.49   Because of the close connection between possession and ownership in the case of moveables, witness the common law requirement for delivery to transfer ownership: there is a legal presumption that the person in possession of moveable property is the owner of that property. This is simply a presumption which can be rebutted. In order to rebut the presumption a person claiming ownership must show:

(1)   that he/she was the owner of the property at the time possession was lost; and

(2)   that his/her possession terminated in circumstances inconsistent with an intention to part with ownership.

4.50   In *Prangnell-O'Neill v Lady Skiffington*[1] the following comment was made by Lord Hunter on the operation of the presumption[2]:

'Whether it may be easy or difficult to rebut the presumption depends on circumstances, which may vary greatly. The method by which the presumption may be rebutted has been expressed as follows: "In overcoming the presumption by proving the property, it must be shown not only that the articles once belonged to the person seeking to recover them, but that his possession terminated in such a way that the subsequent possessor could not have a right in property in them[3]." ... [This] demonstrates ... that the party seeking to rebut the presumption must surmount two obstacles.'

The case concerned a dispute about the ownership of property in a house which had been shared by the parties before the pursuer left. He failed since, on the evidence, even if he was able to prove that he had owned the items at some stage, he could not establish that he had had them in his possession immediately before he left the shared accommodation. In other words, it was not clear that the reason for his loss of possession was his leaving of the shared home, which would be a loss of possession in circumstances where the subsequent possessor could not obtain ownership.

1   1984 SLT 282.
2   1984 SLT 282 at 284.
3   Referring to *Dickson on Evidence* (3rd edn), section 150.

CHAPTER 5

Fixtures and other accessions

FIXTURES

5.1   A tenant attaches heavy machinery to the floor of his/her rented factory premises. Does he/she thereby lose ownership of the machinery to the landlord who owns the heritage? If so, does the tenant have the right to take away the machinery at the end of the lease? (It would seem harsh if the tenant lost ownership of the machinery forever and was not entitled to remove it at the end of his/her tenancy.) The answers are to be found in the law of fixtures which is therefore concerned with two questions:

(a) when does moveable property become heritable by attachment or annexation, ie in what circumstances will it be regarded as a fixture; and

(b) when does a right to remove fixtures exist/arise?

As should be clear from the above, the consequence of formerly moveable property (such as the machinery in the example) being treated as a fixture is that ownership then transfers to the owner of the heritable property to which it has been attached. The answers to these questions can therefore be of considerable consequence to the respective owners of the heritable and moveable property.

When does moveable property become heritable?

5.2   The answer to this depends on a number of factors[1]. These can be organised in a variety of ways. Here they will be organised into three groups: the degree of annexation; the degree to which the heritable property has been adapted to accommodate the moveable; and the intention of the parties.

[1]   *Stair Memorial Encyclopaedia*, vol 18, paras 579–585; Gordon 5–05 to 5–15.

Degree of annexation

5.3   In general something firmly or securely attached to heritage will be regarded as a fixture. However, it is not true that everything affixed firmly to heritage will be treated as a fixture, nor is it the case that all that is necessary to convert moveable property into a fixture is physical attachment to heritage[1].

[1]   *Scottish Discount Co v Blin* 1986 SLT 123, overruling *Cliffplant Ltd v Kinnaird* 1982 SLT 2.

5.4   Though attachment in the sense of some physical nexus (connection) between moveable and heritage is important it is not essential. Items which are simply resting on the ground may be regarded as heritable fixtures if they are substantial and if moving them would be difficult[1]. *Edinburgh & Leith Gas Comrs v Smart*[2] however suggests that the principle that an item could be regarded as heritable by virtue of its size, weight and function even though not actually attached to heritage should be applied with caution. In *Oman v Ritchie*[3] the dispute was about a wooden shed which simply rested on a slab of concrete. The shed was in sections, and so could be removed, and was about 20' by 12' in area. It was held to be a fixture, the sheriff proceeding on the basis of cases relating to assessment for rates and pointing to a principle which they had established[4]:

> 'That principle ... is that, in the case of self-contained structures or erections of the kind referred to, the fact of attachment to the ground is no longer of paramount or primary importance. The initial question now is whether the structure is, in its nature, *prima facie* heritable or moveable ... In the recent cases sectional removal, while not regarded as conclusive, has always been treated as tending to shew permanent or heritable character.'

[1]   *Niven v Pitcairn* (1823) 2 S 270; *Oman v Ritchie* 1941 SLT (Sh Ct) 13.
[2]   1918 1 SLT 80.
[3]   1941 SLT (Sh Ct) 13.
[4]   At 15–16.

5.5 In addition to the caution counselled in *Edinburgh & Leith Gas Comrs v Smart*, there are some cases where items firmly or relatively firmly attached to heritage have, nevertheless, been regarded as remaining moveable. Examples are fitted carpets, which are usually securely fixed, and paintings firmly attached to a wall by metal plates screwed into place[1]. In these cases other factors, principally the intention of the parties, have predominated in the reasoning of the courts.

[1]   *Cochrane v Stevenson* (1891) 28 SLR 848.

5.6   It has sometimes been suggested that if a moveable can be removed without damage to itself or to the heritage, then it is not a fixture. That view, however, is not supported by the leading recent authority on fixtures, *Scottish Discount Co v Blin*[1]. In 1977 and 1979 the pursuers had supplied two sets of scrap shears to Stewart, who operated a scrap business. The shears were supplied on hire purchase, with a term in the agreement to the effect that property in the shears was to remain with the pursuers until the whole price was paid. The shears were substantial, one set weighing 90–100 tonnes, the other 60–70 tonnes. In both case they were affixed to permanent foundations specially created for them and shelters were constructed for both of them. In the case of the larger set the shelter was attached to the machine itself. In 1981 Stewart became insolvent and granted a trust deed for his creditors. Shortly thereafter a dispute arose between the pursuers and the defenders, who included Stewart's trustee in bankruptcy and the holders of a standard security over the property. The question at issue was whether the shears had remained moveable, in which case they were the property of the pursuers, or whether they had become fixtures, in which case the defenders had rights over them. The Inner House, sitting as a specially convened court of seven judges, decided in favour of the defenders. Pending the outcome of the case the shears had been dismantled and removed from Stewart's premises. The fact that this '[d]ismantling and removal ... were effected without any material damage to the shears or their foundations ...'[2] did not prevent the shears being regarded as fixtures.

[1]   1986 SLT 123. For a more recent discussion see *Glasgow City Council v Cannell* 2000 SLT 1023.
[2]   1986 SLT 123 at 126B, per Lord President Emslie.

Adaptation of land to article

5.7   We have already seen this in the *Scottish Discount Co* case, where the specially and individually created foundations for the shears was one element in establishing their character as fixtures. Another example is *Christie v Smith's Executrix*[1] where the article involved was a two tonne summerhouse which rested on specially created foundations. The fact that these foundations had been specially prepared was one factor counting towards the conclusion that it was a fixture. Another factor related to the condition of the surrounding land was that the removal of the summerhouse left a ten foot gap in a fence.

[1]   1949 SC 572.

Purpose of annexation/intention of parties

5.8   The question here is as to the intention of the parties or purpose behind attaching the item to heritage. It is not the parties' subjective intentions which are relevant here, but their 'objective' intentions as disclosed by what has actually happened.

5.9   This test has been elegantly summarised as follows[1]:

'If the item viewed objectively, is, intended to be permanent and to afford a lasting improvement to the building, the thing will have become a fixture. If the attachment is temporary and is no more than is necessary for the item to be used and enjoyed then it will remain [moveable].'

[1]   *Botham v TSB Bank plc* (1997) 73 P & CR D1, per Roch LJ at D2.

5.10   For example, in *Scottish Discount Co* the extent and permanency of the fixing of the shears was a relevant factor. So too was the cost and time involved in the erection of the shears on the site and their subsequent removal, removal taking in aggregate eight days. These factors were taken as evincing an intention that the shears were to be a permanent or semi-permanent feature of the land. A further intention factor in this case was the fact that the shears were installed to allow Stewart 'to make better use of his land for the purposes of his trade'[1].

[1]   1986 SLT 123 at 136F, per Lord President Emslie.

5.11 The question as to purpose of attachment arises often in the context of what have come to be described as ornamental fixtures, ie articles intended to provide some sort of decoration or ornamentation for heritable property. The cases in this area provide examples of both types of intention noted above.

5.12 In *D'Eyncourt v Gregory*[1] two groups of items were regarded as being fixtures. The first comprised tapestries affixed to walls with wooden stretchers, a portrait and a number of carved gilt frames containing satin. They were held to be fixtures on the grounds that they were essentially a part of the building itself. The second group consisted of three carved kneeling figures on a staircase, sculptural marble vases in the hallway, a pair of three foot high stone lions in the garden and 16 stone garden seats. They were held to be heritable on the grounds that[2]:

> 'I think it does not depend on whether any cement is used in fixing these articles or whether they rest by their own weight, but upon this – whether they are strictly and properly part of the architectural design of the hall and staircase itself, as distinct from mere ornaments afterwards added.'

In this instance all the items in the second group were regarded as being part of the architectural design of the house.

[1]   (1866) LR 3 Eq 382.
[2]   At 396, per Rommilly MR.

5.13 Examples of the second type of intention, ie better use and enjoyment of the item, are *Cochrane v Stevenson*[1] and *Leigh v Taylor*[2]. In the former three paintings which were firmly affixed to a wall, which was unfinished behind the paintings, were held to have remained moveable. In the latter case tapestries attached to the walls of a house were regarded as being moveable. Both cases proceeded on the basis that the reason for attaching the items was the better enjoyment of the things themselves rather than of the house to which they were attached.

[1]   (1891) 28 SLR 848.
[2]   [1902] AC 157.

5.14 Perhaps because these types of case often involve disputes between landlord and tenant or liferenter and fiar, there is a confusion in the case law as to whether ornamental fixtures retain their moveable character or whether they become heritable but are subject to a right of removal. We will return to this point later when we consider the right of removal.

5.15   Carpets are treated by Gordon[1] as falling into the second category described above, ie they are attached to the floor for their better use and enjoyment. This seems a rather curious way of looking at this particular question, albeit that it has judicial approval. Most people would probably think the purpose of fitting a carpet was the better enjoyment of the house/ building in which it was placed. It is also usually the case that the carpet is specially adapted to the particular property and would be useless elsewhere without reduction or adaptation. In *La Salle Recreations Ltd v Canadian Camdex Investments Ltd* [2] the question was whether fitted carpets in a hotel should be regarded as fixtures. It was held that they should. Given that the carpets were fixed in the normal way, the decision turned on the purpose of annexation, and it was decided that the purpose of annexation in this case was the better and more effective use of the building as a hotel. The factors leading to this conclusion were: the unfinished plywood floor was unsuitable for hotel use; carpet and underlay resting by its own weight would not provide proper flooring; and that annexation was reasonably required for the completion of the floors as such, having regard to the character and intended use of the areas involved.

[1]   *Scottish Land Law* (2nd edn), at 5–12.
[2]   (1969) 4 DLR (3d) 549.

Conclusion

5.16   The above are some of the elements involved in deciding whether or not an article has, by attachment to heritage, become a fixture. The list is not exhaustive and it has been pointed out that 'each case must depend greatly on its own circumstances'[1]. *Scottish Discount Co* and *Christie v Smith's Executrix* also demonstrate that a wide variety of factors may exist in a single case; it will not necessarily fall simply into one of the categories outlined above. In the latter case relevant factors were the length of time the summerhouse had been up, the site preparation, the hole in the fence, the weight of the building, and on the other side, the possibility of sectional removal. As was also seen in *Oman v Ritchie* this last point is generally counted in favour of treatment as heritage given that modern building methods have made more and more small buildings removable in this way.

[1]   *Scottish Discount Co v Blin* 1986 SLT 123, per Lord President Emslie at 128J.

Constructive fixtures

5.17   These are items which are easily portable and may be quite small and light, but because of their intimate connection with or necessity for the use and/or enjoyment of heritage they are regarded as heritable and as constructive fixtures. Examples are keys, title deeds to property and detachable parts of heritable machinery which are necessary for its use. This last point was made in *Fisher v Dixon*[1], where it was said that the rule relating to fixtures[2]:

> '... not only assigns to the heir the larger machines, but such smaller articles as, though not physically attached to these greater machines, or capable from their use of being so, form part of the general apparatus; provided they be so fitted and constructed as to belong specially to this particular machinery, and not be equally suited for any other.'

[1]   (1843) 5 D 775.
[2]   Per Lord Cockburn, at 801.

Examples of fixtures

5.18   Examples of fixtures include: the electrical system in a house, the electrical wiring down to the bulb holder, built-in cupboards, the central heating and built-in kitchens. Examples of items which remain moveable include: light bulbs, cookers (free-standing as opposed to built-in), washing machines, curtains, and, as we have seen, carpets, including fitted carpets[1].

[1]   Halliday, 30-40.

WHEN DOES A RIGHT OF REMOVAL ARISE?

5.19   In the context of right of removal the relationship between the parties involved is the most important factor, even though it is now clearly established that the relationship is irrelevant to deciding whether an article should be regarded as a fixture or not. Before discussing the possible relationships and their legal consequences two preliminary points must be made. The first of these is that a right of removal is a personal right and can be assigned by the person in whose favour it operates[1]. Because of the personal nature of the right assignation does not give rise to any difficulties of creating a security right without delivery[2].

1   *Miller v Muirhead* (1894) 21 R 658.
2   See CHAPTER 8.

5.20   The second point is that the effect of annexation is that the property which becomes a fixture belongs to the owner of the heritage, and this change of ownership persists, even if there is a right of removal, up until that right of removal is exercised. For example, if I attach machinery to rented premises in such a way that it becomes a fixture, the effect of that is to transfer ownership to the landlord as owner of the heritage, subject to my right of removal. The landlord remains owner of the machinery until I exercise my right of removal of the machinery, and on separation I am once again the owner of the machinery[1].

1   This point is famously made in the judgment of Lord Chancellor Cairns in *Brand's Trustees v Brand's Trustees* (1876) 3 R (HL) 16 at 20.

Landlord and tenant

5.21   This is the principal area in which a right to removal exists. The rationale for permitting the tenant to remove fixtures is the injustice or unfairness of giving the landlord the benefits of the tenant's efforts and machinery at no cost to him/her. In *Syme v Harvey*[1] a tenant was held to be entitled to remove glass houses and other buildings he had erected from a nursery garden which he held on a lease or sub-lease. In the words of Lord Curriehill[2]:

'... it would be a monstrous hardship if the effect of the tenant's making such an erection for his own use, during his own occupation, were to deprive him of those articles belonging to himself, which he placed in the ground for his own temporary accommodation only, and give it to the landlord without any obligation on him to compensate the tenant.'

1   (1861) 24 D 202.
2   At 212.

5.22   This right of removal can be exercised both at the end of the tenancy, or within a reasonable period thereafter, and during the currency of the lease[1]. The right of removal can be exercised even if this will cause some damage to the heritage; however, the tenant must make good any damage so caused[2].

1   *Lloyds Bowmaker Ltd v William Cook Engineering (Evanton) Ltd* 1988 SCLR 676.
2   *Spyer v Phillipson* [1931] 2 Ch 183; though the extent to which the tenant is required to restore the premises to a perfect state will vary: *Foley v Addenbrooke* (1844) 13 M & W 174.

5.23 There are two particular types of fixture worth mentioning: ornamental fixtures and agricultural fixtures.

Ornamental fixtures

5.24 In general this type of fixture is removable. In *Spyer v Phillipson*[1] a tenant was held to be entitled to remove expensive antique wooden panelling which he had put up in his flat even though some minor structural alterations had been carried out to the premises to allow for the incorporation of the panelling[2]. In contrast, if the fixture is essentially part of the building or forms part of the architectural design of the building there will be no right of removal. That was the decision in *D'Eyncourt v Gregory*[3] which we have already discussed, though its correctness was doubted in *In re De Falbe*[4].

1   [1931] 2 Ch 183.
2   In *In re De Falbe* [1901] 1 Ch 523, removal of tapestries fixed to the wall with wooden battens was allowed.
3   (1866) LR 3 Eq 382.
4   [1901] 1 Ch 523.

5.25 While the cases mentioned above by and large treat ornamental fixtures as fixtures in respect of which a right of removal exists, there is a certain ambiguity in the reported judgments. In some cases there are suggestions that these items are, despite annexation, to be regarded as moveable throughout. This was the majority view in *Leigh v Taylor*[1]. The different approaches give rise to the same conclusion in the case of the landlord/tenant relationship, ie that the tenant is entitled to remove the fixture. However in other relationships the view taken of so-called 'ornamental fixtures' will be important. In relationships where there is no right of removal, or a less extensive right of removal than exists in the landlord/tenant relationship, the approach taken will make a real difference to the final destination of the 'ornamental fixture'. For example, as we will see below, the seller of heritable property has no right to remove a fixture in a question with the purchaser. If an ornamental fixture is viewed as remaining moveable then, clearly, the seller would be entitled to keep it. If, on the other hand, it is regarded as a fixture the purchaser will be entitled to it.

1   [1902] AC 157; this was the appeal to the House of Lords of *In re De Falbe*.

Agricultural fixtures[1]

5.26   These are regulated by the Agricultural Holdings (Scotland) Act 1991. The legislation covers agricultural holdings, which are defined as a lease of land for agriculture as part of a trade or business. A tenant in an agricultural holding has, with two exceptions, the right to remove any machinery, engine, fencing or other fixture which he/she has added to the property and also to remove any building he/she has erected. The right of removal exists during the currency of the tenancy and for six months, or such longer period as may be agreed, after the end of the tenancy. Any fixtures or buildings added as a result of an obligation on the tenant to replace something belonging to the landlord are excluded from the right of removal, as are any buildings in respect of which compensation is payable by the landlord[2]. To be entitled to compensation for buildings the tenant must generally have given the landlord notice before erection; if notice has not been given then no compensation is payable and the building can be removed. Compensation may also be available for improvements other than buildings, in which the right to compensation co-exists with a right of removal. In such cases the tenant will have to choose between compensation and removal.

1   Gill, *Law of Agricultural Holdings in Scotland* (3rd edn), ch 9.
2   Agricultural Holdings (Scotland) Act 1991, s 18(1).

5.27   A further restriction is that the right can only be exercised by a tenant who has paid his/her rent and fulfilled the other obligations of the lease. The tenant must also give one month's notice of the intention to exercise the right; notice must be given one month before the earlier of the date when it is intended to exercise the right or the date of termination of the lease[1]. On receipt of the notice the landlord can serve a counter-notice electing to purchase the building or fixture. The counter-notice must be served within one month of receipt of the initial notice[2]. In exercising the right of removal the tenant must not do avoidable damage to the property and must make good any damage caused[3].

1   Agricultural Holdings (Scotland) Act 1991, s 18(2).
2   Agricultural Holdings (Scotland) Act 1991, s 18(3).
3   Agricultural Holdings (Scotland) Act 1991, s 18(4).

Heir and executor

5.28   The division of property into heritable and moveable is now much less important than it was formerly in the context of succession and possible disputes between heir and executor. The executor enjoys no right of removal as against the heir.

Purchaser/seller

5.29   The general principle is that when a purchaser agrees to buy a house they are entitled to all of the fixtures on the property at the time of that agreement[1] and the seller will have no right to remove anything which is a fixture unless there is specific agreement to this effect in the missives. In practice, and for the avoidance of doubt, missives normally make provision for the transfer of certain fixtures, such as fitted kitchens, as well as moveable items such as fitted carpets. Examples of cases involving purchasers and sellers are *Cochrane v Stevenson*[2] and *Christie v Smith's Executrix*[3], both of which we have already discussed.

1   Ie the date of conclusion of missives, see CHAPTER 17; *Cochrane v Stevenson* (1891) 18 R 1208.
2   (1891) 28 SLR 848.
3   1949 SC 572.

Contractual agreement

5.30   Parties may agree that one of them is to have a right of removal. An example would be missives which conferred on the seller the right to remove a fixture which otherwise he/she would not have.

RIGHTS OF REMOVAL AND THIRD PARTIES

5.31   As we have already noted the right or removal is a personal right, and is therefore only available against the other party in the obligation, for example the landlord. The right of removal will not prevail against anyone who acquires a right in the heritable property including the fixtures before the right of removal is exercised. Such a situation might arise, for example, where a heritable creditor realised his/her security before the right of removal was exercised[1].

[1]   As happened in *Scottish Discount Co v Blin* 1986 SLT 123.

5.32   The property consequences of accession to heritage as a fixture cannot be avoided or regulated by contract, even when no third party is involved. That this is the case is illustrated in *Shetland Islands Council v BP Petroleum Development*[1]. A dispute arose about the amount of rent or payment due by the defenders for use of the pursuers land. For the purposes of calculating the rent or other payment it had to be decided who was the owner of the buildings and other fixtures attached to the land. The defenders contended that the fixtures did not belong to the pursuers as owners of the land, but rather to a pipeline group including the defenders as a result of an agreement between his group and the pursuers. This argument was rejected and it was held that no agreement between the parties could alter the property consequences of the operation of the law of fixtures[2].

[1]   1990 SLT 82.
[2]   Per Lord Cullen, at 94G–K.

OTHER INSTANCES OF ACCESSION

Growing crops[1]

5.33   These are regarded as being heritable as being *partes soli*, subject, traditionally, to two exceptions which are important if the land is occupied by someone other than the owner, for example, a tenant. The first concerns trees, shrubs, etc grown as part of a nursery business which are regarded as moveable. The second exception covers annual crops and the first season's crop of hay, which were also regarded as moveable. This second exception was thrown into doubt by the decision of the Inner House in

Chalmer's Trustees v Dick's Trustees[2] where the view was expressed that crops were heritable, but subject to a right of removal on the part of a tenant. In the words of Lord Low[3]:

'... a tenant's right to reap a crop which he has sown is not properly a right of property. The crop until separation is not moveable property of the tenant ... The crop is *pars soli*, but the law recognises the right of the tenant who has sown it, to separate it from the soil, unless he has contracted not to do so.'

Since the decision it has been both approved of[4] and disapproved of[5].

1   D L Carey Miller, *Corporeal Moveables in Scots Law*, 3.04–3.08.
2   1909 SC 761.
3   At 769.
4   For example in *Trinity House of Leith v Mitchell & Rae* 1957 SLT (Sh Ct) 38.
5   For example in *McKinley v Hutchison's Trustee* 1935 SLT 62.

Accession to land[1]

5.34   It is possible for the area of land owned by a landowner to increase in size as a result of the operation of natural forces. In particular, where land adjoins a river or the sea it is possible that it will be added to by the operation of the current or the tides. Where this happens gradually the landowner will become the owner of the added land by the operation of *alluvio*. On the other hand, where a violent event, such as a flood or a storm tears an area of ground away from one property and attaches it to another, eg after washing it down or across a river, ownership of the ground will not change. Such violent upheavals are referred to as *avulsion*. One issue which has not been entirely resolved is the effect of deliberate reclamation of land. Such reclamation may be difficult in rivers for reasons discussed in CHAPTER 9. The issue is considered more fully as regards to reclamation from the sea and tidal rivers in CHAPTER 10.

1   *Stair Memorial Encyclopaedia*, vol 18, 592–594.

Accession to moveables[1]

5.35   Some aspects of this have already been dealt with in the context of industrial accession[2]. More generally the item regarded as the accessory will accede to the principal and so become the property of the owner of the principal. Bell set out three tests for establishing which item is the principal[3]:

'1. That of two substances, one of which can exist separately, the other not, the former is principal.

2. That where both can exist separately, the principal is that which the other is taken to adorn or complete.

3. That in the absence of these indications, bulk prevails; next value.' Miller expresses the view that a better view as far as the third test is concerned is to reverse the elements expressed by Bell[4].

[1]   D L Carey Miller, *Corporeal Moveables in Scots Law*, 3.19–3.22; *Stair Memorial Encyclopaedia*, vol 18, 588–591.
[2]   See CHAPTER 4.
[3]   Bell, 1298.
[4]   D L Carey Miller, *Corporeal Moveables in Scots Law*, 3.19.

5.36   For proprietary consequences to follow accession good or bad faith is irrelevant, all that is needed is a more or less permanent attachment or connection between the two items involved. Finally, in the case of paintings, the finished article belongs to the painter, rather than the paint acceding to the canvas[1]. Other instances of accession to moveable property in the form of *specificatio* and other original forms of acquisition of ownership have already been considered in CHAPTER 4.

[1]   Erskine, II, i, 15.

CHAPTER 6

Incorporeal moveable property

INTRODUCTION

6.1 As we saw in CHAPTER 1, incorporeal property has no physical existence and consists entirely of legal rights. In the context of moveable property these rights can come into existence in a variety of ways. Firstly, by operation of law. Examples of this include the right to compensation for negligently caused injury (arising under the law of delict), rights to aliment, and copyright. Secondly, by agreement. Rights under contracts are examples of this; more specific instances would be the policyholder's rights under an assurance policy and the rights of a hirer under a hire-purchase agreement. Thirdly, rights can arise by virtue of court decree, for example the right to recover money after a court judgment in your favour.

TRANSFER OF RIGHTS

6.2 Certain types of incorporeal right are not transferable; these are rights which are personal to the individual enjoying them. Examples are rights involving *delectus personae*, occupancy rights under the Matrimonial Homes (Family Protection) (Scotland) Act 1981, alimentary rights (eg the rights of financial support enjoyed by children), and rights to various benefits. Conditional rights, for example the rights of a beneficiary under a will where the testator is still alive (known as a *spes successionis*), can be transferred, even though the right may never fully come into existence.

6.3   Transfers of incorporeal rights are effected by assignation followed by delivery and intimation to the debtor. The person making the transfer is described as the cedent, with the person in whose favour it is made being the assignee. The person in whose favour the rights involved exist is described as the creditor in the obligation, the person against whom the rights are enforceable being the debtor.

6.4   We will now consider the various elements required for an effective transfer.

FORM OF ASSIGNATION

6.5   At common law no special form of words is required to effect a transfer. All that is needed is that the words used must be sufficient to indicate a present intention to transfer the property and any directions or authority contained in the deed must be sufficient, if put into effect, to transfer the property.

6.6   In *Carter v McIntosh*[1] the assignation was in the form of a direction to trustees to pay the beneficiary's interest under the trust to a third party. Lord Justice Clerk Inglis expressed the view that[2]:

> '... if anything is settled in the law of Scotland, it is that no words directly importing conveyance are necessary to constitute an assignation, but that any words giving authority or directions, which if fairly carried out will operate a transference, are sufficient to make an assignation, and, therefore, there is no doubt that we have here an assignation.'

[1]   (1862) 24 D 925.
[2]   At 933.

6.7   In *Brownlee v Robb*[1] the assignation was in the form: 'I Joseph Robb hand over my life Policy to my Daughter Elizabeth Scott Robb now wife of George Brownlee, Dairyman, Bonnyfield.' This was held to operate as a valid assignation: it, taken with the surrounding circumstances, indicated an intention to transfer the policy.

[1]   1907 SC 1302.

6.8   Any assignation should be in writing, though it need take no special form. There are statutory provisions which provide specific forms of words to be used in assignations, though there is no legal requirement to use these styles[1]. Other legislation deals with specific types of property, for example, the Policies of Assurance Act 1867 whose provisions are mandatory and the Stock Transfer Act 1963 (dealing with shares in companies) whose provisions are optional.

[1]   Transmission of Moveable Property (Scotland) Act 1862.

6.9   Before a cedent can confer an effective assignation in favour of the assignee, he/she must have title to the property being assigned.

DELIVERY

6.10   To be effective an assignation must be delivered to the assignee. Delivery, however, only confers on the assignee a personal right against the cedent; in order to obtain a real right the assignation must be intimated to the debtor. The consequences of this are that in the period between delivery and intimation the right of the assignee can be defeated by a subsequent assignation, provided that the later assignee intimates and so obtains a real right first. For example if Philo Vance assigns his rights under an insurance policy to Miles Archer on 1 March and Miles does not tell the insurance company until 30 March, his rights in the policy will be defeated if Philo assigns the rights in the same policy to Sam Spade on 3 March and Sam tells the insurance company on 16 March. In that case Sam will have acquired a real right in Philo's interest under the policy, and Miles will be left with a right of action against Philo, ie a personal right.

6.11   A further consequence is that the debtor is entitled to pay the cedent and therefore discharge the debt before intimation[1]. If this happens after an assignation has been made it leaves the assignee with a worthless right since the corresponding obligation has been discharged. Here again the assignee would have a personal right against the cedent.

[1]   *Drummond v Muschet* (1492) M 843.

INTIMATION

6.12   The importance of intimation in conferring a real right in the property transferred has already been established. Section 2 of the Transmission of Moveable Property (Scotland) Act 1862 prescribes two forms of effecting intimation. The first is by delivery by a Notary Public of a certified copy of the assignation and completion by him/her of a certificate of intimation. The second is the sending by post of a certified copy of the assignation by the assignee or his/her agent together with the debtor's written acknowledgement thereof. Sections 5 and 6 of the Policies of Assurance Act 1867 set out a form of intimation to be used in the transfer of insurance policies and impose a duty on insurance companies to acknowledge receipt of intimation.

6.13   Intimation is effective from its date; and the date of intimation, rather than the date of assignation, is the date by which competing claims will be determined. In other words if the same right has been assigned twice, it is the assignation which is intimated earlier which will prevail, rather than the assignation which is earlier.

6.14   As well as a notice of assignation the law considers a number of other activities or situations as being equivalent to intimation. These include: diligence by the debtor against the assignee proceeding on the basis of the assignation; recording of an assignation of a heritable right in the General Register of Sasines or Land Register; and payment by the debtor to the assignee[1].

[1]   *Livingston v Lindsay* (1626) M 860.

EFFECT OF ASSIGNATION

6.15   The effect of a properly completed duly delivered and intimated assignation is to divest the cedent of his/her rights and invest the assignee in his/her place, ie the assignee replaces the cedent as the beneficiary of the right.

6.16   In this process, however, the assignee obtains no better right against the debtor than the cedent had, so that any defence or objection available to the debtor to resist a claim by the cedent will be available against the assignee. An example of this is the case of *Scottish Widows Fund v Buist*[1]. A policy of assurance was take out by a certain Moir with the pursuers. One of the conditions of the policy, which was repeated on the proposal form, was that the policy would be void if there was an untrue statement regarding the health of the assured. The policy was issued and then assigned to the defenders. Moir later died and the defenders applied for payment. The pursuers resisted this and raised an action for reduction of the policy on the grounds that Moir's statements regarding his health made in the proposal form were untrue:

'... Mr Moir had represented himself to be a man of temperate habits, and one who had never suffered from any but slight and childish complaints, while in point of fact he was addicted to drink, and had suffered severely from suppuration and other serious diseases; that the said diseases were amongst those which tend to shorten life; and their tendency in this direction was greatly aggravated by habits of dissipation such as those in which Mr Moir indulged, and which ultimately caused his death.'

He had died of otorrhea, disease of the internal ear, and suppurative arachnitis. Part of the defence to the pursuers' action was that breach of the conditions of the policy was not pleadable against onerous assignees. This was rejected by Lord President Inglis[2]:

'... in a personal obligation, whether contained in a unilateral deed or in a mutual contract, if the creditor's right is sold to an assignee for value, and the assignee purchases in good faith, he is nevertheless subject to all the exceptions and pleas pleadable against the original creditor.'

[1]   (1876) 3 R 1078.
[2]   At 1082.

6.17 In cases like this however, insurance companies may be barred from relying on such a defence if they continued to accept premiums in full knowledge of the defect in the assignee's right and without notifying him/her of the defect. This point was made, but did not assist the assignees, in *Scottish Equitable Life Assurance Society v Buist*[1], a case which shed further light on Mr Moir's health problems. An action for reduction of a policy granted to Moir was raised on the grounds that false statements had been made in the proposal form despite the terms of the form that any policy granted would be void if any matter was not stated fairly thereon. Reduction was granted on the grounds of false statements as to (1) general habits in the matter of sobriety and temperance: the proposal was made in May 1872 and during 1870 and 1871 Moir's intemperance had reached such a pitch that he had suffered bouts of delirium tremens; (2) state of health: from 1869 to 1871 Moir was suffering from syphilis, he was told on 15 May 1872 that he was suffering from the secondary or tertiary stage of this disease; and (3) as to dealings with other insurance companies: he hid the fact that he had made proposals to three other companies. One line of defence was that during the currency of the policy these material facts were known to the insurers, at least before receiving any premiums from the defenders, or at least the pursuers had been put on their enquiry by this stage, and that they were therefore barred from raising the action. The defence failed because there was no evidence to support the contentions as to the pursuers' knowledge. However, Lord President Inglis noted that[2]:

> 'If after a policy has been assigned the insurance company become aware of objections as to its validity, so clear and conclusive that the mere statement of them is enough, I do not say that there may not then be a duty of communication with those whom the company know to be interested in the policy. It would not be consistent with good faith that they should, in such circumstances, go on receiving the premiums on a policy that they intended to challenge in the end.'

[1]   (1877) 4 R 1076.
[2]   At 1081–1082.

6.18   It should be emphasised that if objections or defences are to be used against an assignee they must have been available to the debtor at or prior to the date of intimation. The subsequent actings of the cedent and defences arising subsequently will not affect the assignee's rights. In *Macpherson's JF v Mackay*[1] Macpherson assigned £1,000 from his interest in his deceased father's estate to marriage contract trustees. On his death it was discovered that he was overdrawn on this interest, though there had been more than £1,000 to his account at the date of the assignation. The marriage contract trustees claimed from the judicial factor as the trustee on the deceased father's estate. They were held entitled to claim the sum as the actings of the cedent subsequent to intimation of the assignation could not affect the assignee's claims.

[1]   1915 SC 1011.

6.19   Finally the right of the assignee will not be affected if the cedent held the property under a latent trust of which the assignee was ignorant[1]. This protection is not available in the absence of good faith on the assignee's part, if the assignation was gratuitous, or in the case of the general assignation of a bankrupt's property occurring on sequestration.

[1]   *Redfearn v Sommervails* (1813) 5 Pat App 707.

CHAPTER 7

Intellectual property

INTRODUCTION

7.1 Intellectual property law now covers a wide variety of rights, going beyond products of human imagination and invention. It extends certainly to these types of product in the law of copyright and patents and the law on the protection of designs, but it also extends to trade marks, confidential information and interests protected by passing off. The focus in this chapter will be on copyright, patents and trade marks.

7.2 Although intellectual property rights are a type of incorporeal property, they differ from traditional types of this property in a number of significant ways:
(a) Traditional incorporeal property is debt-based; intellectual property rights are not.
(b) Most intellectual property rights are created and regulated by statutory provisions.
(c) Traditional incorporeal property rights consist of a debt/obligation owed by one person to another; intellectual property rights are rights to prevent others from undertaking certain activities.
(d) Most intellectual property rights are governed by international agreements, and in some cases, eg patents, the rules are the same throughout Europe; others, such as trade marks, have been harmonised inside the European Union.
(e) The property underlying intellectual property rights, unlike most types of property, is non-rivalrous. What this means is that more than one

person can enjoy it at the same time. For example, if I own a patent for a motorised ice cream cone[1] and have made one for my own use, you can copy it and this does not affect my use or enjoyment of my own cone. By contrast, if I own a pencil, only I can use it, and if someone else is using it I cannot.

[1]   See US Patent 5,971,829.

COPYRIGHT

7.3   The law of copyright is largely contained in the Copyright, Designs and Patents Act 1988 (CDPA 1988)[1]. Copyright confers the right on an author or producer of a literary or artistic work (broadly defined) to prohibit certain activities, such as copying the work or translating it into another language. It is important to remember that what is protected by law is the way in which the creator of the work has expressed him/herself, not the idea lying behind the work; anyone is therefore free to write a novel involving a private detective, a jewel encrusted bird of prey and a *femme fatale* provided they do not simply copy out *The Maltese Falcon*. Unlike other forms of intellectual property right, no formalities are necessary to bring copyright into existence; it arises as soon as the work is recorded in some permanent form, eg writing down a story. For example, if a student makes a verbatim transcript of a lecturer's comments in the course of a lecture this creates copyright in the lecture. The copyright belongs in this case to the lecturer who has created the copyright work rather than to the student who has merely recorded it.

[1]   Substantially amended by the Copyright and Related Rights Regulations 2003 (SI 2003/2498) implementing Directive 2001/29/EC on the harmonisation of certain types of copyright and related rights in the information society [2001] OJ L 167/10.

What is covered by copyright?

Original literary, dramatic, musical or artistic works

LITERARY WORKS

7.4 These are defined as: 'any work, other than a dramatic or musical work which is written, spoken, or sung'[1] and specifically include computer programs. As with all the other categories, the work must be original. The threshold for originality is not particularly high and simply requires that it has not been copied from any source. Similarly, the description of this category as literary works could be misleading; the work need have no literary pretensions and copyright has been enjoyed under this category for a football pools coupon[2], a list of horses[3], and the instructions for use of a herbicide[4]. Before a work can enjoy protection it will need to be relatively substantial. In *Francis, Day & Hunter v Twentieth Century Fox Corporation Ltd*[5] it was held that the song title 'The Man Who Broke the Bank at Monte Carlo' was not substantial enough to enjoy copyright protection. In addition, obscene works will not enjoy protection[6].

[1]   CDPA 1988, s 3.
[2]   *Ladbroke v William Hill* [1964] 1 WLR 273.
[3]   *Weatherby & Sons v International Horse Agency and Exchange Ltd* [1910] 2 Ch 297.
[4]   *Elanco Products Ltd v Mandops (Agricultural Specialists) Ltd* [1979] FSR 46.
[5]   [1940] AC 112. But see the comments in *Shetland Times Ltd v Wills* 1997 SLT 669. See also *Scottish Daily Record and Sunday Mail Ltd v News Group Newspapers Ltd* 1998 SLT 1411.
[6]   See *Glyn v Weston Feature Films Ltd* [1916] 1 Ch 261, compared with *Re Masterman's Application* [1991] RPC 89.

DRAMATIC WORKS

7.5 As well as plays this category also includes works of dance or mime[1], but not game show formats which have been held to have insufficient fixed content to enjoy protection[2].

[1]   CDPA 1988, s 3.
[2]   *Green v Broadcasting Corporation of New Zealand* [1989] RPC 700, concerning 'Opportunity Knocks'. For a discussion of this case and its aftermath see S Lane, 'Format Rights in Television Shows: Law and the Legislative Process', (1992) 13 *Stat L Rev* 24.

MUSICAL WORKS

7.6 These are works consisting of music, excluding any words or actions intended to be spoken, sung or performed with the music[1]. One consequence of this definition is that a song will involve two copyrights, one in the music and another in the words as a literary work.

[1]   CDPA 1988, s 3.

ARTISTIC WORKS

7.7 These include graphic works (including paintings, drawings, maps, engravings, etchings, etc), photographs or sculpture or collage, regardless of artistic quality. Also included are buildings and models for buildings and 'works of artistic craftsmanship'[1].

[1]   CDPA 1988, s 4; *Vermaat and Powell v Boncrest Ltd* [2001] FSR 5.

OWNERSHIP OF WORKS IN THIS GROUP

7.8 Regardless of the type of work involved the owner of the copyright will be the person creating the work, unless this is done in the course of employment when the employer will normally own the work produced. Copyright lasts for 70 years from the end of the calendar year in which the author dies.

Sound recordings, films, and broadcasts[1]

7.9 A sound recording is a recording of sounds[2] or recording of a musical, literary or dramatic work, regardless of medium or method by which sounds are produced or reproduced.

[1]   CDPA 1988, ss 5A and 6.
[2]   For example the birdsong broadcast before Radio 5 came on air.

7.10 A film is defined as a recording on any medium from which a moving image may be produced. This definition includes film in the traditional sense as well as digital files containing information which will produce a moving image on screen.

7.11 Broadcast means an electronic transmission of visual images, sounds or other information. The transmission must either be for simultaneous reception by members of the public or at a time determined solely by the person making the transmission. It includes cable, satellite and traditional terrestrial transmissions. Certain internet transmissions are excluded from this definition, for example, transmissions where the time of transmission is determined by the person receiving it.

7.12 For the first two of these the author will be the person making arrangements for the production of the recording/film. For broadcasts the author will be the person making the broadcast. For films and sound recordings copyright lasts, in general, for 70 years from the end of the year of release; for the others the copyright period is 50 years from the end of the year in which the work was first shown.

Typographical arrangement of published works[1]

7.13 This is designed to protect the form rather than the substance of a printed work, in other words it protects the arrangement of the text on the page. Copyright lasts 25 years from the date of publication.

[1]   CDPA 1988, ss 1(1)(c) and 8; *Newspaper Licensing Agency Ltd v Marks & Spencer plc* [2001] 3 All ER 977.

Transfer of rights[1]

7.14 Copyright in fact consists of a bundle of rights. In the case of a novel, for example, this would include rights to control publication, rights to control translations, film and television rights and dramatisation rights. The owner of the copyright can transfer any or all of these rights either for the duration of the copyright or for a more limited period. This transfer can be effected by way either of a licence or an assignation.

[1]   CDPA 1988, s 90.

7.15 A licence effectively permits the licensee to do something which could otherwise be prevented by the holder of the copyright. The licence may cover one or all of the rights covered by copyright, it may be geographically limited or it may be for a particular purpose. For instance, the Walt Disney Corporation[1] may licence the reproduction of characters from its films to different companies in different countries, and within the same country to different companies for different purposes.

1   Walt Disney should not, of course, be confused with Bing Crosby.

7.16   Assignation involves the transfer of rights from the copyright owner to the assignee. Assignations of copyright must be in writing and must be signed by the copyright owner.

Moral rights

7.17   The CDPA 1988 introduced the notion of moral rights into the UK for the first time. The moral rights are:
1   The right of the author of literary, dramatic musical or artistic work or director of a film to be identified as author of that work[1]. To be effective this right must be asserted by the author, either in an assignation of the copyright or in some other notice[2]. The right is limited because of the exclusion from it of computer programs, reports of current events and works produced in the course of employment.
2   An integrity right gives the same people the right to object to derogatory treatment of the work[3]. Treatment will be derogatory if it amounts to a distortion or mutilation of the work or is otherwise prejudicial to the honour or reputation of the author or director.
3   A right not to have work falsely attributed to you[4].
4   A person who commissions a photograph or film for private and domestic purposes has the right to prevent issue of copies of the photograph or film to the public[5].
The first two and the last of these moral rights have the same duration as copyright; the third continues for 20 years from the end of the year in which the author dies.

1   Usually described as the paternity right: CDPA 1988, ss 77–79.
2   Eg the notices now commonly found in books to the effect that: 'The right of X to be identified as Author of this Work has been asserted by her in accordance with the Copyright, Designs and Patents Act 1988'.
3   CDPA 1988, ss 80–83; see the discussion in *Pasterfield v Denham & Anr* [1999] FSR 168 at 180–181.
4   CDPA 1988, s 84; see *Clark v Associated Newspapers* [1998] 1 All ER 959.
5   CDPA 1988, s 85.

Infringement of copyright[1]

Copying

7.18 The most common form of infringement involves simply copying the work protected by copyright. Before infringement will be held to have occurred, however, it must be established that the copying was of a substantial part of the protected work. This is a relative concept, and what is important is the commercial value of the part copied as much as the proportion of the protected work which it forms. For example, in *Spelling Goldberg Productions Inc v BPC Publishing Ltd*[2] it was held that copying a single frame from the television programme *Starsky and Hutch* amounted to infringement of the copyright held in the programme.

1 CDPA 1988, ss 16–26.
2 [1980] RPC 283.

7.19 It follows from what was said above about copyright protecting the way in which an idea is expressed rather than the idea itself that infringement of copyright will only take place where the form of expression in the copyright work is reproduced. It is, however, clear that the courts will sometimes go beyond this and protect more than the form of expression. It has been said that[1]:

'... United Kingdom copyright cannot prevent the copying of a mere idea but it can prevent the copying of a detailed "idea". It is a question of degree where a good guide is the notion of overborrowing of the skill, labour and judgement which went into the copyright work.'

1 *Ibcos v Barclays Mercantile Finance* [1994] FSR 275 at 302.

7.20 An illustration is *Ravenscroft v Herbert*[1]. The plaintiff was the author of a book entitled *The Spear of Destiny* which was partly historical and partly mystical and traced the history of a spear forming part of the Hapsburg treasure. The defendant, the author James Herbert, wrote a novel, *The Spear*, about a neo-Nazi group getting hold of a mystical spear which gave them great power. A prologue to each section of the book recounted the history of the spear, as described by the plaintiff. These prologues made use of some of the same language as the plaintiff's work and also had[2]:

'...the identical incidents of documented and occult history which the plaintiff used in support of his theory of the ancestry and attributes of the spear ... [Herbert] did this in order to give his novel a backbone of truth with the least possible labour to himself. In so doing he annexed for his own purposes the skill and labour of the plaintiff to an extent which is not permissible under the law of copyright.'

1   [1980] RPC 193.
2   At p207

7.21   In some cases the copying will be the result of a deliberate act, but it is no defence to claim that the copying was done subconsciously. In *Francis Day and Hunter v Bron*[1] it was held that copyright infringement could be committed unconsciously where the copier is familiar with the work which it is claimed has been copied (or must be deemed to be so, eg in the case of a well-known song) and there is substantial similarity between the two works (note that they need not be identical). If these two requirements are met a *prima facie* presumption that there has been copying will be created.

1   [1963] Ch 587, though no subconscious copying was found in this case.

Infringement by public performance or showing/playing work in public

7.22   This applies not only to recitals of literary works but performances of music, plays etc. Whether the performance is in public or not will be a matter of degree. Where the performance of a play took place in a hospital, though it was open to patients and relatives, this was not regarded as being in public[1]. In contrast, performances of music in a 'private' club to which members of the public had fairly ready access were held to be performances in public[2].

1   *Duck v Bates* (1884) 13 QBD 843.
2   *Performing Rights Society Ltd v Rangers FC Supporters Club, Greenock* 1974 SLT 151, where it was suggested that an important consideration in deciding whether the performance was in public or not was the role of copyright in preventing the use of an author's work to his/her financial disadvantage.

Infringement by making an adaptation of the work

7.23 This includes translating the work (including translations of a computer program from one programming language to another) and other format changes, such as the dramatisation of a novel and the novelisation of a film.

Infringement by communicating to the public

7.24 It is an infringement of copyright in a literary, dramatic, musical or artistic work, a sound recording or film, or a broadcast to communicate it to the public without the copyright holder's agreement. Communication to the public involves electronic transmission of the work, for example, by broadcasting or by making the work available over the internet.

Defences to infringement

7.25 As a general matter it must be remembered that if what is taken is an insignificant part of a copyright work there is no infringement. The defences set out below are relevant only where a substantial amount of the work is taken. If it were not for the existence of the defences, the taking would otherwise amount to infringement.

Temporary copies

7.26 To reflect the realities of internet use it is now specifically provided that temporary copying of a copyright work is permissible. This is restricted to situations where the copying is an integral and essential part of a technological process and the sole purpose of copying is to enable a transmission of the work in a network between third parties or a lawful use of the work. In addition the copying must have no independent economic significance[1]. This therefore makes it clear that the copying of web pages onto the RAM memory of the user's computer, which is an integral part of accessing web-based material, is permissible. What it does not clearly authorise is caching of web pages.

---

[1]   CDPA 1988, s 28A.

Fair dealing¹

7.27   It is a defence to an action for infringement of copyright to establish that the use of the copyright material amounted to fair dealing either for the purposes of non-commercial research and private study or for the purposes of review, criticism or reporting current events. An example of the last is *BBC v BSB Ltd*² in which it was held that the defence was available to BSB in respect of its use of excerpts of BBC broadcasts of the 1990 World Cup. For the defence of fair dealing for criticism or review to apply there must be some element of this in the use of the copyright material. In *Associated Newspapers Group plc v News Group Newspapers Ltd*³ the plaintiffs had a limited term copyright in letters written by the Duchess of Windsor to the Duke of Windsor and published extracts in the *Daily Mail*. The defendants somehow obtained copies of some of the letters and published them in the *Sun*. The defendants relied on the defences of fair dealing for the purposes of criticism and review and fair dealing for the purposes of reporting current events. The court expressed the view that the question of fairness probably depended, in the end, on the motive for use. They also took the view that, since the letters were written in the 1930s, there was no reporting of current events, nor was there any criticism or review[4]:

> 'They are not criticising the letters in any way, they are not reviewing them in any way, they are merely presenting them and saying: "Look at these passionate love letters between the Duke and Duchess."'

Fair dealing may permit reproduction of the whole of a work, eg a painting or photograph, for one of the authorised purposes.

¹   CDPA 1988, ss 29 and 30; see *Pro Sieben Media AG v Carlton UK Television Ltd* [1999] FSR 610; *Hyde Park Residence v Yelland* [2001] Ch 143.
²   [1991] 3 WLR 174.
³   [1986] RPC 515.
⁴   At 519.

Education¹

7.28   There is a series of defences connected with educational purposes, eg permitting non-reprographic copying for the purposes of instruction or preparation for instruction, allowing performance of works in schools and allowing copying for examination purposes.

¹   CDPA 1988, ss 32–36A.

Libraries[1]

7.29   Another set of defences permits libraries and librarians to do certain things which would otherwise infringe copyright. These include making copies for others who are engaged in non-commercial research or private study and making copies of complete works to replace items lost or damaged.

1   CDPA 1988, ss 37–41.

Public administration[1]

7.30   This covers use for the purposes of parliamentary/judicial proceedings, reports of such proceedings, etc.

1   CDPA 1988, ss 45–50.

Miscellaneous[1]

7.31   These defences permit everyday activities which would otherwise infringe copyright. They allow time-shifting (ie taping broadcasts to be watched at another time), showing broadcasts/cable programmes to an audience which has not paid (eg in a public house), taking photographs of buildings (which would otherwise infringe the architect's copyright) and making back-up copies of software.

1   CDPA 1988, ss 50A and 70.

Public interest

7.32   In addition to the defences set out above there is a residual defence which permits publication in the public interest. This is likely to be available only in a restricted number of situations because normally it will be sufficient to publish the information content of the copyright material (not protected by copyright) rather than the precise way in which the information is expressed (which is covered by copyright)[1].

1   *Ashdown v Telegraph Group Ltd* [2001] 4 All ER 666; contrast *Hyde Park Residence v Yelland* [2001] Ch 143.

Protection of technical measures

7.33   Where a copyright holder seeks to protect a copyright work by use of a technical means (eg encryption) or seeks to embed other information (eg a rights management system) within the copyright work, it is an infringement of copyright to interfere with these measures[1]. One example of this is the combination of hardware within a PlayStation console and software on game discs which only permits the console to play games which have been purchased within the same region as the console. Chipping the console to allow it to play games from other areas would on the face of it amount to interfering with a technical means used to protect a copyright work (the PlayStation game)[2].

[1]   CDPA 1988 Act, ss 296ZA and 296ZG.
[2]   *Sony Computer Entertainment v Owen* [2002] ECDR 27; *Kabushiki Kaisha Sony Computer Entertainment Inc v Ball* [2004] EWHC 1738 (Ch); but see the decision of the Tribunale di Bolzano, 31 December 2003, available at www.ipjustice.org/123103playstationdecision.html.

PATENTS

7.34   A patent allows its owner to exploit an invention for the period of patent protection, which is 20 years. It does this negatively rather than positively, that is it gives the patent holder the right to prevent anyone else from exploiting his/her invention for the duration of the patent. This is perhaps the most international of all intellectual property rights. The current law is contained in the Patents Act 1977 (PA 1977) the provisions of which are based on the European Patent Convention. Most countries in Europe are signatories to this convention which means that the rules as to what can be patented and, in principle, what counts as infringement of a patent are the same in all of these countries.

7.35   Unlike copyright, patent protection only arises once a patent has been granted following an application by the inventor. There are two principal routes for applying for a patent. An application can be made to individual national Patent Offices for a patent applying in the countries covered by these offices. For example, if an inventor wanted to obtain patents in the UK and in France, separate applications could be made to the UK and French Patent Offices. Alternatively, where the inventor wants to obtain patents in a number of countries which have signed up to the European Patent Convention an application can be made to the European

Patent Office. This application will set out the countries in which it is wished to have patent protection and, if successful, the application will result in the grant of a bundle of patents covering these countries. If the inventor also wants patent protection in the USA and Japan then separate applications would need to be made in these countries.

Requirements for patentability[1]

7.36 In order to acquire a patent the applicant must show that they have produced an invention which fulfils a number of criteria. Although it has been argued that it is enough for these criteria to be fulfilled, the courts have taken the view that, in addition, what is to be covered by the patent must be an invention, though they have not been clear on what precisely this involves[2]. The criteria to be met are that the invention must be novel, it must involve an inventive step, it must be capable of industrial application and it must not be excluded from patentability.

[1]   PA 1977, s 1.
[2]   See the comments in *Biogen Inc v Medeva plc* [1997] RPC 1.

Novelty[1]

7.37 This requires that the invention does not form part of the state of the art, which is information, products, processes, etc made available to the public *anywhere in the world* before the application is made for the patent. Making available to the public may take place in a variety of ways, for example by publication or by use in public, provided that the public use allows the public to see how the thing works. An example of public use is *Windsurfing International Inc v Tabur Marine (Great Britain) Ltd*[2] which involved a patent held by the plaintiffs for a sailboard. They claimed patent infringement against the defendants and, as often happens in patent infringement actions, the defendants responded by challenging the validity of the patent. In particular they argued that the invention was not novel. Their argument was based in part on the use of a similar device by a 12-year-old boy during his summer holidays in 1958 and 1959, well before the date of the patent. The court concluded, based on this evidence, that the invention was invalid for lack of novelty.

[1]   PA 1977, s 2.
[2]   [1985] RPC 59.

7.38 The prior disclosure must be an enabling one, ie it must allow use of the invention, though it need not be in the precise technical terms of the patent being applied for[1].

1   *Merrell Dow v Norton* [1996] RPC 422.

Inventive step[1]

7.39 The invention must involve an inventive step. That is, starting with currently available products/processes/knowledge the claimed invention must not be obvious to a person skilled in the field in which the invention is claimed.

1   PA 1977, s 3.

7.40 In the UK the assessment of inventive step is approached through a test identified in *Windsurfing International Inc v Tabur Marine (Great Britain) Ltd*. There the stages were stated to be[1]:

'The first is to identify the inventive concept embodied in the patent in suit. Thereafter, the court has to assume the mantle of the normally skilled but unimaginative addressee in the art at the priority date and to impute to him what was, at that date, common general knowledge in the art in question. The third step is to identify what, if any, differences exist between the matter cited as being "known or used" and the alleged invention. Finally, the court has to ask itself whether, viewed without any knowledge of the alleged invention, those differences constitute steps which would have been obvious to the skilled man or whether they require any degree of invention.'

1   [1985] RPC 59, at pp 73–74.

7.41 A similar approach, known as the problem and solution approach, is used by the European Patent Office. In the problem-and-solution approach, there are three main stages:
(i)   determining the 'closest prior art';
(ii) establishing the 'objective technical problem' to be solved; and
(iii) considering whether or not the claimed invention, starting from the closest prior art and the objective technical problem, would have been obvious to the skilled person[1].

1   European Patent Office Examination Guidelines, §9.8.

Industrial applicability[1]

7.42 Industrial applicability is not, in general, a problem that a patent applicant has to address; indeed it has been argued that the exclusions from patentability in s 1(2) of the 1977 Act render the requirement otiose. It has been applied in some cases, for example applications for perpetual motion machines and recently in *BRITISH TECHNOLOGY GROUP/ Contraceptive method*[2]. More recently it has been suggested that it is not enough that the invention can be made or used in industry; production must also be useful in the sense that the invention has an identifiable purpose for which there is some demand[3].

[1]   PA 1977, s 4.
[2]   [1995] EPOR 279.
[3]   *Chiron Corp v Organon Teknika (No 3)* [1996] RPC 535; *ICOS/Novel V28 seven transmembrane receptor* [2002] OJEPO 293.

7.43 Methods of treatment practised on the human or animal body are deemed not to be capable of industrial application[1].

[1]   PA 1977, s 4(2).

Exclusions from patentability[1]

Innovations classified as non-inventions

7.44 These include discoveries, scientific theories, artistic works, rules for playing games, methods of performing mental acts, computer programs and methods of presenting information. Note that these are only excluded from patentability if they consist of one of these things *as such*. This has permitted the patenting, for example, of computer programs provided that they have a 'technical effect'[2]. In considering whether the invention makes such a technical contribution the courts in the UK will consider the substance of the invention rather than the form of the claims[3].

[1]   PA 1977, s 1(2)–(4).
[2]   Eg *IBM/Computer Programs* [1999] EPOR 301.
[3]   *Hutchins' Application* [2002] RPC 8; compare with the European Patent Office approach in *Pension Benefits System Partnership* [2002] EPOR 52, HITACHI/ Auction method [2004] EPOR 55.

Inventions the publication or exploitation of which would be generally expected to encourage offensive, immoral or anti-social behaviour

7.45   The European Patent Office guidelines give as examples letter bombs and anti-personnel mines[1].

¹   Examination Guidelines, § 3.1.

Plant and animal varieties

7.46   Plants or animal varieties or any method of producing plants or animals by essentially biological process are not patentable. Note that this, in general, does not prevent the patenting of genetically engineered plants or animals[1].

¹   PA 1977, Sch A2, paras 3 and 4. See *Oncomouse/Harvard II* (1993) 1 IIC 103; *PGS/Glutamine synthetase inhibitors* [1995] EPOR 351.

Ownership of inventions

7.47   In general the person making the invention will be the owner of it. There are exceptions, however, for inventions made by employees. An invention made by an employee will belong to the employer either[1]:

(a)   if it was made in the course of the employee's normal duties or in performing duties outwith his/her normal duties which were specifically assigned to him/her and in either case the circumstances were such that an invention might reasonably be expected to result from the carrying out of these duties; or

(b)   if it was made in the normal course of the employee's duties, and because of the nature of his duties and the responsibilities arising from them he/she had a special obligation to further the interests of the employer's undertaking.

In *Harris's Patent*[2] Harris was employed as a manager by a company which manufactured valves under licence from a Swiss company. He was made redundant, but between the period of the notice of redundancy and redundancy taking effect he invented a new improved valve which he sought to patent. The employers sought to establish ownership of the invention, but their attempt was unsuccessful. Harris's duties as a manager were confined to selling the valves and were not such as might be expected to result in an invention[3].

1 PA 1977, s 39.
2 [1985] RPC 19.
3 See also *Greater Glasgow Health Board's Application* [1996] RPC 207.

Transfers of patents

7.48 Patent rights can be licensed and assigned. Any assignation must be in writing and registration of the licence or assignation in the Register of Patents is necessary to protect the rights of the assignee/licensee[1].

1 PA 1977, ss 30–33.

Infringement[1]

7.49 Infringement involves copying the item or process patented or supplying or offering to supply infringing goods. In deciding whether infringement has taken place the courts will ignore minor differences between the patent and the allegedly infringing item. Making this assessment involves the court in applying the Protocol on Interpretation of Article 69 of the European Patent Convention. Most usually in applying this Protocol the courts have adopted the so-called purposive approach set out in *Catnic Components v Hill and Smith Ltd*[2]. The approach set out in *Catnic* was further developed in *Improver Corporation v Remington Consumer Products*[3]. In that case three questions were formulated as an aid to deciding whether there has been infringement:

1 Does the variant have a material effect on the way the invention works? If yes, the variant is outwith the claim.
2 Would the fact that the variant had no material effect have been obvious at the date of publication of the patent to a reader skilled in the art? If no, the variant is outwith the claim. If yes,
3 Would the reader skilled in the art nevertheless have understood from the language of the claim that strict compliance with the primary meaning was an essential requirement of the invention? If yes, the variant is outwith the claim.

1 PA 1977, s 60.
2 [1982] RPC 183.
3 [1990] FSR 181.

7.50 The extent to which this approach accurately reflects the Protocol has been the subject of some debate[1]. It has also been pointed out that the answers to these questions are not necessarily determinative of the issue, but simply function as an aid to interpretation of the patent so as to give fair protection and reasonable certainty[2]. Recently there have been judicial comments that the *Improver* questions may not always be easy to answer or appropriate. It has now been suggested by the House of Lords that in interpreting a patent to determine whether it covers a claimed infringement there is only one compulsory question: 'what would a person skilled in the art have understood the language of the claim to mean?[3]' The focus, therefore, is on whether a person skilled in the art in which the patent is located would interpret the patent as covering the allegedly infringing article or process[4].

1   See *PLG Research v Ardon International* [1995] RPC 287.
2   *Wheatley v Drillsafe Ltd* [2001] RPC 7.
3   *Kirin-Amgen Inc & Ors v Hoechst Marion Roussel Ltd & Ors* [2004] UKHL 46, per Lord Hoffmann at para 69.
4   See also the suggestion that a decision on whether a variation was included within the protection offered by a patent is made by asking if a person skilled in the field of the patent would conclude with reasonable confidence that the patent covered the variant, *Merck & Co Inc v Generics UK* [2004] EWCA Civ 151.

7.51   Certain activities are permitted under the PA 1977 which would otherwise amount to infringement, for example, acts done privately and not for commercial purposes and acts done for experimental purposes. In addition someone who purchases an item covered by a patent has an implied licence to do things which would otherwise infringe the patent in order to repair the item[1].

1   *Solar Thomson Engineering Ltd v Barton* [1977] RPC 537; *United Wire Limited v Screen Repair Services (Scotland) Limited* [2001] FSR 24.

TRADE MARKS

7.52 Trade marks are the signs or indications that manufacturers and service providers use to distinguish and identify the source of their goods or services. They may take the form of a word or design or may be the get-up, the shape or packaging, of goods themselves. Trade marks may be protected at common law under the law of passing off, or they may be registered and protected under the Trade Marks Act 1994 (TMA 1994). In order for a trade mark to be registered it must meet certain criteria, considered below. Trade marks can be used to extend the life of other forms of intellectual property right by building up brand loyalty. An example of this is in the field of medicines where drug companies have tried, with varying degrees of success, to register colours and shapes for particular drugs. The assumption here is that once generic substitutes are available patients will continue to demand tablets which look the same as the ones they are used to[1].

[1]   Eg *Smith Kline & French's Application* [1976] RPC 511.

7.53   When a trade mark is applied for it is not applied for 'at large', that is to cover all conceivable uses of the mark; rather the application is made in respect of certain types of goods set out in an international classification system.

What is a trade mark?

7.54   A trade mark is any sign capable of being represented graphically which is capable of distinguishing the goods and services of one undertaking from those of another. The sign may consist of words, designs, letters, numerals, the shape of goods or packaging or even, in principle, a scent[1]. The requirement for graphical representation means that it must be possible to describe the mark in some way which can be recorded and with sufficient clarity that possible competitors will know what the registered mark is and when they will be likely to infringe it. This requirement means that in practice it will be very difficult if not impossible to register a scent trade mark because of the difficulty of defining the scent precisely enough[2].

[1]   For example the 'smell of fresh cut grass', case R 156/1998-2 OAMI, 2nd Board of Appeal, 11 February 1999.
[2]   *Sieckmann v DeutschesPatent und Markenamt* [2003] RPC 38.

7.55   The final requirement is that the sign is capable of distinguishing. In practice this requirement has been run together with the requirement for distinctiveness considered below. In essence capacity to distinguish means that the sign will be capable of allowing consumers to distinguish the products of one enterprise from those of another. There is a variety of reasons why a sign might not do this. It might be a commonly used descriptive word, eg soap as a trade mark for soap, or it may be a sign, such as the overall shape of a product[1], the name or image of a celebrity[2], or a promotional slogan[3] which the public are not used to regarding as having any trade mark significance[4].

1 *Linde AG TM Application* [2003] RPC 45.
2 Eg Elvis Presley on toilet paper, *Re Elvis Presley TM Application* [1999] RPC 199.
3 Case T281/02 *Norma Lebensmittelfilialbetrieb GmbH & Co AG v OHIM* (2004) 30 June.
4 *Linde AG TM Application* [2003] RPC 45.

7.56 In addition to these general requirements there is a series of further possible grounds on which the Trade Mark Registry might refuse to register a trade mark. These are divided into absolute and relative grounds for refusal.

Absolute grounds for refusal[1]

7.57 The TMA 1994 sets out a number of absolute grounds for refusal, based on the nature of the mark which it is sought to register. Each of these grounds is independent and must be separately considered where relevant. The grounds are:

(a) The sign does not fulfil the requirements for a trade mark set out above.

(b) The mark applied for is devoid of distinctive character[2]. In other words the mark will not be recognised by consumers as indicating the origin of goods or services or as distinguishing them from other goods and services.

(c) The mark applied for is indicative of kind, quality, quantity, intended purpose, value, geographical origin, time of production of goods or other characteristics of goods[3]. There is a public interest in keeping these types of sign available for other enterprises which might have a legitimate interest in using them[4]. It is possible, for example, to imagine that giving exclusive rights to one company to use a geographical name would affect other firms in the same area who might legitimately wish to use the same term. Giving exclusive rights to use the geographical indicator 'Scotch' to one whisky producer would seem, for example, unfair. Before a mark is treated as being descriptive of the goods it must evoke an immediate image of the qualities of the goods or services involved. This has led to some marks which are arguably descriptive being registered on the grounds that they do not evoke such an image, eg BabyDry for nappies[5]. More recently the courts seem to have moved away from allowing such nearly descriptive marks indicating that 'a sign must be refused registration where at least one of its possible meanings designates a characteristic of the goods or services concerned'[6].

(d) The mark applied for consists of signs which have become customary in current language or established practices of a trade or profession.

(e) The following signs cannot be registered: a shape resulting from nature of goods; a shape needed to achieve technical effect; a shape giving substantial value to goods[7].

(f) A trade mark is not to be registered if it is contrary to public morality or public policy[8]; of such nature as to deceive the public, eg as to nature or geographical origin of goods; if its use is prohibited by law; or where application is made in bad faith.

The objections set out in (b) to (d) above are largely based on the inability of the sign to function as a trade mark, eg because it will simply be taken as a description of the goods or their origin. Where the mark has been used it is possible to overcome these objections by showing that the mark has, in fact, become distinctive. In other words, a significant proportion of the public regard it as performing the trade mark function of distinguishing the goods or services of one enterprise from those of another.

[1]   TMA 1994, s 3.
[2]   Eg *Procter & Gamble's Trade Mark Application* [1999] RPC 673; *AD2000 Trade Mark* [1997] RPC 168
[3]   *EUROLAMB Trade Mark* [1997] RPC 279
[4]   Eg *Koninklijke KP Nederland BV v Benelux Merkenbureau* [2004] ETMR 57.
[5]   *Procter & Gamble v OHIM* [2002] RPC 17.
[6]   *OHMI v Wrigley* [2004] RPC 45, § 32.
[7]   *Philips Electronics NV v Remington Consumer Products* [2003] RPC 2.
[8]   *Ghazilian's TM Application* [2002] RPC 33 (application for trade mark 'Tiny Penis' for clothing); *Jesus TM Applications*, UK Patent Office, 20 July 2003, available at http://www.patent.gov.uk/tm/legal/decisions/2003/o21103.pdf.

Relative grounds for refusal[1]

7.58   As well as absolute grounds for refusal, the TMA 1994 sets out relative grounds for refusal, based on a comparison between the mark applied for and existing trade marks. These relative grounds are:

(a) Both the mark applied for and the goods/services in respect of which the application is made are identical with an earlier trade mark.

(b) Granting the application would give rise to the likelihood of confusion on the part of the public, including likelihood of association with earlier trade mark, because either:
   (i) the earlier trade mark and the mark applied for are identical and the goods/services they cover are similar; or
   (ii) similarity between the mark applied for and the earlier trade mark and identity/similarity of goods/services.
   Assessments of similarity of marks and goods and possibility of confusion are carried out on the same basis as in the case of infringement and are considered below[2].
(c) Where the mark applied for is identical or similar to an earlier trade mark, but the goods/services are not similar, registration is to be refused if the earlier trade mark has a reputation in the UK and use of the later mark without due cause would take unfair advantage of/be detrimental to the distinctive character or repute of the earlier mark. Again this ground is mirrored in the provisions on infringement and will be considered more fully there.
(d) Where use in the UK of the mark applied for is liable to be prevented by any rule of law (in particular passing off) protecting unregistered trade marks/signs or by virtue of earlier intellectual property right, eg copyright[3].

[1]   TMA 1994, s 5.
[2]   See PARA 7.60FF.
[3]   Eg the potential situation discussed in *R Griggs Group Ltd v Evans* [2003] EWHC 2914 (Ch) where the copyright in a sign to be registered as a trade mark may not belong to the person seeking the registration.

Trade mark infringement

7.59   A registered trade mark will be infringed by:

Use of an identical sign on identical goods or services in the course of trade[1]

This type of infringement should be relatively straightforward to establish. However, one potential defence which might be open here is that the use of the mark is not a trade mark use. This argument was raised by Mr Reed, a street trader, sued by Arsenal FC for infringing their trade marks, 'Arsenal' and the artillery logo, which they had registered for hats, scarves, etc. The trader argued that use of the word Arsenal on items sold by him did not amount to infringement of these marks because they were not being used as trade marks, ie to indicate the origin of the goods. Instead, he argued, they were being used as a badge of allegiance. This argument was ultimately unsuccessful, with both the European Court of Justice and the English Court of Appeal taking the view that some people who saw Mr Reed's goods would think that they originated from Arsenal FC[2].

[1]   TMA 1994, s 10(1).
[2]   *Arsenal v Reed* [2002] ECR I-10273; *Arsenal v Reed* [2003] 2 CMLR 25.

Confusingly similar marks

7.60   Likelihood of confusion on the part of public, including association with the registered trade mark arising from either:
(i)   use of an identical sign for similar goods/services; or
(ii)   use of a similar sign on similar or identical goods/services[1].

[1]   TMA 1994, s 10(2).

7.61   The questions of similarity and likelihood of confusion are to be assessed separately. There are two possible issues of similarity. First there is the issue of similarity of signs. This has to be assessed taking a global view and taking account of the imperfect recollection of consumers who are not always able to have both signs in front of them for comparison purposes. The similarity may be visual or it may be aural; an example of the latter is a case where the aural similarity of Gerri and Kerry was held to be established[1].

[1]   *Gerolsteiner Brunnen GmbH v Putsch GmbH* [2004] ETMR 40.

7.62   The second element is similarity of goods. Factors relevant to assessment of similarity include the respective users of the goods or services, the trade channels through which the goods or services reach the market and the placement of goods in self-service outlets where they are sold in this way (eg are the goods placed together in supermarkets?)[1].

[1]   *British Sugar v James Robertson & Sons Ltd* [1996] RPC 281; see also *Canon Kabushiki Kaisha v Metro-Goldwyn-Mayer Inc* [1999] RPC 117.

7.63   In *Baywatch Production Co Inc v The Home Video Channel*[1] it was held that there was no similarity for this purpose between the TV shows *Baywatch* and *Babewatch*. The latter was described as follows:

'After a brief introduction reminiscent of the opening scenes of *Baywatch*, the *Babewatch* programme contains sexually explicit material, including scenes of oral and group sex.'

¹   [1997] FSR 22.

7.64   Although UK courts seem to have treated the two aspects of similarity as separate issues, the European Court of Justice has taken the position that they are interdependent and that a lesser degree of similarity between goods and services can be overcome by a greater degree of similarity between the marks[1].

¹   *Canon Kabushiki Kaisha v Metro-Goldwyn-Mayer Inc* [1999] RPC 117.

7.65   Finally, the court will have to assess whether there is a likelihood of confusion. What has to be decided is whether there is confusion in the sense that consumers will think that goods or services are the responsibility of the owner of the trade mark which is allegedly being infringed, rather than whether they make any other kind of association between the two marks. In *Wagamama v City Centre Restaurants plc*[1], it was decided that the names 'Wagamama' and 'Rajamama' applied to restaurants were sufficiently similar as to give rise to the likelihood of confusion. More generally it was decided that the confusion caused had to be confusion as to the origin of goods or services, and that the provisions of the TMA 1994 for infringement where similarity gave rise to the likelihood of an association between goods and services did not go beyond this and create broader grounds for infringement[2].

¹   [1995] FSR 713.
²   This was the approach adopted by the European Court of Justice in *Sabel BV v Puma AG, Rudolf Dassler Sport* [1998] RPC 199.

7.66   In taking decisions about the likelihood of confusion, it has been suggested that where the registered mark is very distinctive there is a greater likelihood of confusion than where this is not the case. Although this might seem to be counterintuitive it has been explained that where a mark is highly distinctive consumers might accept a similar mark without question because they will not look closely at it, whereas if a mark is more descriptive consumers will pay more attention to relatively small differences between marks[1].

¹   *Reed Executive plc v Reed Business Information Ltd* [2004] RPC 40, per Jacobs LJ at paras 83–86.

Taking advantage of a trade mark with a reputation

7.67 This involves use of an identical or similar sign in the course of trade on dissimilar goods or services where the trade mark has reputation in UK and its use is without due cause and is likely to be detrimental to or take unfair advantage of the distinctive character or repute of the trade mark[1].

[1]   TMA 1994, s 10(3).

7.68 The first issue regarding this type of infringement is what is required to establish that a mark has a reputation? In *General Motors Corporation v Yplon SA*[1] it was said that, in order for a trade mark to have a reputation it must be known by a significant part of the public concerned by the products or services covered by that trade mark. Relevant factors will be the market share held by the trade mark, the intensity, geographical extent and duration of its use, and the size of the investment made by the undertaking in promoting it.

[1]   [2000] RPC 572.

7.69 There is no need to establish possible confusion on the part of members of the public although more is required than a simple mental association with the mark having a reputation. There must also be some clear detriment to the mark or some clear intention to take unfair advantage[1].

[1]   *Oasis Stores TM Application* [1998] RPC 631; *CA Sheimer (M) SDN BHD's TM Application* [2000] RPC 484; *GALAXY TM* Trade Marks Registry 19 May 2000 available at: http://www.patent.gov.uk/tm/legal/decisions/2000/o17900.pdf.

7.70 On the face of it, this provision only protects marks having a reputation where the goods or services to which they are applied differ from those in respect of which the reputation is enjoyed, eg using the mark VISA for condoms[1]. However, recent case law in the European Court of Justice has drawn attention to an alleged gap in protection for such marks if they cannot be protected against use on goods or services similar to those for which they enjoy a reputation[2]. The European Court of Justice has therefore decided that the protection also extends to goods or services which are similar to or identical with those protected by the mark having a reputation[3].

[1]   *CA Sheimer (M) SDN BHD's TM Application* [2000] RPC 484.
[2]   Although it may be difficult to imagine a case where such use would not cause confusion and therefore infringe under s 10(2).

3   *Davidoff & Cie SA v Gofkid Ltd* [2003] FSR 28, *Adidas-Salomon AG v Fitnessworld Trading Ltd* [2004] FSR 21.

Infringement of well-known marks

7.71   This involves use of a trade mark similar or identical, as a whole or in an essential part, to a well-known trade mark in relation to identical or similar goods/services, provided that use is likely to cause confusion[1]. Unlike the previous forms of infringement, this protects trade marks which are not registered in the place in which the infringement is alleged to have taken place. For example, it would allow the owner of a trade mark registered in the US which was well known but unregistered in the UK to protect their mark.

1   TMA 1994, s 56(2).

Infringing use

7.72   Infringement as defined above can take place by use of a sign similar or identical to the trade mark in a variety of ways, including:

(a)   Affixing a sign to goods or their packaging.

(b)   Offering or exposing goods for sale, putting them on the market or stocking them for these purposes under the sign or supplying services under the sign.

(c)   Importing/exporting goods under the sign. This ability to object to the importing of trade marked goods does not apply where the goods concerned have been put on the market inside the European Economic Area by or with the consent of the trade mark proprietor[1]. For example, if Christian Dior puts one of its perfumes on sale in Greece where it sells for a low price, they cannot object if an importer in the Netherlands buys the product in Greece, imports it into the Netherlands and sells it below the normal price there[2].

(d)   Using the sign on business papers or advertising[3]. This is subject to exceptions which broadly cover spare parts and comparative advertising[4].

In *Trebor Bassett Ltd v The Football Association*[5] the (English) FA sought to prevent Trebor Bassett from issuing cards featuring England footballers wearing shirts featuring the three lions logo which is a trade mark owned by the FA. It was held that the appearance of the trade mark as an incident of the photograph was not 'use' for the purposes of trade mark infringement. Trebor Bassett could not be said to have affixed the FA's trade mark to their goods or to have put the goods on the market under that sign.

¹   Eg *Zino Davidoff AG v A & G Imports Ltd* [2002] All ER (EC) 55. What is involved in putting goods on the market is discussed in Case C-16/03, *Peak Holding AB v Axolin-Elinor AB*, ECJ, 30 November 2004.

²   Though special restrictions apply to the import of medicines: for an example see *Boehringer Ingelheim KG v Swingward* [2004] EWCA Civ 129.

³   TMA 1994, s 10(4).

⁴   TMA 1994, s 10(6).

⁵   [1997] FSR 211. Though see *Football Association v Panini UK Ltd* [2004] FSR 1 for a successful claim based on copyright.

Defences to infringement

7.73 The principal defences to an infringement action are:

(a) The allegedly infringing trade mark is also registered[1].

(b) The use of the mark is a use, in accordance with honest practices in business/commercial matters, of:
   (i) the user's own name/address;
   (ii) indications of kind, quality, quantity, intended purpose, value, geographical origin, time of production of goods or other characteristics of goods[2];
   (iii) a trade mark to indicate the intended purpose of a product or service (especially, for example to indicate which brands spare parts will fit)[3].

(c) There will be no infringement of a registered trade mark by use of an earlier unregistered trade mark which applies only in particular locality, providing that this use is protected by passing off[4].

¹   TMA 1994, s 11(1).

²   See *Bravado Merchandising Services Ltd v Mainstream Publishing (Edinburgh) Ltd* [1996] FSR 205; *Allied Domecq Spirits and Wine Ltd v Murray McDavid Ltd* [1997] FSR 864.

³   TMA 1994, s 11(2); Case C-63/97 *BMW v Deenik* [1999] ETMR 339.

⁴   TMA 1994, s 11(3).

Comparative advertising

7.74 The TMA 1994 permits comparative advertising[1]. It should be noted that this is not a matter dealt with in the Trade Marks Directive, though it is dealt with in a proposed directive which sets down certain boundaries within which comparative advertising must remain in order to be lawful[2].

[1] TMA 1994, s 10(6); compare the previous law: *Chanel Ltd v Triton Packaging Ltd* [1993] RPC 32.

[2] EU Directive 97/55/EC (OJ L 290, 23.10.97, p 18), amending Directive 84/450/EEC (OJ L 250, 19.9.84, p 17) concerning misleading advertising (implemented in the UK by the Control of Misleading Advertisements Regulations 1988 (SI 1988/915), as amended). Proposed changes can be found in COM (2003) 356 final.

7.75 The restrictions on use of a trade mark in comparative advertising are that if the use is *not* in accordance with honest practices in business and commercial matters it will be infringing if, without due cause, it in addition either:

(a) takes unfair advantage of: or

(b) is detrimental to

the distinctive character or repute of the trade mark.

7.76 The view has been expressed that the elements listed here as (a) and (b) will, in most cases, add nothing to the requirement that use must be in accordance with 'honest practices'[1]. The suggestion has also been made that honesty is to be 'gauged against what is reasonably to be expected by the relevant public of advertisements for the goods or services at issue'[2].

[1] *Barclays Bank plc v RBS Advanta* [1996] RPC 307.

[2] At 316.

The Community Trade Mark

7.77 A Community Trade Mark system came into operation in April 1996, administered by the Office for Harmonisation in the Internal Market (Trade Marks and Designs)[1]. Unlike national trade marks, Community trade marks apply throughout the European Union. The rules as to registrability, term, infringement, etc are very similar to those for UK trade marks.

[1] Council Regulation (EC) No 40/94 on the Community trade mark [1994] OJ L 11/1.

CHAPTER 8

Securities over moveable property[1]

THE NATURE OF SECURITY RIGHTS

8.1 A security right is a real right enjoyed by a creditor in addition to his/her right to raise a personal action against the debtor for recovery of a debt which is due. As such, the security may take one of two forms:

1   a right against a third party (a cautioner) giving rise to a cautionary obligation, allowing the creditor to raise a personal action against the cautioner; or

2   a real right in security over property. It should be noted that this second form of security is a *real* right over property, and not merely a personal right, ie the right to sue someone. It is this second form of security that we will consider in this chapter.

The consequence of obtaining a real right in security is that the creditor holding it obtains a preference over other creditors in the event of the debtor's sequestration. In addition, as we will see below, the creditor also usually has a power of sale, ie the property over which the security is created can be sold to allow the creditor to recover the sum of money owed.

[1]   D L Carey Miller, *Corporeal Moveables in Scots Law*, ch 11.

8.2 Security rights over heritable property will be considered in CHAPTER **15**.

SECURITIES OVER CORPOREAL MOVEABLES

Need for possession

8.3   Subject to the exceptions listed below it is not possible to obtain a security right over corporeal moveable property without possession of the property. This means that the security right normally has to be completed by some form of delivery of the property over which the security is to be held. It has been suggested in the past that this requirement can cause difficulty for small businesses in raising finance. If they wish to raise a loan they might have to provide a security over their property and if this property is moveable it means transferring the property to the lender, which in turn means that they are deprived of the resources needed to run their businesses[1].

[1]   There have been a variety of proposals to change the current system, partly because of this problem: see the discussion in G Gretton, 'The Reform of Moveable Security Law', 1999 SLT (News) 301, which also lists the various proposals.

Exceptions to the need for possession

8.4   Having stated this general principle, there are certain exceptions to it, where a security right can be created without the creditor obtaining possession.

Landlord's hypothec

8.5   Landlord's hypothec is a form of security enjoyed by a landlord for payment of rent. The precise details will be considered in CHAPTER **12**, but, broadly, it gives the landlord a security over goods in the rented premises which can be realised by sequestration for rent.

Floating charges

8.6   These are granted by a company over the whole or part of the property which it owns, and can secure both heritable and moveable property. The charge 'floats' over the company's assets allowing it to deal with them until an event happens which results in crystallisation of the charge. On crystallisation the charge becomes a fixed charge over property belonging to the company as at the date when it happens. A floating charge must be registered in the company's register of charges.

Solicitor's hypothec

8.7 At common law a solicitor has a hypothec over expenses awarded to a client in a court action. The security is to cover the solicitor's expenses in pursuing the action on behalf of his/her client and is made effective by the solicitor moving the court to grant decree in his/her name rather than that of the client. In addition, a court can declare a solicitor entitled to a charge on or to a right of payment out of any property recovered in a court action in order to cover the solicitor's expenses[1].

1   Solicitors (Scotland) Act 1980, s 62(1).

Securities based on agreement

Pledge

8.8 This normally requires the transfer of possession of the security subjects[1] expressly in security. The only exceptions to this are pledges created by delivery of bills of lading and pledges of documents of title to goods by a mercantile agent which are, by statute, deemed to be equivalent to a pledge of the goods to which they relate[2].

1   *Hamilton v Western Bank* (1856) 19 D 152. Despite the adverse comment on this case in Gloag and Irvine, *Rights in Security* at 256–257, and Gloag and Henderson, *Introduction to the Law of Scotland* (11th edn, 2001), 42.12, it has been followed in subsequent cases (eg *Hayman v McLintock* 1907 SC 936), the case cited against it in Gloag and Henderson being concerned with the special case of bills of lading (*North Western Bank Ltd v Poynter* (1894) 22 R (HL) 513).

2   Factors Act 1889, s 3; *Inglis v Robertson & Baxter* (1898) 25 R (HL) 70.

8.9 Unless the creditor is expressly given the power of sale he/she has no automatic right to dispose of the security subjects on default, instead an application would have to be made to court for a warrant to sell the subjects on default by the debtor[1]. The property pledged can only be held as security for the specific debt in respect of which the pledge was made;

it cannot be retained as security against other sums owed by the debtor to the creditor.

1   Bell, 207.

Pawn

8.10   The provisions of the Consumer Credit Act 1974 apply to certain types of pledge – essentially those in which the pledgee lends on security as part of a business. In terms of the Act, the pledger/debtor is referred to as the 'pawner', and the creditor/pledgee as the 'pawnee'.

8.11   When an item is pawned the pawnee must give a pawn receipt in the prescribed form[1]. The pawn is redeemable for six months, or such longer period as the parties may agree, and if the value of the credit received is greater than £75 the pawner can redeem the pawn at any time until it is sold[2]. Redemption is effected by tendering the pawn receipt and the sum due – when this is done the pawnee must deliver the item pawned unless he/she knows or has reasonable cause to suspect that the bearer of the receipt is neither the owner of the pawn nor authorised by the owner[3]. If the pawner has lost the receipt, he/she can still redeem the pawn on making a statutory declaration or statement[4]. If there is no redemption by the due date and the credit given is less than £75 property in the pawn passes immediately to the pawnee. Where the credit is more than £75 there is no immediate transfer of property, rather the pawnee has the power of sale in respect of the pawn. Only if the credit given was greater than £100 must notice of the sale be given to the pawner. Once a sale has taken place, whether following transfer of ownership to the pawnee or exercise of their right of sale, the pawnee must account to the pawner for the proceeds of the sale and remit any surplus within 21 days[5]. If challenged over the sale, the pawnee must be able to show that reasonable care was taken in selling and that the true market value of the pawn was obtained.

1   Consumer Credit Act 1974, s 114(1).
2   Consumer Credit Act 1974, s 116.
3   Consumer Credit Act 1974, s 117.
4   Consumer Credit Act 1974, s 118.
5   Consumer Credit Act 1974, ss 120 and 121; Consumer Credit (Realisation Of Pawn) Regulations 1983 (SI 1983/1568), reg 3.

Ex facie absolute transfer

8.12 Here the transfer to the creditor is *ex facie* absolute, ie on the face of it there is an outright transfer of the security subjects. The creditor therefore becomes the owner of the property and has, deriving from this, an automatic right of sale on default. Unlike pledge, this type of security covers any debt due by the debtor to the creditor. For example in *Hamilton v Western Bank of Scotland*[1] a quantity of brandy had been transferred by a bankrupt to the defenders. The trustee in bankruptcy paid the debts in respect of which the transfer had been granted and sought a reconveyance of the brandy. The defenders refused, and were held by the House of Lords to be entitled to retain the brandy against other debts owed to them by the bankrupt.

[1] (1856) 19 D 152.

8.13 The position as between the creditor and debtor, particularly as regards the creditor's powers of sale, will normally be regulated by an agreement between creditor and debtor. In any event, the debtor retains a reversionary right in the property in the form of a right to a reconveyance on payment of the debt due.

Obligations of the creditor

8.14 In all cases the creditor must take reasonable care of the security subjects but is not liable for accidental loss or damage to them. More importantly, the creditor's right to recover the debt by personal action is not affected by such loss or damage.

8.15 In contrast, if the creditor is unable to return the security subjects through his/her own fault he/she is not entitled to demand repayment from the debtor. This is illustrated in *Ellis & Co's Trustees v Dixon-Johnson*[1] where the defendant opened an account with a firm of stockbrokers and deposited some shares with them as security against a debit balance in his account. Unknown to the debtor, the firm sold the shares, and subsequently became bankrupt; thereafter the trustee in bankruptcy sued for the balance due by the defendant after giving credit for the sale of the shares. It was held that the shares had to be valued as at the date of the account, and doing this the value exceeded what was owed by the defendant. On appeal the Lord Chancellor (Cave) said[2]:

'I have always understood the rule in equity to be that, if a creditor holding a security sues for his debt, he is under an obligation on payment of the debt to hand over the security; and if, having improperly made away with the security, he is unable to return it to his debtor, he cannot have judgement for the debt.'

1   [1925] AC 489.
2   At 491.

8.16   A final obligation is that in exercising the power of sale the creditor must have regard to the interests of the debtor and of other creditors.

SECURITIES IMPLIED BY LAW – LIENS

8.17   Liens are rights to retain property belonging to another against payment of money due to the person retaining the goods. There are two types of lien: special and general, which will be considered more fully below. The main examples of liens are in the context of sale, where under the Sale of Goods Act 1979 the unpaid seller has a lien over goods[1]; and in the context of employment.

1   This will not be further discussed here.

Special lien

8.18   Special liens form an implied term in contracts of employment (in the sense of contracts for services where an individual is hired/contracted to perform a specific task), specifically in the context where the employee comes into possession of something belonging to the employer on which some work is to be done. They are explained in Gloag and Henderson in the following terms[1]:

'The mutual obligations of the parties are on the one hand to pay for the work done; on the other hand to return the article, and the party engaged to provide services is not bound to fulfil his obligation until the obligation due to him, and arising out of the same contract, is fulfilled.'

1   *Introduction to the Law of Scotland* (11th edn, 2001), 42.16.

8.19   The right of retention extends to two categories of case. The first is to secure payment for the work which has been done with or on the property which is in the employee's possession. Examplees are property given to the employee to repair, and the right of an accountant to retain books against payment for work done. There is American authority that an undertaker cannot exercise a lien over a corpse[1]. Secondly a right of retention may arise in respect of property which is in the hands of one party in order to allow them to perform their part of a contract with a second party, against whom the right of retention is then exercised. For example, a distributor held a stock of electrical goods as part of a contact with the manufacturer of the goods under which they were to draw on this stock to deliver and install appliances to end customers. It was held that they could retain appliances in their warehouses against sums owed to them under the contract by the manufacturers[2].

1   *Morgan v Richmond* 336 So 2d 342 (La Ct of App, 1976).
2   *National Homecare Ltd v Belling & Co Ltd* 1994 SLT 50.

General lien

8.20   A general lien must usually be recognised by a custom or usage of a particular trade or profession. In most cases such a general lien confers a right of retention against any debts owed by the debtor, and not just, as in the special lien, a debt connected with a particular piece of work on the property retained. We will consider three examples of general lien.

Stockbroker

8.21   In his/her capacity as a mercantile agent a stockbroker has a right of general lien. This is illustrated in *Glendinning v Hope & Co*[1]. The defenders purchased shares on behalf of the pursuer who subsequently repudiated the transaction. The shares were sold causing a loss to the defenders of £50/2s. The defenders had earlier purchased shares on behalf of the pursuer and had in their hands, as agents for the pursuer, a transfer of these shares. They claimed a lien over this transfer for their losses. The central dispute was whether or not stockbrokers had a lien over such documents in respect of debts due by a customer not arising out of the transaction to which the documents related. It was decided that they did.

1   1911 SC (HL) 73.

Innkeeper

8.22   An innkeeper has security over a guest's luggage for payment of the bill owed by that guest. This security extends to anything forming part of the guest's luggage, even if the item actually belongs to a third party. This point was made in *Bermans & Nathans Ltd v Weibye*[1], where it was said that[2]:

> '... the right of lien emerges where the innkeeper has received into his hotel an individual whom he is, in law, bound to receive there, and that this right is the counterpart of the onerous obligations and strict liability placed by the law upon the innkeeper in relation to such a person and his baggage and to his other possessions, whether these belong to him or not, which accompany him or which are brought by him into the hotel during his stay.'

In this case, costumes hired out to a production company could not be said to form part of the luggage of individual guests in respect of whose bills the defender sought to exercise a lien.

[1]   1983 SC 67.
[2]   At 72.

8.23   The innkeeper's right of lien covers only property in the possession of the innkeeper or left on his premises; it does not confer the right to detain guests and remove their clothing[1].

[1]   *Sunbolf v Alford* (1838) 3 M & W 248; compare *McKichen v Muir* (1849) J Shaw 223.

Solicitors

8.24   The solicitor's right of lien covers all the client's papers in the hands of the solicitor and is available as security for the solicitor's business accounts and any disbursements made by the solicitor in the ordinary course of conducting the client's business. An example might be the payment of registration fees to register the purchase of a house in the Land Register. It has been held that this right of lien can be exercised even where the papers are sought for the purposes of a negligence action against the solicitor[1].

[1]   *Yau v Ogilvie & Co* 1985 SLT 91.

Effect of lien

8.25 In the case of a special lien, other than those involving a right of security over papers, the creditor can petition the court to have the retained goods sold. In the case of innkeepers, they have a statutory power of sale under the Innkeepers Act 1878. In other cases, the lien generally only confers a right of retention and a preference for the creditor in the sequestration or liquidation of the debtor.

Consequences of loss of possession

8.26 A lien over property is lost when possession of that property is lost. Once that happens the creditor clearly cannot physically retain the items which were the subject of the lien. In the case of a general lien there seems no reason why the lien should not revive if the items come back into the possession of the creditor, but it is clear that this rule does *not* apply in the case of a special lien[1]. Where possession is surrendered in error or as a result of fraud or improper means the right of lien will not be lost and the creditor will be able to take action to recover possession[2].

[1] *Morrison v Fulwell's Trustee* (1901) 9 SLT 34; though see the comment in *Goudie v Mulholland* 2000 SLT 303, per Lord Kirkwood at 307.
[2] *Goudie v Mulholland* 2000 SLT 303.

SECURITIES OVER INCORPOREAL MOVEABLES

8.27 Securities over incorporeal moveables are constituted by assignation. The assignation may bear to be in security or may be an *ex facie* absolute transfer of the property. In the latter case it will normally be qualified by a back letter, a separate agreement between the parties setting out the true nature of the transaction and regulating repayments, sale, etc. The same requirements apply to such assignations as apply to assignations on transfer of property[1].

[1] See CHAPTER 6.

RETENTION OF TITLE CLAUSES

8.28   These are clauses in a contract of sale which provide that ownership of the goods is to remain with the sellers, notwithstanding delivery, until the goods are paid for, or, more broadly, until all debts due to the sellers and companies in the same group are paid. The legality of such clauses was established in the House of Lords' decision, *Armour v Thyssen Edelstahlwerke AG*[1]. The clause was in the form:

> 'All goods delivered by us remain our property (goods remaining in our ownership) until all debts owed to us ... are settled ... Debts owed to companies, being members of our combine, are deemed to be such debts.'

[1]   1990 SLT 891.

8.29   We have already discussed these clauses in CHAPTER 4 from the point of view of their effect in preventing the transfer of ownership. The point to note here is that they also effectively give the supplier of goods who uses such a clause a security and a preference over other creditors. In the event of non-payment or default the seller can simply recover the goods, as they are still the property of the seller, instead of having to compete with other creditors for the purchaser's assets.

8.30   Such retention of title clauses, as has been discussed in the context of *Scottish Discount Co v Blin*[1], will not protect the seller where the property is attached to heritage so as to become a fixture, and additional provision is needed to protect the seller where the goods are used in production and so subject to the rules of *specificatio*.

[1]   1986 SLT 123; see CHAPTER 5.

CHAPTER 9

Ownership rights in land

9.1 This chapter is concerned with the rights acquired by an individual as an incident of their ownership of heritable property.

EXCLUSIVE POSSESSION

9.2 The owner has a right of exclusive possession of heritable property. This right of exclusive possession runs *a coelo usque ad centrum*, in other words from the centre of the earth to the outer limits of space. At common law therefore the owner of a piece of land owns everything underneath it and everything above it. There are some statutory exceptions and limitations to this. One example is the Civil Aviation Act 1982 which provides that there should be no liability in respect of trespass or nuisance in respect of the flight of aircraft over property[1]. Another exception is the reservation of rights in coal to the state, and rights in gold and silver to the Crown. In addition it is likely that ownership of other minerals will be vested in someone other than the owner of the land. Therefore although in theory the owner of a piece of land owns everything underneath it, in practice it is likely that there will be separate ownership of the land and of the minerals underneath it[2].

---

[1] Provided that the flight is reasonable having regard to the wind, weather and all the other circumstances of the case: Civil Aviaition Act 1982, s 76(1); see *Lord Bernstein v Skyviews and General* [1978] QB 479.

[2] In the case of coal, silver and gold this is necessarily the case.

9.3   This collision between the common law rule and the situation found commonly in practice can have consequences when a piece of land comes to be sold. On sale the presumption is that the seller sells not only the land but also any minerals which lie underneath it. If a reservation of minerals[1] is not specifically mentioned in the missives for sale of the land the purchaser can withdraw from the contract on discovering that minerals are reserved on the ground that he or she is not acquiring everything which he or she had contracted to purchase[2].

[1]   Other than those reserved to the state/Crown.
[2]   *Campbell v McCutcheon* 1963 SLT 290.

9.4   This right of exclusive possession can be interfered with in a number of ways. First, however, it is necessary to consider who is entitled to take an action to protect exclusive possession of a piece of land. The owner can take such action, provided that he or she still has the right of exclusive possession. The tenant of a piece of land is also able to take action to protect their exclusive possession, the nature of the relationship of landlord and tenant means that the tenant is entitled to exclusive possession even as against the landlord. Finally, somebody who is merely in possession of a piece of land without any title either as owner or as tenant may be entitled to take steps to protect that possession[1].

[1]   See the discussions in Gordon at 14–14 and in the *Stair Memorial Encyclopaedia*, vol 18, at 138–141.

9.5   The most extensive form of interference with exclusive possession is denial of possession by unlawful occupation of the property. The person who is unlawfully occupying may be removed by an action either of ejection or of removal. Ejection is the appropriate form of action to take to remove someone where their possession is violent, fraudulent or precarious. On the other hand, an action of removing is appropriate where someone has been entitled to occupy the land, but their entitlement to occupy has expired. An example of this would be the case of a tenant whose lease has expired.

9.6   A *bona fide* possessor who is removed from possession of a piece of land is in a special position. A *bona fide* possessor must fulfil three requirements:

1   He or she must have a reasonable but mistaken belief in the right to possess the property[1].
2   That right must be based on an *ex facie* valid title.

3   He or she must possess in good faith, in other words in ignorance of the fact that they are not entitled to possess the property.

1   *Lord Napier v Livingstone* (1765) 2 Pat App 108; *Houldsworth v Brand's Trustees* (1871) 10 M 304.

9.7   The special position of the *bona fide* possessor means three things:
1   On removal he or she is entitled to recompense for any improvements made to the land.
2   He or she is entitled to the fruits of the property during their possession, for example crops or rents payable in respect of use of the land by others.
3   He or she is not liable to the person legally entitled to possession for what are known as violent profits. Violent profits in an urban setting are twice the annual rental of the land possessed[1]. In a rural setting violent profits are the maximum likely profit which could have been derived from the land during the period of possession. The corollary of this is that possessors who are not acting in good faith are liable for violent profits.

1   *Jute Industries Ltd v Wilson & Graham Ltd* 1995 SLT (Sh Ct) 46.

9.8   Aside from interference with the right to exclusive possession by depriving the owner of possession, this right may be interfered with by trespass. This involves temporary incursions over the property by someone who is not authorised by the owner to be there, for example somebody walking over the property. The ability of an owner to prevent individuals from coming onto his or her land is now restricted because of the public right of access created by the Land Reform (Scotland) Act 2003[1]. This right of access must be exercised reasonably otherwise it will not be available; it is also excluded from certain areas and for certain purposes. Where the right of access is excluded anyone entering onto land will be a trespasser[2]. If an owner finds a trespasser on his/her land then he/she can ask the trespasser to leave and may be able to use reasonable force to assist his removal[3]. Where a trespasser causes damage to the land the owner will be entitled to claim compensation. Any repeated trespass can be prevented by obtaining an interdict, though an interdict will only be granted if the intrusion is material[4].

1   Land Reform (Scotland) Act 2003, ss 1, 2, 6 and 7, considered more fully in CHAPTER 13.
2   Unless they are exercising some other right, eg a public right of way.

3   *Stair Memorial Encyclopaedia*, vol 18, 184; Gordon 13–10.
4   See for example *Winans v Macrae* (1885) 12 R 1051.

9.9   A further type of interference is by way of encroachment. This is of a longer lasting nature and requires a more permanent intrusion into the owner's property or air space. Examples of this are intruding branches of trees[1], buildings, or in one case, the boom of a tower crane[2]. The courts do, however, have an equitable power to refuse a remedy in cases of encroachment. This power would be exercised where three criteria are fulfilled:

1   The encroachment has been placed on or over the owner's property in good faith.
2   The inconvenience and or damage caused to the owner is minimal.
3   The loss caused by removal of the encroachment is disproportionate to the remedy[3].

The normal remedy in cases of encroachment is for the court to grant an order requiring removal of the offending encroachment; only in cases where such an order is refused on the equitable grounds explained above will damages be ordered[4]. As well as a judicial remedy the owner has the right of self-help to remove the encroachment, for example by cutting back the branches of an overhanging tree[5].

1   *Halkerston v Wedderburn* (1781) Mor 10495.
2   See *Brown v Lee Constructions Limited* 1977 SLT (Notes) 61.
3   *Anderson v Brattisani's* 1978 SLT (Notes) 42; though the Brattisanis have now retired from the business underlying this dispute, see 'The Brattisanis are cashing in their chips', (2004) *Edinburgh Evening News* 22 June.
4   *Strathclyde Regional Council v Persimmon Homes (Scotland) Ltd* 1996 SLT 176.
5   See the discussion in the *Stair Memorial Encyclopaedia*, vol 18, 178.

FREEDOM FROM INTERFERENCE WITH ENJOYMENT OF PROPERTY

9.10   The owner's freedom to enjoy his or her property is protected in three ways.

Nuisance

9.11 The law of nuisance can be used to protect the owner's enjoyment of his or her property against unjustified interference. A useful definition of common law nuisance is given by Bell in his *Principles*[1]:

> 'Whatever obstructs the public means of commerce and intercourse, whether in highways or navigable rivers; whatever is noxious or unsafe, or renders life uncomfortable to the public generally, or to the neighbourhood; whatever is intolerably offensive to individuals, in their dwelling-houses, or inconsistent with the comfort of life, whether by stench (as the boiling of whale blubber), by noise (as a smithy in an upper floor), or by indecency (as a brothel next door).'

There may be more modern examples of offensive practices, but this still gives the general idea. However, a point to note at the outset is that Bell's definition extends beyond the reciprocal rights and obligations of neighbouring property owners and involves the public at large. Thus the right of an owner to use his/her property as he/she pleases is restricted by his/her obligation to refrain from carrying on a nuisance that would interfere not only with his/her neighbours, but also members of the public. Likewise, where an owner's right to enjoy his/her property is being interfered with, his/her redress is not limited to nuisances perpetrated by a neighbouring owner; a member of the public may also be liable, eg where the owner of a traction engine was held liable for nuisance when sparks from his vehicle caused damage to property adjoining the road[2]. However, most examples of nuisance arise between nearby property owners or their tenants. A nuisance is something that happens on a regular basis, and there can be no liability for a one-off occurrence[3]. The most usual examples of nuisance involve noise and air pollution but nuisance has also been extended to other areas, for example in *Lord Advocate v The Reo Stakis Organisation*[4] nuisance provided a remedy for removal of lateral support for a building.

[1]   Bell, 974.
[2]   *Slater v McLellan* 1924 SC 854, 1924 SLT 634.
[3]   *Gray v Dunlop* 1954 SLT (Sh Ct) 75, (1954) 70 Sh Ct Rep 270.
[4]   1981 SC 104, see also *Kennedy v Glenbelle* 1996 SC 95, per LP Hope at 101D–G.

9.12 In considering whether the activities complained of amount to a nuisance the area in which the activity is taking place will be a consideration. What amounts to a nuisance in a residential area might be acceptable in an industrial area. As Rankine notes[1]:

'It must not, however, be supposed that the standard of purity and tranquillity of the atmosphere is constant, or can be determined by scientific analysis irrespective of considerations of locality. It would be folly to expect the fresh breezes of Ben-y-Gloe in the slums of Cowgate.'

Even in an industrial area with substantial noise and other pollution it is possible to object to the introduction of new nuisances or the extension of existing potential nuisances[2], particularly where this might affect brainworkers[3].

1   *The Law of Landownership in Scotland* (4th edn, 1909), 403.
2   *Charity v Riddell*, Mor 'Public Police' App No 6.
3   *Maguire v Charles McNeil Ltd* 1922 SC 174.

9.13   It is irrelevant that the nuisance was known to exist before the complaining owner bought his property, and it is no defence to the perpetrator to say that the party complaining willingly moved into the area where the nuisance already existed[1]. However, failure to object over a period of time may bar an owner from taking action against nuisance under the principle of acquiescence, and his right of action and that of any future owners of his property will be extinguished by the long negative prescription if the nuisance has continued unchallenged for 20 years or more[2]. Neither is it a defence that the use causing the nuisance is a legitimate use of the land which has been granted planning permission[3].

1   *Fleming v Hislop* (1886) 13 R (HL) 43, per Lord Halsbury at 49; 23 SLR 491.
2   Prescription and Limitation (Scotland) Act 1973, ss 7 and 8.
3   *Shanlin v Collins* 1973 SLT (Sh Ct) 21.

9.14   The appropriate remedy in cases of nuisance will usually be interdict to prevent the repetition of the activity causing the nuisance. In some cases damages may also be appropriate, though where these are sought it will be necessary to prove that there was fault on the part of the person responsible for causing the nuisance[1].

1   *Rank Hovis McDougall v Strathclyde Regional Council* 1985 SC (HL) 17; though in some cases the activity may be such that fault will be readily implied: see, for example, *Kennedy v Glenbelle* 1996 SC 95.

9.15   In addition to claims based on common law nuisance an owner or occupier may be able to take action in the sheriff court to seek to have work undertaken to remove or prevent the recurrence of a statutory nuisance[1]. Nuisances in respect of which such action can be taken include any premises in such a state as to be prejudicial to health or a nuisance; any accumulation or deposit which is prejudicial to health or a nuisance; and any noise emitted from premises[2]. This provision has been used, for example, by local authority tenants to try to force their landlords to take action or to recover compensation for loss resulting from the nuisance[3]. In such cases it is still necessary either to establish the existence of a nuisance in the common law sense, in other words something substantial and intolerable to the ordinary person[4], or that there is potential danger to health.

1   Environmental Protection Act 1990, s 84.
2   Environmental Protection Act 1990, s 79.
3   For example, *Adams v Glasgow City Council* 2000 Hous LR 3; *Robb v Dundee City Council* 2002 SLT 853.
4   See, for example, *Anderson v City of Dundee Council* 2000 SLT (Sh Ct) 134 at 143.

Aemulationem vicini

9.16   Where a land owner makes a lawful use of his/her property it may still be struck at as being in *aemulationem vicini*, in other words designed to cause harm to a neighbour. To establish this it will need to be proved that 'the predominant motive for use is the harm of a neighbour, the gratification in spite, or other oblique motive'[1]. Use of this remedy is very unusual.

1   D M Walker, *Delict,* p 993.

Non-natural use of property

9.17   This provides a remedy for damage caused by a neighbour making a non-natural use of their property. What is involved is the bringing of an innovation or new work onto land which then escapes causing damage on neighbouring land. The familiar examples involve damage caused by dammed water which breaches the dam and escapes[1]. Another example involves damage caused by drifting weed killer[2].

1   *Caledonian Railway Company v Greenock Corporation* 1917 SC (HL) 56.
2   *D McIntyre & Son v Soutar* 1980 SLT (Sh Ct) 115.

MINERAL RIGHTS[1]

9.18   The right to minerals is a separate tenement in the law of Scotland, that is, it is an interest in land which is capable of being separately owned from the ownership of the land itself and the, non-mineral, subsoil.

[1]   See on this Rennie, *Minerals and the Law in Scotland* (2001).

Separation from the surface

9.19   The ownership of the surface and the ownership of the minerals underlying the surface may be separated in two ways. First of all there may be an express grant of the mineral rights by somebody who at the time of the grant owns both the surface and the right to the minerals underlying the surface. Secondly there may be a grant of ownership of the surface of the land by the person owning both rights under reservation of the mineral rights. In addition, the minerals may be the subject of a minerals lease.

What is a mineral?[1]

9.20   In *Borthwick-Norton v Gavin Paul and Sons*[2] three criteria were set out:

1   The mineral must not form part of the normal subsoil, but must be exceptional in use, character or value[3].

2   At the time of separation of the interests the claimed mineral must be known as a mineral in the vernacular of mining engineers, commercial men and land owners. In *Marquis of Linlithgow v North British Railway Company*[4] the question arose as to whether or not oil shale was included in the general term 'mineral'. The court was of the view that the question had to be answered as at the date when the interests in ownership of the land and ownership of the minerals were separated, in this case 1818. Addressing that question the court took the view that at that date oil shale was not 'in the opinion of the mining or commercial world' a mineral. The views of geologists were discounted as irrelevant.

3   The conveyance or reservation of minerals must not swallow up the grant of land. In other words there must be some land left which can be used after the mineral rights have been fully enjoyed by the person to whom they are reserved or to whom they are granted.

What does ownership of minerals involve?

9.21 Ownership of mineral rights gives the owner the right to work these minerals underground subject to the obligation to provide support to the surface of the ground. It does not give the owner of the minerals the right to enter on to the surface of the land in order to exercise their rights to minerals unless there is express authority for this to take place in the deed conferring or reserving ownership of the mineral rights. One exception to this, however, is a reservation of minerals in terms of the Crofting (Scotland) Act 1993[1].

1   *Anderson v Williamson* 1997 SLT (Land Ct) 46.

Statutory provisions

MINES (WORKING FACILITIES AND SUPPORT) ACT 1966

9.22 This allows individuals to apply for the rights needed to work minerals as efficiently as possible[1]. These rights include rights ancillary to the working of minerals, eg, the right to lower the surface or the right of access over land to work or transport minerals[2]. The rights applied for are not to be granted unless it is in the national interest to do so, or unless it is not reasonably practicable to obtain the rights by private agreement[3]. An application for the right to lower the surface will only be granted after weighing up the comparative values of the minerals required to provide support and any buildings or works on the land, or, if the land is not built on, the comparison will be with the prejudice caused to the existing use of the surface[4]. It is also possible for someone who has no right of support to apply for such a right[5]. Applications are made in the first instance to the Scottish Ministers. If a *prima facie* case is made out the application is referred to the Court of Session for decision.

1   Mines (Working Facilities and Support) Act 1966, s 1.
2   Mines (Working Facilities and Support) Act 1966, s 2.
3   Mines (Working Facilities and Support) Act 1966, s 3.

⁴   Mines (Working Facilities and Support) Act 1966, s 2.
⁵   Mines (Working Facilities and Support) Act 1966, s 7.

COAL INDUSTRY ACT 1994

9.23   This is the most recent piece of legislation to follow on from the nationalisation of coal in 1946. It created a new body, the Coal Authority, in which rights in unworked coal are vested, and this body now issues licences to operators to carry out coal mining operations[1]. The Act also gives the licensed operators of coal mines the right to withdraw support from land as a result of coal workings on giving three months' written notice of their intention[2].

1   Given the later consideration of the issue of support (at PARA **9.24**FF) it should be noted that at the date of writing there were no underground coal mining operations in Scotland.
2   Coal Industry Act 1994, s 38.

COAL MINING (SUBSIDENCE) ACT 1991[1]

9.24   This replaces earlier legislation in similar terms. It imposes on the licensed operator, or, where there is no licensed operator the Coal Authority, the duty to take remedial action in respect of 'subsidence damage', ie any damage to land or buildings resulting from the withdrawal of support in connection with coal mining. This withdrawal of support can be active withdrawal because of current workings or passive withdrawal, for example where material used to infill old mine workings collapsed[2]. It should be noted that it does not matter when the working of coal took place or who did it, the operator at the time the damage is caused on the surface or the Coal Authority is responsible. The remedial action can take three forms. In the first place it can be the execution of remedial works[3]. Secondly, it can involve paying the costs of remedial work done by others. This is appropriate where the repairs are undertaken by a public body (eg a local authority) or statutory undertaker, where the claimant wishes to do the work him/herself, or where the remedial works will form part of other works of repair/improvement to the property[4]. Finally it can involve the operator or Coal Authority in paying an amount equal to the depreciation of the property. This is appropriate where the costs of repair exceed the amount of depreciation by 20 per cent or more, where the property is not a dwelling house and the owner agrees, or where the property is likely to be subject to compulsory purchase or a demolition order as a result of the subsidence damage. The operator, or the Authority, is also liable to pay for any emergency work undertaken to allow continued use of the property or to prevent further subsidence damage[5].

1   Rennie, *Minerals and the Law in Scotland* (2001) 4.14.
2   *British Coal Corporation v Netherlee Trust Trustees* 1995 SLT 1038.
3   Coal Mining (Subsidence) Act 1991, s 7.
4   Coal Mining (Subsidence) Act 1991, ss 8 and 9.
5   Coal Mining (Subsidence) Act 1991, s 12.

Rights of support[1]

9.25 Owners of the surface of land enjoy a right of support which is both subjacent (in other words from below) and adjacent (in other words from neighbouring property). The nature of this right of support is the subject of some disagreement at least in the context of the working of minerals, and there are two main views which, as will be seen, have different consequences[2].

1   For a fuller discussion see Rennie, *Minerals and the Law in Scotland* (2001), ch 4. Note also the specific statutory provisions for coal mining at PARA **9.24**.
2   Though Rennie argues that there are three positions.

9.26 The first view draws a distinction between land in its natural state and land which has been built on. In the case of the former there is a natural right of support; for the latter any right of support has to be created as a servitude. This is the view taken by Rankine[1], and also by the House of Lords, where it was said to be based on principles common to all systems of jurisprudence[2]. On this view land with buildings erected on it will only enjoy a right of support in three circumstances:

1   Where a right of support is expressly granted by the owner of the mineral rights or where it is expressly reserved by the owner of the surface when the minerals are separated.

2   Where there is an implied grant or reservation of a right of support. This seems to be considered to exist either where the buildings already existed at the time of the separation of the interest in the minerals and in the surface of land or in the situation where, at that date of separation, the buildings were in the contemplation of the parties. It is not entirely clear in this context what the phrase 'in the contemplation of the parties' actually means. On the one hand it might mean that the parties

might vaguely contemplate that it would be not unreasonable at some undefined point in the future for buildings to be erected on the land, in which case the right is very similar to that described in the second view considered below, or it may mean that the buildings have to be in the fairly imminent contemplation of the parties. An example of this latter view would be where land is sold off reserving the minerals and the sale is made to a builder who it is known to the seller intends to build on the land which has been sold.

3   Prescriptive acquisition where the building has been standing for a period of 20 years.

1.   J Rankine, *The Law of Landownership in Scotland* (4th edn, 1909), pp 495–503.

2   By the Lord Chancellor (Cranworth) in *Caledonian Railway Co v Sprot* (1856) 2 Macq 449 at 461. This is the view taken in the most recent Scottish case: *Rogano Limited v British Railways Board* 1979 SC 297.

9.27   In contrast, and as indeed acknowledged by Rankine[1], there is a second line of authority which indicates that the natural right of support extends to land which has been built on. Rankine suggests that at least some of these authorities are in fact consistent with his view because they indicate that buildings will only enjoy support if they do not materially increase the burden on the mineral owner[2]. It is true that there are some comments in the case law to the effect that the buildings erected in each case have not increased the subsidence complained of, but there are also clear statements of general principle that the owner of land is entitled to support for buildings which were not in consideration at the time the minerals were leased out or sold off:

'When the minerals are constituted into a separate property from the surface, the proprietor of the surface is not thereby disabled from building houses any more than from any other legal use of his property. Every legitimate use of his property remains open to him the same as before.[3]'

'[E]ven where the owner of the surface is himself the seller of the minerals, he is not restrained from building, although no buildings may have existed at the time the mineral lease was entered into. He is not, on the other hand, entitled so to occupy the ground, by building large factories or towns, as to prevent the tenant from working with any profit; but the mineral tenant, on the other hand, must not restrain him beyond what is reasonable, and must use every care to protect his property from injury, whether it still remains an agricultural subject, or is occupied by buildings.[4]'

The apparent restriction noted in the second extract on the types of building to be erected has not been acted on in any reported case to negative the existence of a right of support.

1   J Rankine, *The Law of Landownership in Scotland* (4th edn, 1909), pp 503–505.
2   *Bain v Duke of Hamilton* (1867) M 1 at 3; *Hamilton v Turner* (1867) 5 M 1086; *Dryburgh v Fife* (1905) 7 F 1083.
3   *Hamilton v Turner* (1867) 5M 1086 at 1091, per Lord Kinloch.
4   *Hamilton v Turner* (1867) 5M 1086 at 1095, per Lord President (Inglis).

9.28   Where a right of support exists the duty imposed on the minerals' proprietor is not an active duty which implies a positive action to maintain support in the surface of the land. Rather it is a negative obligation not to damage or remove support[1]. This duty can be enforced prospectively by seeking interdict to prevent works which are likely to cause damaging loss of support.

1   See *Rogano Limited v British Railways Board* 1979 SC 297 for an example of the consequences of this distinction.

9.29   Where damage has been caused by withdrawal of support then the remedy is a claim for damages. If the damage to the surface has been caused by coal mining the provisions of the Coal Mining (Subsidence) Act 1991 discussed above will apply; otherwise a common law claim for damages will be available. Such a claim can only be made for damage caused to the land and buildings on the surface and the owner of the surface cannot claim compensation for personal injury[1]. In addition, the current owner of the mineral rights is not liable for actions undertaken by their predecessors which result in damage during the period of their ownership[2].

1   *Angus v National Coal Board* 1955 SLT 245.
2   *Geddes's Trustees v Haldane* (1906) 14 SLT 328.

9.30   Exceptionally the deeds separating ownership of the minerals and the surface may specifically exclude the right to support or the ability to claim compensation for any damage caused by withdrawal of support[1]. Any such exclusion must be clear. In the absence of such a specific exclusion the right of support and the ability to claim damages are implied by law. Where there is specific provision in the deeds for the properties for compensation to be paid this does not function to authorise withdrawal of support[2].

1   *Buchanan v Andrew* (1873) 11 M (HL) 13.
2   *White v Wm Dixon Ltd* (1883) 10 R (HL) 453.

9.31   In addition to any natural support offered by minerals underground, the owner of the surface will have a right to the support generated by the hydrostatic pressure of underground water and any artificial underground support (eg filling or props put in after the extraction of minerals)[1].

1   *Bald's Trustees v Alloa Colliery Co* (1854) 16 D 870 at 875, per Lord President McNeill; contrast this with the position in England: see *Stephens v Anglian Water Authority* [1987] 3 All ER 379.

WATER RIGHTS

9.32   This section is designed to consider the rights in water which are not affected by Crown rights. In other words there is no consideration of rights in the sea, foreshore or tidal waters, which are considered in CHAPTER **10**.

Non-tidal rivers and streams – the common law

9.33   Where a river or stream falls completely within the property of one proprietor, that river or stream belongs to him or her. Where a river forms the boundary between two properties, one on either side of the river, the boundary line will normally be the middle (or *medium filum*) of the riverbed (or *alveus*). There is no ownership in the water itself, but rather the opposing proprietors have a common interest which affects what the owner of the opposing bank can do either with the water or on his or her share of the riverbed. The common interest can effectively prevent building on the riverbed if the opposite owner can show potential damage to his or her interests resulting from this building. It is very likely that this will be the case, as the courts have taken the view that the consequences of a change in the flow of the river which might be caused by such building are unpredictable[1]. This common interest will even operate to prevent works undertaken on the opposing proprietor's own land where this might adversely affect the other proprietors. An example of this is *Menzies v The Earl of Breadalbane*[2]. The owner of land on one side of the river intended to erect works to prevent flooding of his land. The difficulty was that these floods were a fairly common or normal event and the opposing proprietor sought to prevent the works. The basis of his claim was that if the works were completed the result would be that more water would be thrown on to his land in times of flood and this would adversely affect his interests. The court agreed and granted interdict to prevent the flood prevention works. It should be noted that the authority of this case only extends to cases where the floods are 'normal'; it does not extend to flood protection works undertaken by individuals to prevent abnormal or unusual floods.

1   *Morris v Bicket* (1864) 2 M 1086.
2   (1828) 3 W & S 1086.

9.34   In the case of successive proprietors of land bordering rivers or streams there is again no ownership in the water which passes their respective properties; instead, as with opposing proprietors, there is common interest. This common interest restricts what proprietors can do with the water as it passes through their property. In general proprietors have a right to remove water for primary purposes. These primary purposes are drinking, cooking and watering animals. Aside from such removal a general rule is that the proprietor must allow the water to run through his/her property undiminished in flow or quality. There is some disagreement over whether there is a right at common law to remove water for what is described as secondary purposes, ie for anything which is not contained in the definition of a primary purpose[1]. Where use for such purposes involves insignificant amounts of water there will be no remedy available regardless of the absence of a right of use.

1   Compare Gordon, 7–32, suggesting that a reasonable quantity can be withdrawn for such purposes with *Stair Memorial Encyclopaedia*, vol 18, 288.

9.35   The right to withdraw water for secondary purposes can be acquired either by agreement with downstream proprietors or by prescriptive use. As well as restrictions on use, the requirement to allow the water to flow downstream undiminished in quantity means that upstream proprietors cannot dam the river and thereby alter or vary its flow. Again the right to dam can be acquired by agreement or through the operation of prescription.

9.36   Two cases illustrate how strictly courts have in the past dealt with this issue of allowing undiminished flow of water. In *Hood v Williamsons*[1] the court ruled that where water was removed for primary purposes any excess of water which was not actually used for those purposes must be returned to the river within the boundaries of the property of the proprietor who removed it. In *Stevenson v Hogganfield Bleaching Company*[2] the view was taken that it was not permissible for an upstream proprietor to remove water for secondary purposes and then to replace it with water drawn from the mains water supply.

1   (1861) 23 D 496.
2   (1890) 30 SLR 86.

9.37   Abstraction of water from rivers and the building of dams or other obstructions across them will in future be regulated by the Water Environment and Water Service (Scotland) Act 2003, considered below[1].

1   See PARA **9.42**.

Rights of navigation

9.38   Members of the public have a right of access to non-tidal waterways[1]. In addition a more extensive public right of navigation in a non-tidal river can be established by use from time immemorial, which is defined as being use for a period of 40 years. Once the right of navigation is established it is not restricted to the means by which it was originally established, so that in the leading case on the subject in Scotland, the right of navigation was originally established by floating logs down the river but was subsequently held to extend to canoes. In addition once the right is established it extends to the whole navigable width and capacity of the river. However, the right of navigation does not extend to navigation which is more in the form of acrobatic feats, navigation involving a new type of vessel, or navigation which causes damage to or destruction of the vessel used in the navigation[2]. The right of navigation also gives a limited right to use the shores of the river, but not to walk on the river bed[3].

1   See PARAS **13.37–13.41**.
2   On all of these points see *Wills Trustees v The Cairngorm Canoeing and Sailing School* 1976 SLT 162.
3   *Scammell v Scottish Sports Council* 1983 SLT 462.

Lochs

9.39 Lochs which are entirely within the property of one proprietor are the property of that proprietor. Otherwise ownership of the *solum* of the loch is divided up amongst the proprietors of the land surrounding it by extending their land boundaries out into the water. In addition fishing rights are shared amongst the surrounding proprietors[1].

1   *Mackenzie v Banks* (1878) 5 R (HL) 192.

Water outside a definite channel/surface water

9.40 Such water belongs to the landowner who is entitled to make use of it as he or she wishes. This includes the right to withdraw underground water, even if this affects the presence of water under neighbouring properties or abstracts water which would otherwise run into a river or stream[1]. The introduction of statutory control over such abstractions is discussed below.

1   *Milton v Glen-Moray Glenlivet Distillery Co Ltd* (1898) 1 F 135.

Drainage rights

9.41 The owner of land is entitled to have the land drained on to lower property and there is nothing that the owner of the lower property can do about it. This right also permits the superior proprietor to gather the draining water at one point (eg by new drainage on his/her land) as long as the burden of suffering the draining water is not increased[1]. The inferior proprietor will be entitled to object if the owner of the higher ground unduly and unnecessarily presses this right with damaging consequences for him/her[2].

1   *Campbell v Bryson* (1864) 3 M 254.
2   *Logan v Wang (UK) Ltd* 1991 SLT 580.

Statutory control of water abstraction

9.42 The Water Environment and Water Services (Scotland) Act 2003 introduces a new framework for the control of abstraction of both surface and underground water. As originally passed the Act applies only to mechanical abstraction[1], leaving, for example, abstraction by laying a pipe to withdraw water from a river outwith the control. The Act will also regulate impounding works, that is dams, weirs or other methods for retaining water[2]. The precise detail of the framework is still being developed at the time of writing, but is expected to come into effect in 2005. Once it does all new abstractions of water will be subject to a new licensing regime. The licensing requirements are likely to depend on the amount of water being abstracted. Small abstractions will be required simply to notify the regulatory body[3], with larger abstractions subject to General Binding Rules and the largest abstractions requiring a licence. Existing abstractions will be covered by transitional provisions until 2012 when they will have to be fully incorporated into the licensing regime.

[1]   Water Environment and Water Services (Scotland) Act 2003, s 20(6). Though it is proposed to amend this definition to include non-mechanical abstraction, for example by a pipe or mill lade leading off a river: see Scottish Executive Environment Group, *Controlled Activities Regulation: A Consultation* (2004), 1.5.

[2]   Water Environment and Water Services (Scotland) Act 2003, s 20(6). See the consultation cited in the previous footnote for a proposed amendment to this.

[3]   The Scottish Environmental Protection Agency.

FISHING RIGHTS

9.43   Rights to fish for salmon are, of course, part of the *regalia minora*. Rights to fish for other fish run with the ownership of the land. The riparian proprietor is entitled to stand up to the centre line of the river, in other words to stand on his/her property, and cast from there[1].

[1]   *Arthur v Aird* 1907 SC 170.

RIGHTS TO GAME

9.44   The owner of land has a right to take game on the land. Ownership of land does not on its own confer an ownership of the game of that land, only a right to take the game[1]. Both fishing rights and shooting rights can be the subject of a lease granted by the proprietor of land.

[1]   *Wilson v Dykes* (1872) 10 M 444.

RIGHT OF ACCESS

9.45 The owner of land has an implied right of access to his/her land. This is only likely to be relevant where a piece of ground is landlocked, that is surrounded by land belonging to other owners across which there is no established right of access. Such cases have normally been considered as involving the creation of a servitude right of access[1]. More recent case law has suggested that such rights of access are in fact incidents of ownership[2]. The case law suggests that such a right of access will only exist where the land requiring the access and the land over which this is to be taken were previously owned by the same proprietor, though the authorities on which this conclusion is reached seem to suggest that the scope of the right of access should extend beyond this[3]. Unlike a servitude right such an implied right of access will exist only for as long as it is necessary and will not prescribe with the passing of time.

[1]   See CHAPTER 13.
[2]   *Bowers v Kennedy* 2000 SC 555; *Inverness Seafield Development Co Ltd v Mackintosh* 2001 SC 406.
[3]   See the passages from Erskine and Bankton cited in the judgment of Lord President Rodger in *Bowers v Kennedy*. See R Paisley, 'Bower of Bliss?', (2002) 6 Edin LR 101.

CHAPTER 10

Crown rights

10.1 Crown rights fall into three categories. In the first place, there are rights of ownership. Secondly, there are *regalia maiora*. These are rights which are held by the Crown in trust for the general public and which cannot be alienated by the Crown. In other words the public's right of use etc cannot be denied by any action on the part of the Crown. The final type of Crown right is *regalia minora*. These are property rights belonging to the Crown which can be alienated by the Crown; an example discussed below is rights to salmon fishings, although when they are alienated they may be subject to public rights held by the Crown *regalia maiora*, such as in the case of the foreshore.

PROPERTY RIGHTS

10.2 The only ownership right to be discussed here is the Crown's ownership of the sea and the seabed, at least up to the limit of territorial waters. Although this was at one time regarded as being part of the *regalia maiora* it is now clear that this right is a proprietary one and that the Crown has the power to sell or let parts of the seabed[1], though where this is done public rights remain exercisable over the area sold or let. The seabed, along with other areas owned by the Crown, for example the foreshore, is managed by the Crown Estates Commissioners.

1   *LA v Clyde Navigation Trust* (1891) 19 R 174; *Shetland Salmon Farmers v Crown Estates Comrs* 1991 SLT 166, involving leases granted to salmon farmers.

See also Scottish Law Commission Discussion Paper 113, *Law of the Foreshore and Seabed* (2001), 3.2–3.8.

10.3 Given that the seabed and foreshore (see below) belong to the Crown unless sold off to a third party, what happens in the case of land reclaimed from the sea where the foreshore and seabed have remained in Crown ownership? The question is whether the reclaimed land belongs to the Crown as owner of the foreshore or accresces to the owner of the adjacent land as would happen in a non-tidal river through *alluvio*. There are two views on this[1]. Reid[2] treats reclamation as a form of alluvion and states that: 'When tidal waters retreat, whether naturally or as the result of a human act, the land which is reclaimed accedes to the adjacent dry land.' He cites authority in support of this. It is fair to say that, as Reid points out, the authority is not all one way and in *Smith v Lerwick Harbour Trustees*[3] Lord Kinnear firmly states the view that a claim over the foreshore requires an *ex facie* valid title followed by prescriptive possession, in other words the view that reclaimed land on the foreshore vests in the Crown. This also seems to be Gordon's view[4]. Although there is the possibility of acquisition of ownership through prescription based on recording or registering an *a non domino* title[5] this would need to be followed by possession for the 20-year period required to obtain a good title in a question with the Crown.

1   See also Scottish Law Commission Discussion Paper 113, *Law of the Foreshore and Seabed*, (2001) 8.2-8.7.
2   *Stair Memorial Encyclopaedia*, vol 18, 594.
3   (1903) 5 F 680.
4   Gordon, 4–21; this is the rule proposed by the Scottish Law Commission Report 190, *Law of the Foreshore and Seabed* (2003), 6.1–6.5.
5   See CHAPTER 3.

REGALIA MAIORA[1]

Navigation and fishing

10.4 The Crown rights involved here are rights of navigation and of fishing in the sea and in tidal rivers. The right of navigation includes the rights which are necessarily incidental to navigation, for example a right of passage and of temporary, but not permanent[2], mooring. As well as a right of navigation the public also has a common law right to fish in the sea for white fish[3].

[1]   Some possible changes are discussed in Scottish Law Commission Report 190, *Law of the Foreshore and Seabed* (2003), Part 3.

[2]   *Crown Estate Comrs v Fairlie Yacht Slip Ltd* 1977 SLT 19; *Walford v David* 1989 SLT 876; Scottish Law Commission Discussion Paper 113, *Law of the Foreshore and Seabed* (2001), 3.2–3.8.

[3]   *Bowie v Marquis of Ailsa* (1887) 14 R 649; for a discussion of statutory restrictions on fishing see Gordon, 8–11 to 8–18.

Foreshore

10.5   The foreshore describes that part of the beach which lies between the high and low water marks of the ordinary spring tides. The foreshore is the subject of a variety of public rights: these include rights connected with fishing, for example the drying of nets; rights connected with navigation, including the right to anchor and to load and unload goods; and, a public right to use the foreshore for the purposes of recreation[1]. The public right of recreation includes the right to discharge a shotgun[2] but not the right to sell ice-cream[3]. It has been proposed[4] that these public rights should be extended beyond the foreshore to cover that part of the shore above the high tide mark, as there will be a public right of access[5] over this. It will be noted, however, that the rights conferred by the *regalia maiora* both over the foreshore and over the sea are much more extensive than those conferred by the public right of access.

[1]   On this last point see *Marquis of Bute v McKirdy & McMillan Ltd* 1937 SLT 241.
[2]   *McLeod v McLeod* 1982 SCCR 130.
[3]   *Marquess of Ailsa v Monteforte* 1937 SLT 614.
[4]   Scottish Law Commission Report 190, *Law of the Foreshore and Seabed* (2003), 3.17.
[5]   See CHAPTER 13.

Tidal navigable waters

10.6   The same considerations apply to tidal navigable waters as apply to the sea. In consequence there are public rights of navigation, but by analogy the Crown owns the river bed.

REGALIA MINORA

Gold and silver mine

10.7   As mentioned in CHAPTER **9**, the Crown has rights to all gold and silver lying underground. These rights can be sold or leased in exchange for a royalty of 10 per cent[1].

[1]   Mines and Metals Act 1592.

Salmon fishings

10.8   Salmon fishings form a separate tenement, ie a property interest which can be owned separately from the ownership of land. Where rights to salmon fishing are owned separately from ownership of the river bank, the owner of the salmon fishings has the right to access to the river to exercise these rights and the right to use the bank of the river as a base for fishing. The right to fish allows the owner of the right to salmon fishing to cast as far as is reachable from the territory over which he/she has the right[1]. There is extensive statutory regulation of salmon fishing, for example as to methods of fishing[2] and periods when fishing is prohibited or restricted[3]. Salmon fishings are subject to both the community right to buy and the crofting community right to buy[4].

[1]   *Fothringham v Passmore* 1984 SLT 401.
[2]   Salmon and Freshwater Fisheries (Protection) (Scotland) Act 1951, s 2 (to be replaced by the Salmon and Freshwater Fisheries (Consolidation) (Scotland) Act 2003, s 1).
[3]   For example the Annual Close Time (Lossie Salmon Fishery District) Order 1999 (SI 1999/1363).
[4]   See CHAPTER **17**.

Foreshore

10.9   As well as forming part of *regalia maiora* the foreshore also forms part of *regalia minora.* The consequence of this dual membership is that the foreshore can be alienated by the Crown; in other words its ownership can be sold to an individual land owner. however, when this land owner becomes owner, his/her ownership is subject to the public rights discussed above.

Treasure and lost property

10.10   These matters have already been dealt with in CHAPTER 4. The Crown's prerogative right in respect of treasure was confirmed in *Lord Advocate v Aberdeen University*[1].

[1]   1967 SLT 361.

CHAPTER 11

Tenement properties

11.1 Before 28 November 2004 the common law set out certain rules as to ownership, maintenance and common interest in tenement properties. It was common in practice for these to be varied by agreement, usually set out in a deed of conditions covering the tenement property. As a result the rules governing a tenement property were a combination of the common law rules and the specific burdens imposed on that particular tenement. Wide variation is found in practice between the burdens imposed in tenement properties. For example, some make provision for the management of the tenement building, others do not; in some, parts of the building are declared to be common property, in others there might instead be an obligation to contribute towards the maintenance of these parts.

11.2 The common law position was not without its difficulties[1]. One of these was the wide variety of burdens affecting different tenements. Another was that there is little case law in this area and, partly as a result, doubt over the ownership status of some parts of tenements. There was also, as we discussed in CHAPTER 2, a lack of clarity over the operation of the positive aspect of common interest in tenement buildings. The most important practical difficulty, however, was the general lack of satisfactory mechanisms for securing the maintenance and repair of tenement properties. Declaring part of the building, for example the roof, to be common property simply imports the problem that unanimous agreement is required before any work can be done to it. On the other hand, if nothing is said about the roof it would be up to the owners of the top flats to pay for most of its maintenance, a burden which they were unlikely to be able to afford. The

Tenements (Scotland) Act 2004 addresses these problems. It does this by clarifying the ownership of parts of the tenement building and by setting up a management scheme to allow decisions to be taken about maintenance of the tenement.   As regards management, however, the scheme will normally only apply where it does not conflict with any real burdens relating to management and repairs[2]. It will therefore still be necessary to check such burdens to be certain about the management scheme and responsibility for costs of repairs existing in respect of any tenement. Finally, the Act replaces the common law provisions regarding common interest as these applied to tenement properties.

[1]   See Scottish Law Commission Report 162, *The Law of the Tenement*, ch 2 for a discussion of these.

[2]   Tenements (Scotland) Act 2004, s 4.

11.3   The definition of tenement in the Tenements (Scotland) Act 2004 is a building or part of a building comprising two or more flats provided that at least two of the flats are designed to be in separate ownership and are divided from each other horizontally. Traditional tenement closes will be included in this definition, but it would also extend to other types of building, for example substantial single dwellings which have been subdivided into flats or four in a block of houses.

OWNERSHIP

11.4   Within a tenement building some parts of the building will be in the sole ownership of proprietors of individual flats and other parts will be the common property of all of the owners in the tenement. In some cases the parts of the building which are common property and the extent of sole ownership will be set out in the titles to the property. Where the titles are silent the following rules will apply.

Sole ownership[1]

11.5   The following are in the sole ownership of the proprietors of individual flats within the tenement. All sole ownership rights are, of course, subject to common interest:

1   *Solum*. The *solum*, or ground, on which the tenement is built is the property of the ground floor proprietors. Each proprietor will own the ground under their flat as well as the ground in front of and behind it.

The proprietor of the *solum* is free to use it as he/she wishes, subject to the application of common interest. As with other property ownership, the owner of the *solum* also owns the air space above it. One consequence of this is that the interests of the other flat owners are seen as exceptions from this and the owner of the *solum* also owns the air space above the tenement roof line[2]. The only exception to sole ownership is that the ground under the common passage and stairs is owned in common by all proprietors in the close.

2   *Roof and roof space.* Aside from the roof and roof space above the common stairs, which is common property, the roof and roof space belong to the proprietor(s) of the top floor flat(s). Where there is more than one such owner, each will own the roof and roof space above their flat. One consequence is that subject to common interest, they can extend their flat up into the roof space[3].

3   *The flat and external walls.* Each proprietor of a flat obviously owns the space within the flat itself. Subject to the exceptions noted below he/she will also own the external walls of the flat. In addition, if the tenement is demolished, the flat owner will continue in ownership of the air space previously occupied by the flat[4].

4   *Floors/ceilings.* These are separately owned by the proprietors of the adjoining flats to the mid-point between the two flats.

5   *Walls.* Walls between adjoining flats are separately owned to the mid-point between the two flats. The position as regards a wall between a flat and the common close is not entirely clear.

6   *Common gables.* Common gables are owned to the mid-point between the adjoining properties[5].

[1]   Tenements (Scotland) Act 2004, s 2.
[2]   *Arrol v Inches* (1864) 14 R 394.
[3]   *Taylor v Dunlop* (1872) 11 M 25.
[4]   *Watt v Burgess's Trustees* (1891) 18 R 766
[5]   *Trades House of Glasgow v Ferguson* 1979 SLT 187.

Common ownership[1]

11.6   The common stairs and passageways in a tenement are common property. By extension the roof above these stairs and the *solum* under the close are also common property. All proprietors in the tenement who need to use the close to access their flat have an equal share in the stairs and passage. The walls in the close are in common ownership to the mid-point between close and individual flats and thereafter the property of the owner of the flat. Doors and windows letting out onto the close are the property of the owner of the flat which they serve.

¹   Tenements (Scotland) Act 2004, s 3.

11.7   Pertinents such as flues, chimneys, cables etc., are in the common ownership of those flats which they serve, and, except for chimneys, the flats served will have equal shares in the common property.¹ For example if a water tank serves only one side of a close the ownership will be shared between the flats on that side. In addition, it is made clear that common property in the close is shared only by the flats served by the close and that each flat has an equal share of that common property.

¹   S 3(4), 3(5).

Common interest

11.8   The Tenements (Scotland) Act 2004 contains a statutory restatement of the rules of common interest as they apply to tenement properties. First of all the owner of a flat has a negative duty not to do anything which would impair, or which would be likely to impair, the support provided to, or the natural light enjoyed by, any part of the tenement to a significant extent¹. Secondly, a positive duty of maintenance is imposed. This extends to any part of the tenement building which provides support or shelter to another part and is directed to ensuring that this support or shelter is continued. The obligation is limited in that the owner cannot be obliged to undertake maintenance where this would be unreasonable. In making the judgement as to what is reasonable the age and condition of the building and the cost of maintenance are relevant considerations².

¹   Tenements (Scotland) Act 2004, s 9.
²   Tenements (Scotland) Act 2004, s 8.

THE TENEMENT MANAGEMENT SCHEME¹

11.9   The tenement management scheme will apply to all tenements subject to two exceptions. The first of these is where a development management scheme applies to the flat². The second set of exceptions applies where specific provision in burdens affecting the tenement runs contrary to the provisions of the scheme.

¹   Tenements (Scotland) Act 2004, s 4 and Sch 1.
²   See CHAPTER 14.

11.10   The scheme applies to what the Bill describes as 'scheme property'. Scheme property includes any property which by virtue of either common law or the titles to the tenement is common property as well as a number of parts of the building which at common law were in sole ownership. These include the *solum*, the foundations, the roof and load bearing walls. The scheme then provides a structure for taking decisions about the maintenance and inspection of the scheme property, the appointment of a manager (except in cases where there is a manager burden¹), arrangement of a common insurance policy and decisions that an owner in the tenement will not have to contribute towards maintenance costs. The scheme permits the appointment of someone to manage maintenance work and the taking of deposits prior to the commencement of such work. Maintenance in general excludes works of improvement, unless the improvement is incidental to work falling within its definition. It includes repairs and replacement, cleaning, painting and reinstatement of a part (but not most) of the building.

¹   See CHAPTER 14.

11.11   In general, decisions on any of these matters are to be taken by a majority, with each flat having one vote. Decisions can be annulled by an owner or owners who have not voted in favour of scheme works and who have an obligation to pay 75 per cent of the costs of the works (for example under the terms of the tenement titles) serving a notice of annulment¹. It is also possible to apply to the sheriff to annul a decision if it is not in the best interests of the owners as a whole or if it is unfairly prejudicial to one or more owners².

¹   Tenements (Scotland) Act 2004, Sch 1, r 2.11.
²   Tenements (Scotland) Act 2004, s 5; under s 6, application can be made to the sheriff to resolve other disputes about the operation of the scheme.

11.12   The costs of implementing any scheme decision are known as the scheme costs. The incidence of these between flat owners depends on the nature of the costs:

(a) *Maintenance and running costs*. Where the work is on common property the costs are payable in proportion to the shares in that common property. In other cases the scheme costs are payable in equal shares by the flats in the tenement. The only exception to the equal shares' rule, which also applies to the roof over the common close, will be in cases where the floor area of the largest flat is one and a half times or more the area of the smallest. In this case the costs will be apportioned in proportion to the floor areas of the flats in the tenement.

(b) *Management and insurance costs*. These are always shared equally, in the absence of contrary provision in the titles to the tenement.

There will be no liability to contribute towards scheme costs where, because of a procedural irregularity, the owner was not aware that costs were being incurred, or when he/she became aware of this he/she objected[1].

1   Tenements (Scotland) Act 2004, Sch 1, r 5.3.

11.13   Not all repairs must be instructed as a result of a scheme decision; any owner can instruct emergency repairs and recover the costs from the other owners[1].

1   Tenements (Scotland) Act 2004, Sch 1, rr 6.1–6.3.

MISCELLANEOUS PROVISIONS

11.14   Owners have an obligation to maintain insurance for their flat and its pertinents on a reinstatement basis[1]. Owners also have a continuing liability for work decided on when they were owners. The owner who sells (the old owner) is severally liable with the new owner for scheme costs arising out of such a decision, and if the new owner pays, recovery can be made from the old owner[2].

1   Tenements (Scotland) Act 2004, s 17.
2   Tenements (Scotland) Act 2004, ss 11–14.

11.15   Owners have an obligation to allow access to their properties to allow maintenance works to be carried out[1]. Finally, there is a series of provisions relating to demolition of the tenement[2]. These provide that ownership is not to be affected by demolition. They further provide that any redevelopment or rebuilding on the site can, unless this is required by a real burden affecting the tenement, only be undertaken with the agreement of the owners of all of the flats in the tenement. In the absence of such agreement or requirement any owner can apply to the sheriff for the power to sell the site. On sale the proceeds are shared equally except in the case of a size disparity between different flats identical to that noted above in connection with sharing scheme costs. Where this applies the proceeds will be shared in proportion to the floor areas of the flats.

[1]   Tenements (Scotland) Bill, s 16.
[2]   Tenements (Scotland) Bill, ss 18–21.

CHAPTER 12

Leases

12.1 A lease confers a right of use and enjoyment of a property on the tenant. The tenant has an exclusive right of possession, enforceable against everyone, including the landlord. A lease is to be distinguished from other arrangements which permit the occupation or use of property, for example a license[1]. This last is simply a permission to occupy, which can be terminated at any time without any legal formalities. A lease of property, on the other hand, can normally only be brought to an end by the service of notice by one of the parties, and the tenant can only be removed following appropriate court proceedings.

1   In deciding into which category an agreement falls the intentions of the parties as disclosed in the agreement and in their action will be relevant: *Scottish Residential Estates Development Co Ltd v Henderson* 1991 SLT 490.

CREATING THE LANDLORD/TENANT RELATIONSHIP

12.2 Leases for a period in excess of a year must be in writing; those for a year or less need not be in writing, and it is therefore still possible to have oral leases for up to one year[1]. Aside from this, the normal formalities of any contract apply, with some additional specialties, which are considered below. Thus the parties must have title and capacity, and there must be consensus between the parties. One specialty regarding the landlord should be noted: owners of common property cannot grant a lease to one of their number[2].

¹   Requirements of Writing (Scotland) Act 1995, s 1(7).
²   *Clydesdale Bank plc v Davidson* 1998 SLT 522; *Stair Memorial Encyclopaedia*, vol 18, 28.

12.3   On the face of it the tenant under a lease acquires only a personal right, based on the continuing contract between landlord and tenant. However, based on the Leases Act 1449, tenants can acquire a real right under a lease. Acquisition of a real right means that the tenant's interest is protected if the landlord sells or otherwise transfers his/her interest in the property. In order for the tenant to acquire a real right, certain requirements, developed by the courts, must be fulfilled[1]:

1   The lease must be in writing; therefore a tenant who has an oral lease will not acquire a real right under the 1449 Act.

2   The subjects of the lease must be heritage. The heritage involved must be identifiable; in a case involving a hostel resident who had a bed in a shared room it was not clear what heritage was the subject of the claimed lease[2].

3   There must be a specific continuing rent[3]. The amount of the rent must not be elusory though the rent can be in kind[4].

4   The lease must have a definite ish. The ish is simply the date on which the lease is to come to an end[5]. Where the other requirements for a valid lease are fulfilled but no period of let has been stated in the agreement between the parties, the court will construe the lease as being a lease for one year, or for any longer period indicated by the lease terms[6].

5   The landlord must have recorded or registered their title to the land which is the subject of the lease.

6   The tenant must have entered into possession of the subjects. Occupying under the equivalent of a license will not count as possession for these purposes[7].

¹   The special position of long leases is considered at PARA **12.5**.
²   *Conway v Glasgow City Council* 1999 SCLR 248.
³   *Mann v Houston* 1957 SLT 89.
⁴   *Lundy v Smith of Lundy* (1610) Mor 15166; *Scottish Residential Estates Development Co Ltd v Henderson* 1991 SLT 490.
⁵   Though, of course, it can be continued beyond this date by tacit relocation, considered more fully PARA **12.32**.
⁶   *Gray v University of Edinburgh* 1962 SLT 173; *Shetland Islands Council v BP Petroleum Developments* 1990 SLT 82.
⁷   *Millar v McRobbie* 1949 SLT 2.

12.4   While the requirements set out above are those which are necessary
to endow the tenant with a real right, there is a simpler set of requirements
for the validity of a lease as between the landlord and the tenant. These
are simply that there is consensus between the parties, that the lease is for
the occupation of identified heritage[1], that there is some consideration
payable in return for the tenant's interest, and that the lease is stated to be
for a certain period. As we have noted above, the courts will imply a lease
term of one year if this is not agreed between the parties; however, where
the parties to the lease, the subjects of the lease, and the duration of the
lease are agreed the court will not supply the missing element and set a
rent[2]. The nature of occupation required in order for there to be a lease has
been the subject of some discussion. Currently the view appears to be
that exclusive possession is required[3].

[1]   See the discussion of this point in *Brador Properties Ltd v British
Telecommunications plc* 1992 SCLR 119.
[2]   *Shetland Islands Council v BP Petroleum Developments* 1990 SLT 82.
[3]   *Brador Properties Ltd v British Telecommunications plc* 1992 SCLR 119; *Conway
v Glasgow City Council* 1999 SCLR 248.

12.5   Long leases, that is leases for a period in excess of 20 years, are
subject to certain specialties created by statute. First of all, such leases
contain an implied condition prohibiting the use of the subjects of the
lease as a private dwelling house. This requirement was introduced at the
same time as the ban on creating new feu duties was created by the Land
Tenure Reform (Scotland) Act 1974[1]. The purpose of this prohibition was
to prevent individuals circumventing the abolition of new feu duties by
simply creating long leases over heritable property. Breach of this implied
condition allows the landlord to give notice to terminate the use and, if
this does not happen, to then raise an action for removal of the tenant. The
tenant has a defence if the landlord expressly or by implication approves
of use of the premises as a private dwelling house. If removal is ordered
this cannot be until the end of the lease or until 20 years pass if this is a
longer period. Note that if the landlord does not invoke this implied
condition, the lease is perfectly valid in a question between landlord and
tenant.

[1]   Land Tenure Reform (Scotland) Act 1974, ss 8–10; see the discussion in
A McAllister, *Scottish Law of Leases* (3rd edn) 7.29–7.40.

12.6   The second specialty to do with long leases relates to the
acquisition of a real right by the tenant: the *only* way in which a tenant can

now acquire a real right under a long lease is by registering it in the Land Register[1]. This requirement only took effect when the area in which the subjects of the lease are situated was brought under the umbrella of the Land Register. As a result there will still be long leases which were granted when the area in which the subjects are situated was still covered by the Register of Sasines and where real rights will have been obtained as described above.

[1]   Land Registration (Scotland) Act 1979, s 3.

12.7   Finally, leases entered into after 9 June 2000 must be for less than 175 years[1]. The rationale is to prevent the use of very long leases to effectively re-create the relationship of superior and vassal[2].

[1]   Abolition of Feudal Tenure (Scotland) Act 2000, s 67.
[2]   See PARAS **1.15–1.19**.

12.8   Certain types of lease are taken out of the common law provisions and are governed by their own specific statutory regime: the main examples are residential tenancies[1] and agricultural holdings[2].

[1]   See Housing (Scotland) Act 1988 and Housing (Scotland) Act 2001.
[2]   Agricultural Holdings (Scotland) Act 1991; this type of lease is not discussed further here, though see PARAS **5.26–5.27**; see A McAllister, *Scottish Law of Leases* (3rd edn), ch 14.

LANDLORD'S OBLIGATIONS

12.9   The landlord has a number of obligations under the lease:
1   To give possession of the whole subjects let and to maintain the tenant in possession.
2   To ensure that the property is in a tenantable and habitable condition at the commencement of the tenancy and that it is reasonably fit for the purposes of the let. This requirement of reasonable fitness is a general one. In other words, the subjects have to be fit for occupation as commercial premises, residential premises etc depending on the subjects of the lease. The requirement does not mean that the landlord is obliged to make the premises fit to meet any specific requirements that the tenant might have. Where the tenant knows about specific difficulties which might affect their ability to use the premises, it is up

to the tenant to satisfy him or herself that the subjects are suitable for the purposes for which they intend to lease them[1].

3   To keep the property in tenantable condition throughout the lease. This includes an obligation to keep the premises wind and water tight. It should be noted that the landlord's obligation to repair does not cover damage caused by *damnum fatale* or caused by a third party[2], nor does it cover damage caused by the tenant's own negligence[3]. The obligation does not arise until the landlord is notified of the defect and fails to take action to remedy it[4]. Where damage is caused by *damnum fatale* or by a third party, neither the landlord nor the tenant has an obligation to carry out repairs. It is important to note that in commercial and industrial tenancies there is usually specific provision made imposing the obligation to insure and repair on the tenant[5].

[1]   *Paton v MacDonald* 1973 SLT (Sh Ct) 85.
[2]   *Allan v Robertson's Trustees* (1891) 18 R 932.
[3]   *Hardie v Black* (1768) Mor 10133.
[4]   *Woolfson v Forrester* 1910 SC 675.
[5]   A McAllister, *Scottish Law of Leases* (3rd edn), 3.3 and 10.11–10.15.

TENANT'S OBLIGATIONS

12.10   The tenant also has a number of obligations under the lease:

1   To take and maintain possession. The tenant is required to enter into possession of the property and to remain in possession throughout the duration of the lease. If the tenant fails to do this he/she may be liable to the landlord for loss of goodwill where commercial premises are left unopened and unoccupied for a period of time. The leading case in this area is *Graham & Black v Stevenson*[1]. The tenant of an inn closed the premises for a period towards the end of his tenancy. He was found liable in damages, with the judgment proceeding 'on the breach of the bona fides of the lease, by shutting up the house for several months, to the injury of its business and character as an inn'. A reclaiming motion which, among other things, argued that the tenant had no obligation to use the subjects let was rejected. The possession must involve possession in the form contemplated by the lease. The tenant may be liable for what is known as inversion of possession, in other words, use of a property other than for the purposes of the lease[2]. Doubtless to the relief of residential tenants, it has been held

that rearranging the furniture or making other decorative changes does not amount to inversion of possession[3].

2 To take reasonable care of the premises, and to make good any damage caused by his own negligence. The tenant may be liable for any damage to the property caused by his/her own negligence[4] or for damage caused by the property being left unoccupied[5]. Aside from this the tenant has no liability for repairs at common law though, as mentioned above, in commercial leases the obligation of repairing and insurance is normally put on to the tenant.

3 To plenish the subjects. This essentially means that the tenant has an obligation to furnish them with fittings and trade goods appropriate to the activities being carried out on the premises by the tenant. The purpose of this obligation is to ensure that there are sufficient goods and fittings in the subjects in case the landlord wishes to exercise their right of hypothec. The obligation can be enforced by court order, even in circumstances where the contents of the property have been sold off because of the landlord's exercise of his/her remedies[6].

4 To pay the rent due in respect of their occupation of the property. As we have already seen, agreement on a rent to be paid is a prerequisite for creation of a lease. In commercial and industrial leases it is unlikely that the rent will remain the same for the duration of the lease. Instead there will usually be a rent review clause which creates a mechanism for periodically revising the rent[7].

[1] (1792) Hume 781.
[2] *Miln v Mitchell* (1787) Mor 15254.
[3] *Miller v Stewart* (1899) 2F 309.
[4] *Hardie v Black* (1768) Mor 10133.
[5] *Mickel v McCoard* 1913 1 SLT 463.
[6] *Macdonald v Mackessack* (1888) 16 R 168. A recent example is *Co-operative Insurance Society Ltd v Halfords Ltd* 1997 SCLR 719.
[7] A McAllister, *Scottish Law of Leases* (3rd edn), ch 11.

ASSIGNATION AND SUB-LETTING

12.11 Assignation involves the transfer of the entire tenancy interest to a new tenant. In other words the assignor severs their relationship with the property and the effect of the assignation is to set up a new relationship of landlord and tenant between the landlord and the assignee. Sub-letting, however, involves the tenant letting out the whole or part of the tenancy interest. In this case the tenant becomes in his/her turn a landlord to the sub-tenant. At common law the rule is that the consent of the landlord is not necessary for any assignation or sub-letting in a case where the lease does not involve *delectus personae*. *Delectus personae* exists in agricultural tenancies, though not where these are of extraordinary duration or in cases where the lease terms can overcome this presumption[1], and in furnished lettings of residential accommodation[2].

[1]   *Scottish Ministers v Drummond's Trustees* 2001 SCLR 495, also holding that *delectus personae* did not extend to forestry leases.
[2]   *Earl of Fife v Wilson* (1864) 3 M 323; this matter is, of course, now regulated by the statutory schemes covering residential tenancies.

12.12   In cases where assignation or sub-letting is permitted by common law it may be specifically excluded in the contract of lease. It should be noted, however, that an exclusion of the power to assign does *not* exclude the power to create sub-tenancies[1]. Where there is a provision excluding assignation or sub-letting without the consent of the landlord the landlord need give no reason for refusing to consent to such a transaction; indeed in one case it was said that the landlord was entitled to withhold consent arbitrarily and out of mere caprice[2]. Because of this it is common in practice to find a provision that the landlord's consent is not to be unreasonably withheld.

[1]   *Trotter v Dennis* (1770) Mor 15282.
[2]   *Marquis of Breadalbane v Whitehead & Sons* (1893) 21 R 138.

12.13   An assignation is completed in a question with the landlord by serving notice to the landlord, and in a question with third parties by the assignee taking up possession of the subjects of the lease.

12.14   It is also possible for a landlord to sell the landlord's interests to a third party and then to lease it back, thereby interposing themselves in between the head landlord and the tenants[1]. The effect of this is that any tenants of the original landlord now become sub-tenants, and there is a new ultimate landlord above the original landlord. This sort of transaction can be used where the original landlord wishes to raise a large capital sum by sale of the property. If the original landlord wishes to maintain an interest in the property, for example from an investment point of view, the property can then be leased back. For example a developer invests in building a shopping center. After the centre is let the developer wants an injection of capital, but also wants to retain an income stream from the centre. The centre could be sold off to a pension fund or similar organisation and the developer would then become their tenant. The purchase price would give the developer capital and they would continue to obtain income from the rents paid by the tenants in the centre.

1   Land Tenure Reform (Scotland) Act 1974, s 17.

LANDLORD'S REMEDIES

Rescission

12.15   In the case of material breach on the part of the tenant the landlord can terminate the lease by rescission. It is, however, not possible for the landlord to do this unless a reasonable landlord would terminate the lease in all the circumstances of the case[1].

1   Law Reform (Miscellaneous Provisions) (Scotland) Act 1985, s 5.

Interdict/implement

12.16   Breaches of lease conditions can be enforced by the landlord by way of interdict or by way of implement.

12.17   It is common to find a clause to the effect that the tenant is obliged to carry on a particular business in the premises for the duration of the lease or until the lease is assigned (referred to as 'stay open clauses') in commercial leases, particularly involving leases of retail premises. The question of what remedy the landlord has if the tenant breaches this condition or indicates an intention to stop trading has occupied the Scottish courts over recent years. The case law has focused on two main issues.

Interdict

12.18   It is clear that once a tenant has left the premises interdict cannot be used to force the tenant to keep trading; this would result in a double negative in the interdict which has been held to be legally impossible[1]. In effect what the pursuer in such a case would be seeking is an order from the court ordering the defender not to not trade.

1   *Church Commissioners for England v Abbey National plc* 1994 SLT 959.

12.19   On the other hand, the landlord can successfully obtain an interdict to prevent the tenant from leaving where the tenant is still trading from the premises. An example of this is *Retail Parks Investments Ltd v Our Price Music Ltd*[1]. Initially two interim interdicts were granted against the defenders who wished to cease trading following their purchase by Virgin. The first was to prevent the removal of stock, fittings, sales equipment and advertising. The second was to prevent the tenants vacating or removing from the premises or taking steps to vacate or remove. At a recall hearing the first interdict was recalled on the grounds that it related to actings which could be consistent with the normal management of the unit. The second was varied to delete the reference to taking steps to vacate/remove, leaving in place the interdiction of removal or vacating.

[1]   1995 SLT 1181.

12.20   An interdict is a purely negative order and cannot require the defender to do anything positive such as continuing to trade. Landlords have therefore sought to enforce stay open clauses through the mechanism of specific implement.

Specific implement

12.21   The first case in which an order for specific implement was granted to enforce a stay open clause was *Retail Parks Investments Ltd v Royal Bank of Scotland (No 2)*[1] a decision of the Inner House of the Court of Session after the order was refused at first instance. This decision has been followed in a number of other cases[2]. One factor of importance to a court in deciding whether to grant the order is how specific the order sought is[3]. It has been held that references to a 'high class store' and to 'normal opening hours' are not too vague[4]. The order need not specify in detail the steps required of the tenant, but can follow the wording of the clause in the lease, as this has been agreed between the parties in terms which they found clear enough at the time of agreeing the lease[5]:

> '… it must be presumed that, when they agreed the terms of their contract, the parties considered the expressions used by them to be sufficiently precise to let them know what had to be done. Consequently, if the order for implement essentially repeats the provisions of the contract, it is inherently likely that the parties will

know what the [order] means and what must be done to comply with
its terms.'

1   1996 SLT 669.
2   Eg *Co-operative Wholesale Society v Saxone Ltd* 1997 SLT 1052; *Highland and
     Universal Properties Ltd v Safeway Properties Ltd (No 2)*, 2000 SLT 414; *Oak
     Mall Greenock Ltd v McDonald's Restaurants Ltd* (9 May 2003, unreported),
     OH. Note that in England and Wales an order for specific performance will not
     be granted in such circumstances: *Co-operative Insurance Society Ltd v Argyll
     Stores (Holdings) Ltd* [1997] 3 All ER 297.
3   Compare *Co-operative Insurance Society Ltd v Halfords Ltd* 1997 SCLR 719
     and *Co-perative Wholesale Society Ltd v Saxone Ltd* 1997 SCLR 835.
4   *Highland and Universal Properties Ltd v Safeway Properties Ltd (No 2)* 2000
     SLT 414.
5   *Oak Mall Greenock Ltd v McDonald's Restaurants Ltd* (9 May 2003, unreported),
     OH, per Lord Drummond Young at [6].

12.22   Another factor which has been considered relevant is the length
of time the lease still has to run because of possible changes over time in
the retail environment; though in a recent case an order was to be granted
although there were still almost 17 years of a 25-year lease still to run[1].

1   *Britel Fund Trustees Ltd v Scottish and Southern Energy plc* 2002 SCLR 54.

12.23   A final factor which is relevant is the nature of any losses accruing
to the tenant as a result of continued operation of the premises. Substantial
losses might be an indicator that the court should use its discretion to
refuse the order for implement because granting the order would be
inconvenient and unjust[1]. However, in order for refusal of an order for
implement to be justified by reference to losses suffered by the tenant, the
loss must be severely disproportionate to any corresponding benefit to
the landlord arising from the tenant keeping their business open: it is not
enough that it is clear that the tenant will operate at a loss for the remainder
of the lease[2].

1   *Stewart v Kennedy* (1890) 17 R (HL) 1.
2   *Oak Mall Greenock Ltd v McDonald's Restaurants Ltd* (9 May 2003, unreported),
     OH.

Irritancy[1]

12.24   Irritancy involves the revocation of the tenant's interests in
property by the landlord: in simple terms it has the effect of bringing the

lease to an end. There is provision for legal irritancy, which is incurred on two years' non-payment of rent[2]. Most irritancies, however, are conventional irritancies: that is, they are specifically provided for in the lease itself. A tenant has no automatic right to purge a conventional irritancy. In other words there is no right to take steps to remedy the breach, for example by paying arrears of rent or by complying with the lease condition which has been breached. The courts, though, do have a residual equitable power to refuse a landlord's action for decree of declarator of irritancy if the landlord is acting oppressively[3].

[1]   See Scottish Law Commission Report 191, *Irritancy in Leases of Land* (2003) for proposed changes to the current rules.
[2]   Though the scope of this is now restricted by the Leasehold Casualties (Scotland) Act 2001, ss 5 and 6.
[3]   *McDouall's Trustees v McLeod* 1949 SC 593.

12.25   There are statutory restrictions on the landlord's exercise of their right to irritate the lease. These statutory restrictions contain two sets of rules, one for monetary breaches of the lease (for example non-payment of rent) and one for non-monetary irritancy, that is breach of any other condition.

1   In addition to the legal irritancy which applies in non-payment of rent it is common for leases to specify that if the tenant is late in paying any instalment of the rent that will entitle the landlord to irritate the lease. Where the tenant incurs such irritancy by non-payment by a particular date the landlord must serve a notice on the tenant giving him/her 14 days' notice requiring payment of the arrears and warning of the possibility of termination of the lease through the landlord's exercise of their right to irritate. If the rent is still not paid within the period specified by the landlord, then there is no defence to the ensuing action for decree of declarator of irritancy[1]. This conclusion was reached, albeit with serious reservations as to its equity, in *CIN Properties v Dollar Land (Cumbernauld) Ltd*[2].

2   In the case of non-monetary breaches, the landlord is only entitled to irritate the lease if, in all the circumstances of the case, a fair and reasonable landlord would rely on the breach to terminate the lease[3]. This test has been held to be concerned with how the landlord would act rather than with the penal consequences for the tenant[4].

[1]   Law Reform (Miscellaneous Provisions) (Scotland) Act 1985, s 4.
[2]   1992 SCLR 820.
[3]   Law Reform (Miscellaneous Provisions) (Scotland) Act 1985, s 5.

4   *Blythswood Investments Ltd v Clydesdale Ltd* 1995 SLT 150; *Aubrey Investments Ltd v D S C (Realisations) Ltd (in receivership)* 1999 SC 21.

Landlord's hypothec

12.26   The landlord's hypothec is a security over the moveables (or *invecta et illata*) which are on the leased premises. At present it covers both residential and non-residential premises. Certain items are excluded from the landlord's hypothec, for example, tools of the trade, money, clothing and certain household furniture. The security is enforced by the landlord raising a court action for sequestration for rent[1]. On the basis of this a warrant is issued to list the goods on the premises. Once listed the goods cannot be removed, and if the tenant fails to pay the arrears of rent, the items can be sold at auction.

1   Though the Scottish Executive consultation, *Modernising Bankruptcy and Diligence in Scotland: Draft Bill and Consultation* (2004) proposes abolition of sequestration for rent, but not of the landlord's hypothec.

12.27   The security only covers the current year's rent, but it does cover a wide range of different types of property. In particular it includes items on the premises belonging to third parties[1], for example goods which have already been sold but which have been left on the premises[2], items being acquired under hire purchase[3], and may also include items which are only on the premises temporarily[4]. One specific exclusion from the landlord's hypothec is property belonging to lodgers or members of the tenant's family[5] and property which is on the premises for repairs. The claim under the landlord's hypothec has priority over the claim of the liquidator or receiver under liquidation or receivership. It has also been held that landlords could exercise their right of hypothec even against tenants who had succeeded to the tenant who owed the arrears of rent[6].

1   Though the Scottish Executive consultation, *Modernising Bankruptcy and Diligence in Scotland: Draft Bill and Consultation* (2004) proposes that third party goods should be excluded from the hypothec.
2   *Ryan v Little* 1910 SC 219.
3   *Ditchburn Organisation (Sales) Ltd v Dundee Corporation* 1971 SLT 218, though here it was indicated that property would be excluded from the hypothec if the third party gave appropriate notice to the landlord.
4   *Scottish & Newcastle Breweries Ltd v Edinburgh District Council* 1979 SLT (Notes) 11.
5   *Bell v Andrews* (1885) 12 R 961.

⁶   *Grampian Regional Council v Drill Stem (Inspection Services) Ltd* 1994 SCLR 36.

Other remedies

12.28   The landlord may also have certain other remedies, for example it is possible for the landlord to recover arrears of rent by way of a normal action for payment.

TENANT'S REMEDIES

Rescission

12.29   The tenant, like the landlord, can withdraw from the lease if there is a material breach of contract by the landlord.

Interdict/implement

12.30   Again in common with the landlord, the tenant has the right to seek enforcement of particular lease terms by way of an action for interdict or implement. An action for implement might, for example, be appropriate where the landlord had failed to carry out their repairing obligations.

Retention/abatement of rent

12.31   In some circumstances the tenant may respond to a landlord's breach of contract, for example failure to carry out repairs, by retaining rent which is due. The ability to retain rent may be excluded by the terms of the lease. Once the landlord has remedied the breach of contract, for example by carrying out the repairs, the arrears of rent must be paid in full, unless the tenant is able to argue that the rent for the period of the landlord's breach should be abated (reduced). In some cases the court might take the view that the abatement should be total, for example, where the premises were essentially uninhabitable during the period of the landlord's breach[1].

¹   *Renfrew District Council v Gray* 1987 SLT (Sh Ct) 70. Compare *Paccitti v Manganiello* 1995 SCLR 557, though in this case the issue of abatement does not seem to have been argued.

TERMINATION OF LEASE

Tacit relocation

12.32   Even although a lease has a definite ish, it can only be brought to an end on that ish by one of the parties serving a notice of termination on the other. If this is not done the lease will automatically be continued for a further period of one year by tacit relocation, unless the lease contains an express provision to the contrary[1]. The period of notice depends on the type and length of lease. For residential leases over four months and for other types of lease over one year the notice must be communicated to the other party 40 days before the lease is due to terminate to be effective[2]. If the lease is continued by tacit relocation it will be on the same terms as previously, except for any terms which are inconsistent with an annual lease, for example a clause providing for a three-yearly rent review[3]. There will be no tacit relocation if a new lease is entered into prior to the ish.

[1]   *McDougall v Guidi* 1992 SCLR 167.
[2]   Sheriff Courts (Scotland) Act 1907, ss 37 & 38; *Signet Group plc v C & G Clark Retail Properties Ltd* 1996 SLT 1325; see also *Glass v Klepczynski* 1951 SLT (Sh Ct) 55. There is a minimum 28-day period for other types of residential tenancy and separate rules for agricultural tenancies.
[3]   *Commercial Union Insurance Company Ltd and Watt & Cumine*, Special Case 1964 SLT 62; *Sea Breeze Properties Ltd v Bio-Medical Systems Ltd* 1998 SLT 319.

Breaks

12.33   The lease may provide for breaks at certain periods. These will entitle either the landlord or the tenant to bring the lease to an end on these dates. A tenant is entitled to exercise their right to terminate the lease under a break clause even if they are in breach of other terms of the lease[1].

[1]   *Allied Dunbar Assurance plc v Superglass Sections Ltd* 2003 SLT 1420.

Irritancy etc

12.34   Leases can also be brought to an end by irritancy, rescission etc. These are discussed above.

Destruction of the subjects of let

12.35   The lease will be brought to an end if the subjects are destroyed. This is described as termination by way of *rei interitus*. There is no doubt that total destruction of the subjects will bring the lease to an end[1], though it is common in commercial and industrial leases to provide for continuation of the lease even despite this happening. Where the subjects are destroyed without fault, the landlord is not obliged to rebuild, and the tenant cannot be forced to return and take up the tenancy if the subjects are restored to their former state.

[1]   *Lindsay v Home* (1612) Mor 10120.

12.36   In addition to total destruction, the lease may be brought to an end by partial destruction of the subjects of lease. This will happen if the destruction is sufficient to amount to constructive total destruction, in other words if the destruction in part of the premises effectively renders the premises useless for the purposes of the let[1].

[1]   Compare *Duff v Fleming* (1870) 8 M 769 and *Allan v Markland* (1882) 10 R 383.

Removing and ejection

12.37   As noted earlier the landlord can only remove the tenant if a court order of removing or ejection is obtained. Before such action can be raised the landlord must serve notice on the tenant: for it to be effective this notice must be in the correct statutory form; if not then the action of removing is incompetent[1]. An action of this type might be needed to recover possession of the subjects of the lease after termination of the lease, for example following on a declarator of irritancy.

[1]   *Glass v Klepczynski* 1951 SLT (Sh Ct) 55.

RESIDENTIAL TENANCIES

12.38   There are separate provisions for tenancies in the private sector and in the social rented sector. Before going on to consider these, however, there are certain rules which apply to all residential tenancies. The general rules considered above as to the formation of a lease and the obligations of landlord and tenant apply to residential leases as they do elsewhere. Thus, for example, it is quite possible to have an oral lease of residential property where the let is for one year or less, provided that all of the necessary matters as to parties, property and rent have been agreed.

12.39 The landlord's common law obligations to provide accommodation which is in a tenantable and habitable condition apply to residential leases. This obligation to have the premises in a tenantable condition has been used as the basis for claims for compensation for illness caused by damp or otherwise unsuitable housing[1]. In addition, there are a number of statutory obligations imposed on landlords:

1   Properties let for a rent of less than £300 per week (ie most properties) must be in all respects fit for human habitation at the start of the tenancy and must be maintained in that condition by the landlord. In deciding whether the property is fit for human habitation consideration is given to the extent to which the house falls short of the requirements of the building regulations[2]. In *Quinn v Monklands District Council* [3] the local authority was held to be in breach of this obligation. As a result of condensation a number of rooms in a flat were affected by black mould, treatment of which required the tenant to leave the property for a period. She was awarded compensation for property damaged by the mould and for inconvenience and the general depression caused by the state of the premises[4]. It has been held that the obligation to provide a habitable house at the start of the tenancy involves a broad meaning of habitability in the sense that the house is not in such a condition that damage might be caused to the occupier by ordinary use of the premises[5].

2   For properties let for less than seven years the landlord must keep the structure and exterior of the house in good repair and inside the house must keep the gas, water and electricity supply, the sanitary appliances, and space and water heaters in good repair and working properly[6]. The restriction on the length of tenancies has little practical effect as most tenancies, including those in the public sector, are for less than seven years.

3   Where the landlord is responsible for the maintenance and repair of the premises they must take reasonable care in carrying out this responsibility so as to prevent danger to people coming into the premises[7].

[1]   *McArdle v Glasgow District Council* 1989 SCLR 19; *Nielson v Scottish Homes* 1999 SLT (Sh Ct) 2.

2   Housing (Scotland) Act 1987, Sch 10.
3   1995 SCLR 393.
4   Most of the reported cases in this area concern problems with dampness or condensation, usually caused by poor building design.
5   *Mearns v Glasgow City Council* 2002 SLT (Sh Ct) 49, landlord's obligation breached where prior to the commencement of the tenancy there was a temporary repair on a burst pipe which could have given way at any time.
6   Housing (Scotland) Act 1987, Sch 10.
7   For example, *Hughes Tutrix v Glasgow District Council* 1982 SLT (Sh Ct) 70, where a mother successfully sued for damages for her daughter who was injured on a defective toilet bowl.

Scottish secure tenancies

12.40   With effect from 20 September 2002 all tenants of social landlords became Scottish secure tenants. Social landlords are local authorities, Scottish Water and registered social landlords (mainly housing associations). Prior to this local authority tenants, as well as those of Scottish Homes had secure tenancies and housing association tenants had assured tenancies (at least if their tenancy started in 1989 or later)[1].

1   For discussion of secure tenancies see P Robson and S Halliday, *Residential Tenancies* (2nd edn).

12.41   Certain types of accommodation are excluded from being Scottish secure tenancies; these include accommodation provided with employment, decant accommodation, educational lets, accommodation within the curtilage of another building and accommodation let on a short Scottish secure tenancy[1]. The landlord is required to prepare a written tenancy agreement and have it signed before the beginning of the let and must also provide the tenant with certain other information, for example about allocation rules, tenant's right to buy and repairs and maintenance[2]. Once the tenancy agreement has been entered into there are restrictions on the ability of the landlord to change the lease terms without agreement[3]; and the landlord must consult tenants on any proposed increase in rent and must give four weeks' notice of the increase[4].

1   Housing (Scotland) Act 2001, s 1 and Sch 1.
2   Housing (Scotland) Act 2001, s 23. The right to buy is discussed in CHAPTER 17.
3   Subject to what is said below about conversion to a short Scottish secure tenancy.
4   Housing (Scotland) Act 2001, s 25.

Landlord's repairing obligation

12.42   Schedule 2 of the Housing (Scotland) Act 2001 repeats the common law obligation to have and keep leased premises in a tenantable condition explained above. In addition, it requires the landlord to inspect houses before they are let to identify any repairs that are necessary and to notify the tenant of any necessary work. The landlord is also required to carry out any work needed to bring the house into a tenantable condition within a reasonable time of being notified by the tenant or otherwise becoming aware that such work is necessary.

Tenant's rights

12.43

1   The tenant has the right to seek variation of the lease terms by application to the sheriff court[1].

2   The tenant can also apply to the landlord to be allowed to assign the tenancy, sub-let the property or arrange an exchange with another tenant. The landlord must consent in writing, but may only withhold consent if to do so is reasonable. Refusal will be reasonable, for example, where the proposal would result in overcrowding, where an order for recovery of possession has been made against the tenant or where the landlord has served a notice of their intention to raise proceedings for possession based on the conduct of the tenant[2].

3   Tenants have certain rights to instruct repairs themselves if their landlord fails to do them and to recover the costs and a small compensation payment from the landlord. This power only arises in respect of a limited list of repairs, including blocked drains, loss of electrical power and insecure doors and windows, and then only if the landlord fails to carry out repairs within a specified time after being notified (usually one day)[3].

4   Finally, tenants have rights to compensation for any improvements they have carried out to the house[4].

[1]   Housing (Scotland) Act 2001, s 26.
[2]   Housing (Scotland) Act 2001, s 32.
[3]   Scottish Secure Tenants (Right to Repair) Regulations 2002 (SSI 2002/316).
[4]   Housing (Scotland) Act 2001, s 30; Scottish Secure Tenants (Compensation for Improvements) Regulations 2002 (SSI 2002/312).

Termination of the tenancy

12.44   The ways in which the tenancy can be terminated are restricted. It can be brought to an end by agreement, by the tenant giving the landlord four weeks' notice, by being converted into a short Scottish secure tenancy, if there is no-one entitled to succeed to the tenancy who wishes to take up this option[1], if the house let is abandoned[2] or if an order for recovery of possession is granted by the sheriff[3].

1   Housing (Scotland) Act 2001, s 22.
2   Housing (Scotland) Act 2001, ss 17 and 18.
3   Housing (Scotland) Act 2001, s 12.

12.45   Before an action for recovery of possession can be initiated by the landlord they must send the tenant and any qualifying occupier a notice setting out the grounds on which proceedings for recovery of possession are to be raised and specifying a date on or after which these proceedings may be raised[1]. The date will normally be four weeks after the service of the notice. From this it will be seen that it is not enough that notice is served on the tenants, but qualifying occupiers must also be notified. A qualifying occupier is any member of the tenant's family over 15, anyone to whom the tenancy has been assigned or sub-let either in whole or in part or anyone who the tenant has taken in as a lodger with the consent of the landlord. 'Family' has an extended meaning and includes couples who live together as husband and wife or in a relationship which has the characteristics of the relationship between husband and wife except that the persons are of the same sex[2]. If a notice is not served on a qualifying occupier any order for recovery of possession will be open to recall because of their absence from the court hearing even though the tenant was present at the hearing[3].

1   Housing (Scotland) Act 2001, s 14.
2   Housing (Scotland) Act 2001, s 108.
3   *City of Edinburgh Council v Porter* 2004 Hous LR 46, contrast *North Lanarkshire Council v Kenmure* 2004 Hous LR 50.

12.46   If an application is made for recovery of possession the grounds on which the sheriff can grant an order for possession are limited[1]. They fall into two broad categories.

1   Housing (Scotland) Act 2001, Sch 2.

Conduct grounds

12.47 These are grounds relating to the behaviour of the tenant. More specifically they are:

1 rents arrears or breach of any other obligation of the tenancy;
2 a conviction for using the premises for illegal or immoral purposes or a conviction for an imprisonable offence committed in or near the house;
3 deterioration in the house, including any common areas because of neglect or fault of the tenant;
4 deterioration of any furniture provided as part of the tenancy because of ill-treatment by the tenant;
5 absence from the house for at least six months or ceasing to use it as the tenant's principal home;
6 the tenancy was induced by fraud;
7 the tenant or anyone living in or visiting the house has engaged in anti-social behaviour towards neighbours or has pursued a course of conduct amounting to harassment and it is not reasonable in the circumstances that the landlord be required to make other accommodation available[1].

[1] *Edinburgh City Council v T* 2003 Hous LR 74.

12.48 Before making an order based on any of these grounds the sheriff must be satisfied that it is reasonable to do so. In deciding what is reasonable the sheriff is directed to consider the nature frequency or duration of the conduct complained of or, in the case of ground 2 above, the conduct resulting in the conviction; the extent to which people other than the tenant are to blame; the effect the conduct has had, is having or is likely to have on people other than the tenant; and, any action taken by the landlord to try to stop the conduct[1].

[1] Housing (Scotland) Act 2001, s 16(3).

Management grounds

12.49 These grounds refer more to the management of the landlord's housing stock than to the actions of the tenant. They are:

8 the tenant or someone living in the house has been guilty of conduct amounting to a nuisance or harassment and it is appropriate to require the tenant to move to other accommodation;

9   the house is overcrowded;
10   it is intended either to demolish or carry out work on the house and this cannot proceed without recovery of possession;
11   the house is designed or adapted for special needs and is no longer occupied by a person with such needs;
12   the house is part of a group of houses designed or provided with or located near facilities for people with special needs and the landlord needs it for such a person;
13   the landlord holds under a lease which is coming to an end;
14   the house is held by any of the island authorities for educational purposes and is needed for a teacher;
15   the tenant and his/her spouse (or spouse equivalent) are splitting up and the landlord wishes to transfer the tenancy to the spouse (or spouse equivalent).

Again there are restrictions on the sheriff's discretion to grant an order for possession. In the case of grounds 8 to 14 possession must only be ordered if there is suitable alternative accommodation[1]. In the case of ground 15 making the order must be reasonable and there must be suitable alternative accommodation.

[1]   Housing (Scotland) Act 2001, s 16(2)(b); for the definition of 'suitable' see Sch 2, Pt 2.

Short Scottish secure tenancies

12.50   These are tenancies for a fixed period of six months or more where, before the creation of the tenancy the landlord has served a notice to the effect that the tenancy is to be a short Scottish secure tenancy[1]. The tenancy may be continued beyond its term by tacit relocation or by agreement between landlord and tenant. Before a landlord can let a property on a short Scottish secure tenancy a number of requirements must be fulfilled. These include: an order for possession against the tenant on certain grounds has been made within the past three years; the house is let pending development affecting it; the house is let on a temporary basis to an intentionally homeless person with priority need; and, the tenant or someone residing with them is the subject of an anti-social behaviour order[2]. To terminate the tenancy a notice must be served giving at least two months' notice, and the sheriff must grant an order for possession provided that the notice requirements have been complied with, the tenancy has reached its ish, tacit relocation has not operated and there is no new contractual tenancy in operation[3]. It is possible for a Scottish secure tenancy to be converted to a short Scottish secure tenancy. This is done by service of a notice by the landlord in circumstances where the tenant or someone else living in the house has been made subject to an anti-social behaviour order. The reverse process may also operate. This can happen only in respect of some of the grounds on which a tenancy can be a short Scottish secure tenancy and will take place automatically if the tenancy has been held for 12 months without the landlord serving a notice of intention to start proceedings[4].

[1] Housing (Scotland) Act 2001, s 34.
[2] Housing (Scotland) Act 2001, Sch 6; for anti-social behaviour orders see the Criminal Procedure (Scotland) Act 1995, s 234AA and the Antisocial Behaviour etc (Scotland) Act 2004, s 4.
[3] Housing (Scotland) Act 2001, s 36.
[4] Housing (Scotland) Act 2001, s 37.

Assured tenancies

12.51   These are the dominant form of tenancy in the private sector and have been in existence since the beginning of 1989. There may still be some people who were tenants before then who have other types of tenancy, but these cases will be rare and are not considered here. There are, as with Scottish secure tenancies, a number of cases where those occupying residential accommodation do not qualify as assured tenants, which include: tenancies where the rent is less than £6 per week; lettings to students by educational institutions; and lettings where there is a resident landlord.

12.52   The landlord in an assured tenancy has a statutory obligation to provide a written lease, though the failure of the landlord to comply with this obligation will not affect the validity of any agreement which qualifies as a lease between the landlord and tenant. One of the implied terms of any lease is a prohibition on assignation or sub-letting without the consent of the landlord.

12.53   Assured tenancies are of two types, contractual and statutory. A tenancy is contractual during the period of the contract between the landlord and tenant, including any period during which it is continued by tacit relocation. A statutory tenancy begins when the agreement is brought to an end, most usually by service of a notice to quit. In the former case the basis of the tenant's continued occupation of the house is the contract with the landlord; in the latter it is the protection conferred by statute. There are a number of areas where statutory and contractual tenancies are treated differently:

1   There are differences in the grounds on which a sheriff can order possession of the property. As we will see below the grounds are more limited in the case of a contractual tenancy.

2   There are differences in the steps that have to be taken prior to raising proceedings for recovery of possession. In the case of a statutory tenancy there is no need to serve a notice to quit[1].

3   There are slight differences in the terms of the tenancy as between a contractual tenancy and that tenancy converted into a statutory tenancy. A statutory tenancy is continued on the same terms as the previous contractual tenancy except for provisions relating to the termination of the lease and certain provisions relating to rent increases.

4   In a contractual tenancy any changes to the lease terms or to the rent must be agreed between the parties. The landlord can propose changes to the terms of a statutory tenancy or changes to the rent payable for such a tenancy, subject to the tenant's right to refer any such proposal to the Rent Assessment Committee.

[1]   Housing (Scotland) Act 1988, s 16(3).

Security of tenure

12.54   Before starting proceedings to recover possession of the property the landlord must, where the tenancy is a contractual one, serve a notice to quit at least 28 days before the date on which the lease is to be terminated. The period of notice is 40 days if the lease is for four months or more. In addition, in all cases, he must serve a notice of intention to raise an action for possession which specifies the grounds on which the application is to be made. The minimum period of notice required for his second notice is two weeks, but for certain grounds it is two months[1]. There are rules regarding the form and content of both types of notice. If these are not complied with the notice cannot be used as the basis for a subsequent action for recovery of possession, though the sheriff has the power to dispense with the requirement for a notice of intention to start proceedings if he/she thinks it reasonable to do so.

1   Housing (Scotland) Act 1988, s 19.

12.55   The only grounds on which an order for possession can be granted are those listed in Sch 5 to the Housing (Scotland) Act 1988. The grounds are divided into mandatory and discretionary grounds. If one of the mandatory grounds is established then, subject to an exception in relation to ground 8 noted below, the sheriff must grant an order for possession. Where one of the discretionary grounds is established the order can only be granted if the sheriff is satisfied that it is reasonable to do so. Within the mandatory grounds there is a further subdivision between those grounds which can only be relied on if the tenant has been given notice that this may be done no later than the beginning of the tenancy. This requirement for prior notice can only be dispensed with in respect of grounds 1 and 2 listed below but only where the sheriff considers that this is reasonable. Finally, it must be noted that only grounds 2, 8 and 11–16 can be relied on to seek an order for possession where the tenancy is a contractual tenancy, and then only if the tenancy agreement makes provision for it to be brought to an end on that ground[1]. This means that where the contract of lease makes no reference to any of these grounds the landlord, in order to obtain an order for possession, would first of all have to serve a notice terminating the tenancy so that the contractual tenancy came to an end at the ish and then, once the tenancy had become a statutory tenancy, use any of the grounds for recovery of possession which might be available.

1   Housing (Scotland) Act 1988, s 18(6).

MANDATORY GROUNDS FOR POSSESSION REQUIRING NOTICE

12.56

1   The property is required as a residence by the landlord or a member of their family, provided that they had previously occupied the property or that they did not buy it with a sitting tenant.

2   There is a heritable security over the house which was created before the tenancy started and the creditor requires vacant possession in order to sell it.

3   The tenancy is for less than eight months and the house has, within 12 months previous to the tenancy, been let as a holiday home.

4   The tenancy is for less than 12 months and the house has, within 12 months previous to the tenancy, been let as a student let.

5   The house is required for occupation by a minister of religion or a missionary.

MANDATORY GROUNDS FOR POSSESSION NOT REQUIRING NOTICE

12.57

6   The landlord requires vacant possession to carry out major works to the premises; this ground is not available if the tenant was in the property when the landlord bought it unless the landlord did not pay for the property.
7   The former tenant has died and proceedings are started within 12 months of this.
8   The tenant is at least three months in arrears with payment of rent both at the time notice of intention is served and at the date of the hearing in court. Where the sheriff is satisfied that the arrears are due to delay or failure in payment of housing benefit an order for possession can only be made where the sheriff considers it is reasonable to do so.

DISCRETIONARY GROUNDS FOR POSSESSION

12.58

9   Suitable alternative accommodation is available[1].
10   Notice to quit has been given by the tenant.
11   Persistent delay in payment of rent.
12   Rent due was unpaid on the date of service of the notice of intention to start proceedings and on the date when proceedings were started. For both this ground and ground 11 consideration must be given as to the extent to which these problems are due to late payment, or failure in payment, of housing benefit.
13   Breach of a tenancy obligation other than payment of rent.
14   Deterioration in the condition of the fabric of the building due to the tenant's fault.
15   Use of the house for immoral or illegal purposes, causing a nuisance or anti-social behaviour.
16   Deterioration in the condition of furniture due to the tenant's fault.
17   The house was let in connection with an employment which has come to an end.

18 The tenant has remained in occupation of the property after service of the notice to quit, proceedings must start within six months of the expiry date of the notice.

Where an order for possession is sought on one of the discretionary grounds (including, where appropriate, ground 8) the sheriff has the power to adjourn the case or postpone the date of possession. This could be done, for example, to monitor behaviour or payment of rent for a period.

[1] Housing (Scotland) Act 1988, Sch 5, Pt II lists the considerations relevant to deciding if the available accommodation is suitable.

Short assured tenancies

12.59 These are assured tenancies for a specified period of six months or more where, before the creation of the tenancy, the tenant has been served with a notice to the effect that it is a short assured tenancy. The main features of this form of tenancy are that the tenant has no security of tenure, they can be removed once the contractual tenancy is finished[1], and that there is some control over the rent that can be charged. The tenant can apply to the Rent Assessment Committee at any time for them to assess a market rent for the property.

[1] Perhaps because of this research suggests use of short assured tenancies is widespread, D Houston et al, *Research on the Private Rented Sector* (Scottish Executive Social Research, 2002), paras.4.13 and A2.29.

Wrongful eviction

12.60 It is an offence for a landlord to evict someone without following the correct procedure or to harass a tenant into leaving accommodation[1]. Tenants evicted in this way will also have a claim for damages against the landlord. Such a claim can arise, first of all, where the landlord or someone acting on their behalf unlawfully deprives the tenant of their occupation of the premises[2], for example, by changing the locks. The landlord need not have specifically instructed the illegal activities giving rise to eviction: it is enough that the person responsible was acting as a direct agent of the landlord, was employed by the landlord to do a particular act, or was employed to undertake the management of the property with no particular fetter on that management[3]. In the second place there will be a claim if the landlord or someone acting on their behalf behaves in way that they believe will cause the tenant either to give up their occupation of the premises or not to exercise any right or claim any remedy open to them under the tenancy[4]. An example of this is where a tenant moved out of a cottage to allow refurbishment. Once the work was completed the landlords tried to impose a new lease and rent on the tenant, knowing that she would refuse these terms. Because of her unwillingness to accept the new terms the tenant did not move back in and was therefore caused to give up occupation of the property because of the landlord's actions. She was held to be entitled to damages under this provision[5]. The tenant is entitled, in addition to any other compensation rights, to claim damages assessed as the difference in the value of the property concerned with and without a sitting tenant[6].

[1]   Rent (Scotland) Act 1984, ss 22 and 23.
[2]   Housing (Scotland) Act 1987, s 36(1).
[3]   *Scott v Thomson* (6 December 2002, unreported), IH.
[4]   Housing (Scotland) Act 1987, s 36(2).
[5]   *Anderson v Cluny Investment Services Ltd* 2004 SLT (Sh Ct) 37.
[6]   Housing (Scotland) Act 1987, s 37.

Statutory registration and rented accommodation

12.61   Houses in multiple occupation must be licensed by the local authority; for these purposes a house is in multiple occupation if three or more unrelated people occupy it. There is also provision in the Antisocial Behaviour etc (Scotland) Act 2004 for a registration scheme for landlords and for notices to be served on landlords requiring them to take steps to prevent anti-social behaviour by their tenants[1].

[1]   See PARA **16.37**.

CHAPTER 13

Servitudes and public rights of way

WHAT ARE SERVITUDES?[1]

13.1   A servitude imposes an obligation or burden on the owner of one piece of land (the servient tenement) for the benefit of the owner of another piece of land (the dominant tenement). Servitudes have the following important characteristics:

1   The servitude must confer some benefit on the dominant tenement. Where an express servitude right of prospect had with the passing of time come to protect a view of a corner of a field where silage bales were stored at certain times of year, it was held that there was no benefit to the dominant tenement[2].

2   A servitude runs with the land. In other words the benefit/burden attaches to the land itself irrespective of individual owners and it will continue to affect the servient and benefit the dominant tenement regardless of changes in ownership.

3   As already indicated the land which benefits from the servitude is described as the dominant tenement and the land burdened as the servient tenement.

4   Servitudes in general only require inactivity on the part of the proprietor of the servient tenement, unlike real burdens which can impose positive obligations on the person who is bound by them.

The creation of a servitude requires the existence of two pieces of land in separate ownership. In other words a landowner cannot create a servitude over his/her own land. A deed creating such a servitude can be registered, but the servitude so created will only take effect on separation of ownership of the land[3]. For example, a builder developing an area of land could register a deed creating a right of way in respect of a number of the plots being developed on that land. The right would only come into existence when these plots were actually sold by the builder.

1   D J Cusine & R M Paisley, *Servitudes and Rights of Way*, ch 1.
2   *McAlister v Wallace* 2003 SCLR 773.
3   Title Conditions (Scotland) Act 2003, s 75(2).

CLASSIFICATION OF SERVITUDES

Positive/negative

13.2   A positive servitude allows the owner of the dominant tenement to exercise a right over the servient tenement; an example of this is a servitude right of way which allows the owner of the dominant tenement to travel across the servient tenement. A negative servitude simply requires the owner of a servient tenement to refrain from some action; an example of this is the servitude of light or prospect considered at PARA **13.10**.

13.3   No new negative servitudes can be created after 28 November 2004 (the appointed day)[1]. In future a landowner who wishes to benefit from a negative servitude when selling off a piece of land will have to achieve this objective by including a real burden in the disposition of the property. Existing negative servitudes are automatically converted into real burdens on the appointed day and will continue in existence only for a further period of ten years. Continuation beyond this period can be achieved either by ensuring that the servitude appears on the title sheet for the servient tenement before the appointed day or registering a notice of the servitude against both dominant and servient tenement within ten years after that date[2].

1   Title Conditions (Scotland) Act 2003, s 79.
2   Title Conditions (Scotland) Act 2003, s 80

Urban/rural

13.4   This distinction is quite straightforward. Urban servitudes relate to buildings irrespective of where they are placed, and rural servitudes relate to land irrespective of where the land is situated. It is therefore quite possible to have a rural servitude right of way in a town or city.

THE PRINCIPAL SERVITUDES

13.5 The types of servitude listed below are those traditionally recognised by Scots law. They are not necessarily the only ones, however, and there is authority for the view that new servitudes could arise provided they exhibit the necessary characteristics that distinguish the existing ones. As Lord Ardmillan said in the case of *Patrick v Napier*[1]:

'The habits and requirements of life varying and extending with advancing civilisation, improved agriculture, and multiplying necessities, may render the introduction of a new servitude possible and legitimate. But it must, in my opinion, be of a truly praedial character, similar in nature and quality to the praedial servitudes which the law has already recognised.'

Although a long period had passed since this opinion was offered and despite the changes in society since then, there had, until recently been no recognition of new servitudes. The issue was raised, however, in a sheriff court case which concerned, amongst other issues, whether there could be a servitude right of parking[2]. The sheriff took the view that such a servitude right could exist[3]. In passing he expressed a view that the argument that the categories of servitudes were more or less closed was greatly overstated[4]. Although future servitudes created in a registered deed need not be of a type known to the law[5], this case confirms the possibility, if the reasoning is followed, of new types of servitude being created by implication or by prescription[6].

---

[1]   (1867) 5 M 683, 39 Sc J 346. The requirement that the servitude be praedial reflects the first characteristic set out at the beginning of this chapter.

[2]   *Moncrieff v Jamieson* 2004 SCLR 135. Though see the differing view on the 'servitude' of parking in *Nationwide Building Society v Walter D Allan Ltd*, Outer House, 4 August 2004.

[3]   Though this was *obiter* as the sheriff found that it was ancillary to an established servitude right of way.

[4]   At 171.

[5]   Title Conditions (Scotland) Act 2003, s 76(1).

[6]   See also D J Cusine & R M Paisley, *Servitudes and Rights of Way*, 3.45–3.53

Way

13.6   This is a right of the owner of the dominant tenement to pass across the servient tenement. It must be distinguished from a public right of way (considered below); the latter can be enjoyed by the public at large, whereas a servitude right of way only belongs to the owner of the dominant tenement. Traditionally, a right of way could be either a footpath, a horse road or a carriage road; in modern times, probably only the last of these could be used for motor vehicles. Which of the three exists in a particular case will depend upon the terms of the servitude grant. If the servitude has been created by prescription, the nature of the possession (ie usage) by the owner of the dominant tenement will determine the type of right. For example, if the dominant owner has habitually driven motor vehicles across the servient tenement for the required period, a right of carriage will have been created; if he/she has only walked across it, it will be a footpath. A more burdensome servitude will include a lesser one, but not the other way about; for example, the dominant owner will be entitled to walk on a carriage road, but not drive a car on a footpath[1].

[1]   Though see *Aberdeenshire County Council v Lord Glentanar* 1999 SLT 1456, where the view was expressed that cycling was permitted on a footpath.

Aqueduct and aquaehaustus

13.7   The servitude right of aqueduct is a right to run water over or under land belonging to somebody else, for example by having pipes running under or over their land. There is a related servitude of aquaehaustus allowing the dominant proprietor to draw water from a source, eg a stream or well, on the servient land.

Pasturage

13.8   This is the right to feed cattle or sheep on the ground of the servient tenement. The extent of the right may have been defined in the servitude grant, but otherwise will be the amount of stock the servient tenement can winter. If there is any surplus pasturage, the servient owner can use it.

Fuel, feal and divot

13.9   This gives the right to enter the servient land and take away material forming part of the land for fuel, for example peat, or for other purposes, such as fencing.

Light or prospect

13.10   This is a negative servitude right allowing the person benefiting from it either to prevent building on the land affected, or to prevent building over a certain height or to prevent building which will interfere with the light reaching the dominant tenement or interfere with the view.

Stillicide

13.11   This is a servitude right allowing the owner of the dominant tenement to let water run off their building onto land belonging to another. An example of this would be where a building adjoins the boundary between two properties. In normal circumstances the owner of the building would not be allowed to let the water run off the roof of the building on to the neighbouring property; however, if the owner of the building had a servitude right of stillicide that would permit this to happen.

Support

13.12   In some circumstances properties may enjoy a servitude right of support. In CHAPTER 9 we have discussed this in relation to mineral rights, but there are also obligations involved in supporting buildings.

Underground pipes

13.13   In order to resolve a doubt as to whether there was a recognised servitude which conferred a right to lead pipes, cables, wires, etc over or under land, this is now expressly provided for by statute[1]. The provision is retrospective.

[1]   Title Conditions (Scotland) Act 2003, s 77.

CREATION OF POSITIVE SERVITUDES

Express grant

13.14   Express grant involves the express creation, in writing, of a servitude right. Since this involves the grant of a servitude right, the grant is made by the owner of the servient tenement in favour of the owner of the dominant tenement. The grant may be incorporated in the transfer of property, for example, where a larger plot of land is being split up, or may be in the form of a separate agreement[1]. An example of the former would be where a plot of land was divided in two. If the area being sold had no direct access to the nearest public road the disposition of the property might include a right of access to this road across the land retained. As from 28 November 2004 any deed creating a new servitude right must be registered against both the dominant and the servient properties if it is to have the effect of creating the desired servitude[2].

[1]   For example, *Moss Bros Group plc v Scottish Mutual Assurance plc* 2001 SLT 691.
[2]   Title Conditions (Scotland) Act 2003, s 75.

Implied grant[1]

13.15   In some cases the law will imply a grant of a servitude right. Implied grant will arise in the situation where the owner of an area of land divides up the land and sells off part of it. In these circumstances the law will imply the grant to the purchaser of any servitude rights which are necessary for the comfortable enjoyment of the property[2]. Examples of this might be a right of way for access to the property, or a right of aqueduct to allow water supplies to reach the property which has been purchased. Where land would otherwise be landlocked, a servitude right of access will normally be implied, for instance in the example given above, if there was no express grant of a servitude right and the land would otherwise have no access to the public road a servitude right would be implied. Recent authority suggests that the right of access to landlocked property is an incident of ownership and that the doctrine of implied grant was a fiction rationalising this rule[3].

[1]   D J Cusine & R M Paisley, *Servitudes and Rights of Way*, ch 8.
[2]   *Ewart v Cochranes* (1861) 23 D (HL) 3.

3   *Bowers v Kennedy* 2000 SLT 1006; see also *Inverness Seafield Development Co Ltd v Mackintosh* 2001 SLT 118. This issue is also considered in CHAPTER 9.

13.16   Where access has expressly been granted to the owner of the dominant tenement, the courts will not generally imply additional, greater rights of access[1].

1   *Louttit's Trustees v Highland Railway Co* (1892) 19 R 791.

Express reservation

13.17   Express reservation is the converse of express grant, and describes a situation where, in the sale of part of a larger parcel of land, the seller retains servitude rights in his/her favour. The same requirements for registration of new servitudes created in deeds apply as in the case of express grant.

Implied reservation[1]

13.18   This again covers the situation where the seller of part of a larger area of land wishes to argue that servitude rights have been created in his/ her favour over the land which has been sold. The courts are more reluctant to imply the existence of servitude rights in these circumstances than they are in the case of arguments about creation of servitude rights by implied grant. In the latter case the courts appear to take the view that the purchaser is entitled to all the rights which he or she could reasonably be expected to be granted to allow the comfortable use of their property. In the former case the courts take the view that the seller should have reserved any necessary servitude rights expressly and that the purchaser should not be in the position of discovering after the sale that they have in fact a lesser or more restricted right than he or she originally thought. An example of this is *Murray v Medley*[2] where the court approved of the view that a servitude right would only be implied by reservation where the right is absolutely necessary for the use and enjoyment of the property retained by the seller. In this case the court took the view that a water supply was not absolutely necessary to the enjoyment of a house. On the other hand, a second right of access to the rear of premises has held to be necessary and therefore created by implied reservation where the only alternative way of providing such access was demolition of part of the dominant tenement[3].

1   D J Cusine & R M Paisley, *Servitudes and Rights of Way*, ch 8.
2   1973 SLT (Sh Ct) 75.
3   *Union Heritable Securities Co Ltd v Mathie* (1886) 13 R 670.

Prescription[1]

13.19   A servitude right can be created by possession and use for a period of 20 years. It is clear that only positive servitudes can be created by way of prescription. The nature of possession required depends on the type of servitude involved; in any case, however, it must be possession 'as of right', a concept discussed more fully below in the context of public rights of way. It may also be possible to create a servitude right by acquiescence involving knowledge of the use and failure to take action to prevent it over a shorter period[2].

1   See CHAPTER 3; D J Cusine & R M Paisley, *Servitudes and Rights of Way*, ch 10.
2   D J Cusine & R M Paisley, *Servitudes and Rights of Way*, 11.37–11.46; *Moncrieff v Jamieson* 2004 SCLR 135.

13.20   It was generally accepted that negative servitude rights could only be created by express grant or express reservation[1]. As we have seen, it will not in future be possible to create such rights as servitudes.

1   Though see D J Cusine & R M Paisley, *Servitudes and Rights of Way*, ch 9.

ENJOYMENT OF SERVITUDE RIGHTS[1]

13.21   In general terms the servitude right must be exercised for the benefit of the dominant tenement and not for other purposes[2]. The servitude right must be exercised *civiliter*, that is with minimum inconvenience and interference caused to the proprietor of the servient tenement. The owner of the dominant tenement cannot increase the burden on the owner of the servient tenement. For example the owner of the dominant tenement cannot start to use a servitude right of way which was originally created for pedestrian access for vehicular traffic[3]; though where an unrestricted right of access is granted this may be used for any lawful purpose and is not limited to the use in existence at the time the grant as made[4]. Where continued exercise of a servitude right would involve a serious risk of damage to the servient tenement or personal injury to the inhabitants thereof, continued exercise of a servitude will be unreasonable and can be interdicted[5].

1   D J Cusine & R M Paisley, *Servitudes and Rights of Way*, ch 12.
2   *Murray v Magistrates of Peebles* (8 December 1808, unreported), FC.
3   See the comments in *Crichton v Turnbull* 1946 SLT 156. See also *Aberdeenshire County Council v Lord Glentanar* 1999 SLT 1456.
4   *Alvis v Harrison* 1991 SLT 64.
5   *Cloy v T M Adams & Sons* 2000 SLT (Sh Ct) 39, where continued use of a right of way over a dam threatened to breach it.

13.22   The servient proprietor is entitled to use his/her property as long as this use still allows the owner of the dominant tenement to exercise their servitude right[1]. In particular the owner of the servient tenement is entitled to take steps by way of erection of gates, etc, to prevent the ingress or escape of livestock[2]. However, such gates must not prevent the exercise of a servitude right by someone of normal strength or ability.

1   *Fraser v Secretary of State for Scotland* 1959 SLT (Notes) 36.
2   *Drury v McGarvie* 1993 SLT 987.

13.23   A particular issue may arise in the context of rights of way, and the right of the owner of the servient tenement to divert the route of the right of way. In cases where the right of way has been created by prescription, or where the precise route has not been specified in a deed creating the right, the answer appears to be that the route can be diverted, provided that the new route is as convenient for the owner of the dominant tenement. On the other hand, where the route of the right of way is specifically set out in the deed creating it, no diversion of the route is permissible, even though the diversion would not significantly inconvenience the owner of the dominant tenement[1].

1   *Munro v McLintock* 1997 SLT (Sh Ct) 97.

13.24   The owner of the servient tenement is not obliged to maintain any right of way[1]. The dominant proprietor has the right of access to the servient land in order to carry out any necessary works, including repairs and maintenance, to protect their enjoyment of the servitude[2].

1   *Allan v MacLachlan* (1900) 2 F 699.
2   *Drury v McGarvie* 1993 SLT 987.

EXTINCTION OF SERVITUDE RIGHTS[1]

13.25   Servitude rights can be extinguished in a variety of ways.

[1]   D J Cusine & R M Paisley, *Servitudes and Rights of Way*, ch 17.

Confusion

13.26   Where the dominant and the servient tenement come into the ownership of the same individual any servitude right will be extinguished. For example if I enjoy a servitude right of way over a neighbour's land, that right will be extinguished if I buy the neighbour's land. It further seems to be the case that if ownership of the two tenements is later separated a servitude right does not automatically revive, but would have to be created again[1]. Such creation would not necessarily have to be express; it is possible to imagine the situation where a servitude right of way for access would be created by implied grant or reservation on separation of the two tenements.

[1]   *Union Bank of Scotland Ltd v The Daily Record (Glasgow) (Ltd)* 1902 10 SLT 71, though see the discussion in *Stair Memorial Encyclopaedia*, vol 18, 476 and Gordon, 24-96 to 24-98.

Renunciation

13.27   Renunciation describes the situation where the owner of the dominant tenement renounces their right over the servient tenement.

Prescription[1]

13.28   Servitude rights can be lost by non-use for a period of 20 years in the case of positive servitudes and breach of a negative servitude, eg building in breach of a servitude obligation not to build, which lasts for this period. Non-use in the face of interference with a servitude right can, of course, give rise to acquiescence, which would personally bar the proprietor of a dominant tenement from enforcing the servitude right.

[1]   See CHAPTER 3.

Acquiescence

13.29 This is an application of the principle of personal bar, ie a situation whereby a person by his action (or inaction) may lose the right to enforce an obligation, usually because to do so in the situation that has arisen would not be in accordance with justice. Acquiescence occurs where a person sees his rights being infringed over a period of time and does nothing about it, thereby giving others the impression that he/she does not object to the infringement. And so, if a servient owner blocks a servitude right of way, or builds higher than he/she was supposed to, the dominant owner could lose his/her right to object by acquiescence if he/she does not object or take steps to enforce his/her right; if he/she changes his/her mind later, he/she may find that he/she is personally barred from exercising the servitude.

13.30 There is no hard and fast rule regarding the amount of contravention or degree of delay that is required for acquiescence, though it is unlikely that it would need to persist for the 20-year period required for the right to be wiped out by prescription. On the other hand, acquiescence only bars the person who has acquiesced and not their singular successors[1]. For example, the owner of the dominant tenement may lose their right to enforce a servitude by acquiescence, but if he/she sells the property the new owner will have the right to enforce the servitude since he/she has not agreed to the contravention. The only exception would be if the original owner's acquiescence persisted for 20 years, because then of course the servitude would be extinguished by prescription, and this would be binding on the singular successors of the dominant owner.

[1]   Though see D J Cusine & R M Paisley, *Servitudes and Rights of Way*, 17.20.

Lands Tribunal

13.31 As discussed in CHAPTER **14**, servitude rights fall within the definition of title conditions under the Title Conditions (Scotland) Act 2003 and as such they can be varied or discharged by the Lands Tribunal. The same procedures and grounds of application apply as for real burdens.

PUBLIC RIGHTS OF WAY

13.32   Unlike a servitude right of way which confers a right of passage on the owner for the time being of the dominant tenement, a public right of way gives any member of the public the right to use the way. The requirements for creation of such a public right are set out fairly concisely in *Richardson v Cromarty Petroleum Co Ltd*[1]. These four requirements are:

1   The right of way must have been in existence for a period of 20 years. In order to establish this evidence of use over the 20-year period will be necessary.

2   The right of way must connect two public places. In *Richardson* this requirement was fulfilled because the right of way connected a public road and the foreshore. This latter was a public place by virtue of the Crown rights enjoyed by the public over this area of land. The right of way can be established both over land and over artificial structures[2].

3   There must be sufficient use by the public to set the route up as a public right of way. The point has been made in a number of cases that the nature and quantity of use varies according to the nature of the right of way. For example, in the *Richardson* case, which involved a right of way going to a beach, it would be natural to expect that there would be seasonal variation in use, and that it was not necessary for the same volume of use to occur consistently throughout the years.

4   The use by the public must be of such a nature as to show that they are using it as a matter of right, as opposed to use by the tolerance of the proprietor. This requirement has usually been taken to refer more to the actions of the landowner than the intentions or views of the public using the route. It is now fairly clear that the landowner must take some steps to make the public aware that their use is taking place with his/her permission:

> 'A proprietor who allows a way over his land to be used by the public in the way the public would be expected to use it if there was a public right of way cannot claim that use must be ascribed to tolerance, if he did nothing to limit or regulate that use at any time during the prescriptive period[3].'

Such public use need not be in conflict with the interests of the landowner, for example in *Cumbernauld & Kilsyth District Council v Dollar Land (Cumbernauld) Ltd*[4] the dispute was over a public right of way through a shopping centre where such public access was clearly in the interests of landowners as owners of the centre. Although this case law suggests that an objective approach is to be taken in deciding whether use is as of right, a recent sheriff court case considering establishment of a servitude right placed some emphasis on the actual beliefs and intentions of those involved[5].

In this context it should be noted that where the public cross land in exercise of their public right of access this cannot be founded on to create a public right of way.

1   1982 SLT 237; see also *Strathclyde (Hyndland) Housing Association Ltd v Cowie* 1983 SLT (Sh Ct) 61.
2   *Cumbernauld & Kilsyth District Council v Dollar Land (Cumbernauld) Ltd* 1993 SC (HL) 44.
3   *Cumbernauld & Kilsyth District Council v Dollar Land (Cumbernauld) Ltd* 1992 SLT 1035 at 1042, per Lord President Hope. Approved on appeal 1993 SC (HL) 44 and in *R v City of Sunderland, ex p Beresford* [2004] 1 All ER 160.
4   1993 SC (HL) 44.
5   *Webster v Chadburn* (9 May 2003, unreported), Sh Ct Grampian Highlands and Islands at Inverness, available through: www.scotcourts.gov.uk.

13.33   Once a public right of way has been established the nature and quantity of use needed to keep it in existence is less than that required to create it in the first instance[1], nor is it the case that use of it is restricted to use from one terminus to another[2]. It is not clear, however, whether the public right of way can survive if one of the termini ceases to be a public place, though intermediate landowners would continue to have a servitude right of way[3].

1   *North East Fife District Council v Nisbet* 2000 SCLR 413.
2   *McRobert v Reid* 1914 SC 633.
3   *Lord Burton v Mackay* 1995 SLT 507.

PUBLIC RIGHTS OF ACCESS

The right of access

13.34   Members of the public have a right of access to land for recreational or educational purposes, with the right extending to commercial activities which could be carried on non-commercially (eg acting as a paid mountain guide)[1]. This right allows people to be on, over or under land for these purposes as well as to cross land, this last right being, subject to what is said below about responsible exercise of access rights, unlimited in terms of purpose[2].

1   Land Reform (Scotland) Act 2003, s 1.
2   Land Reform (Scotland) Act 2003, s 1(2)(b).

13.35   The land to which these rights extends is broadly defined and includes non-tidal waters, such as lochs and rivers, the foreshore and bridges or other structures built on or over land[1]. Some land is excluded from the access right[2]. Examples are buildings, caravans and tents, school playgrounds, gardens[3], building sites, land open to the public on payment for more than 90 days per year, land developed or set out as a sports or playing field[4], and land on which crops have been sown or are growing. This last restriction does not prevent access on unsown parts of a field, eg the field margins. As well as these permanent restrictions, it is also possible for the local authority to make an order temporarily exempting particular land from the access right for a particular purpose. The maximum duration for such an order in the first instance is two years, though it can then be renewed. Where this exemption is to last for more than six days it must be approved by a Minister[5]. Although it was originally suggested that landowners would themselves have the right to restrict access to allow, for example, for crop spraying, this power is not found in the final legislation. Instead, the Scottish Outdoor Access Code requires that members of the public exercising their right of access respect any notices restricting access because of this type of activity[6]. As we will see below anyone who does not act in accordance with this Code is likely to be treated as having no right of access.

1   Land Reform (Scotland) Act 2003, s 32.
2   Land Reform (Scotland) Act 2003, ss 6 and 7.
3   Though the Land Reform (Scotland) Act 2003, s 6(1)(b)(iv) refers to 'sufficient adjacent land to enable persons living there to have reasonable measures of privacy in that house or place and to ensure that their enjoyment of that house or place is not unreasonably disturbed'.
4   Though this is subject to certain limitations: Land Reform (Scotland) Act 2003, s 7(7).
5   Land Reform (Scotland) Act 2003, s 11.
6   Scottish Outdoor Access Code, 3.24–3.28; and guidance for landowners at 4.11–4.17.

13.36   A further restriction on the existence of a right of access is the requirement to exercise the right responsibly. The corollary of this is that if someone purporting to exercise the right acts irresponsibly the access right will not exist. Responsible exercise requires that the person exercising the right acts reasonably and lawfully and in a way which takes account of the interests of others and the features of the land[1]. There is a list of conduct which is not responsible exercise and in respect of which the right of access cannot be claimed[2]. This includes being on or crossing land for criminal purposes, hunting, shooting, or fishing, crossing land with a motorised vehicle or being on a golf course except for the purpose of crossing it. It also includes any conduct which contravenes byelaws which local authorities are empowered to make in relation to land over which access rights exist[3]. In addition, in deciding whether access is being exercised responsibly regard will have to be had to the Scottish Outdoor Access Code which contains further guidance for the public and for landowners. Where a landowner comes across someone behaving irresponsibly, their remedy is simply to require that person to leave their land. This, of course, is the same remedy which exists at common law in cases of trespass, and there is no additional assistance provided to the landowner by the legislation, although at an earlier stage there was a proposal to give the police specific powers to require a person behaving irresponsibly to leave the land[4].

[1] Land Reform (Scotland) Act 2003, s 2.
[2] Land Reform (Scotland) Act 2003, s 9.
[3] Land Reform (Scotland) Act 2003, s 12.
[4] Section 15 of the original draft Bill, also making failure to comply with such a requirement an offence: Scottish Executive, *Draft Land Reform (Scotland) Bill: Consultation Paper*, February 2001.

13.37 Landowners also have the general responsibility of managing their land in a way which takes proper account of the interests of those seeking to exercise the access right[1]. In particular a landowner may not undertake certain activities whose sole or main purpose is to deter the exercise of the right[2]. The activities covered include putting up signs, fences or walls, ploughing across a path or leaving animals at large. Where any of these activities[3] has been undertaken by the landowner, the local authority may serve a notice requiring that remedial action is taken; if this is not complied with the authority can take the action themselves and recover the costs from the owner[4]. Local authorities also have a general duty 'to assert, protect and keep open and free from obstruction or encroachment any route, waterway or other means by which access rights may reasonably be exercised'[5]. In addition, members of the public who consider that their access rights have been unlawfully interfered with will be able to seek their own remedies. The legislation specifically provides for applications for declarator to be made to the sheriff [6]. The declarator sought may be as to whether land is covered by the access right, as to whether either the landowner or those seeking to exercise access have behaved responsibly, or as to the existence and scope of a right of way. In addition, though, there is no reason why an individual, either landowner or member of the public, should not be able to seek additional remedies, such as interdict or specific implement, to ensure that the right of access can be responsibly exercised.

[1]   Land Reform (Scotland) Act 2003, s 3.
[2]   Land Reform (Scotland) Act 2003, s 14.
[3]   Or any others set out in Land Reform (Scotland) Act 2003, s 14(1).
[4]   Land Reform (Scotland) Act 2003, s 14(2), (3).
[5]   Land Reform (Scotland) Act 2003, s 13(1).
[6]   Land Reform (Scotland) Act 2003, s 28.

13.38 Finally the legislation also anticipates the establishment of a system of core paths [1]. These core paths are intended to provide a network of paths sufficient to give the public reasonable access to the countryside.

[1]   Land Reform (Scotland) Act 2003, ss 17–20.

Relationship to other public rights of access

13.39 As well as the right of access, the public may have or acquire other rights over land or water under pre-existing law. Examples of these are public rights of way, public rights of navigation and public rights over the foreshore. These will continue to exist and their scope is unaffected by the new access right [1]. In some cases the existing public rights will be more extensive than the access right, for example the public's rights on the foreshore extend to fishing, an activity which is incompatible with exercise of the access right. In some cases the access right may be more extensive, for example it permits use of waters where no public right of navigation exists; and also appears to permit activities, such as walking on the riverbed, which are not included in the navigation right.

[1]   Land Reform (Scotland) Act 2003, S 5(3), (4).

13.40 Exercise of the access right is specifically stated not to amount 'of itself' to the exercise of possession for the purposes of constituting a public right of way or navigation [1]. At face value this would seem to make the establishment of new public rights difficult, though this may not matter given the right of access.

1   Land Reform (Scotland) Act 2003, s 5(5).

CHAPTER 14

Real burdens

INTRODUCTION

14.1 Since the late Eighteenth century it has been common for landowners selling land for building or development to impose certain obligations and restrictions on the use of the land sold[1]. In turn, builders or developers would impose obligations and restrictions on the end purchaser of the flat or house. In the context of the original sale of land these might contain specifications for the houses to be built on the land, for example size of building and type of materials to be used. The sale to the end purchaser might impose obligations in relation to repair and maintenance, insurance and use of the property. This type of obligation and restriction came to be referred to as 'real burdens'. Real burdens are real in the sense that they apply to the land regardless of who owns it. Thus if a real burden is effectively created (the requirements for this are discussed below) it will be effective against all owners of the land until it is brought to an end in one of the ways discussed below. A real burden in this sense can be contrasted with a personal burden[2] which is binding as a contractual term on the first purchaser on whom an obligation or restriction is imposed. For example, if Grant were to buy a new house from a volume housebuilder, the housebuilder would impose a variety of burdens on Grant's use of the house in the disposition of the house. If these burdens were merely personal, they would cease to be effective once Grant sold the house. Once the house is sold there is no longer a contractual relationship between the new purchaser, Greg, and the housebuilder and therefore Greg cannot owe the builder a personal obligation based on that contract. In contrast, if a real burden is created that burden will be enforceable not only against Grant, but also against Greg and against Bob, a purchaser from Greg. Real burdens also have the characteristic that enforcement rights derive from the ownership of property. The result of this is that any owner of the property to which the enforcement right attaches has the right of enforcement, not just the owner who imposed the burden in the first place.

1   For the development of real burdens see *Stair Memorial Encyclopaedia*, vol 18, 376–385.
2   Not to be confused with the new category of personal real burdens introduced by the Abolition of Feudal Tenure (Scotland) Act 2000.

14.2   Personal burdens and real burdens could run in parallel. This would have happened most obviously in the case of the first purchaser to whom the burdens were applied. The person imposing the burden would be able to enforce these against him/her either as a real burden or as a personal burden arising from their contractual relationship. From 28 November 2004 this is no longer the case as once a real burden is effectively created the personal burden will be extinguished[1]. It could and can also happen in a case where an attempt to create real burdens fails in part because a burden does not fulfil the criteria for recognition as a real burden. That obligation might continue as a personal burden against the first purchaser with the other burdens being real.

1   Abolition of Feudal Tenure (Scotland) Act 2000, s 9.

14.3   Real burdens could be imposed both in cases where a feudal grant was made[1] or where property was being sold outright[2]. In addition, although these burdens have long historical roots they are still part and practice of the sale of land and houses today. Anyone buying from a volume housebuilder will, for example, be made subject to a wide range of real burdens. Purchasers of older properties will discover that they are also subject to a variety of restrictions; the author, for example, is prohibited from erecting a steam engine on his property, and it is common to find restrictions on using a house other than as a single family residence and prohibitions on further building. These last two restrictions can cause problems, for example where it is desired to convert a house which is now too big for a single family or where a householder wants to build an extension. The possibility that neighbours might be able to enforce these conditions[3] would cause additional problems in these cases, and these problems were partly behind the reform of the law of real burdens which took place in parallel with the abolition of the feudal system.

1   Though, of course, this is now impossible; see CHAPTER 1.
2   As in the leading case on real burdens before reform of the law, *Tailors of Aberdeen v Coutts* (1840) 1 Rob App 296.
3   See below PARA 14.29FF.

14.4   The law relating to real burdens has been substantially rewritten following the passage of the Abolition of Feudal Tenure (Scotland) Act 2000 ('the 2000 Act') and the Title Conditions (Scotland) Act 2003 ('the 2003 Act'). Between them these pieces of legislation redefine real burdens, provide for the restricted continuation of burdens existing prior to 28 November 2004, provide for new means of discharge and variation of burdens and extend the classes of person who can enforce burdens and against whom burdens can be enforced.

WHAT ARE REAL BURDENS?

14.5   The 2003 Act defines a real burden as: 'an encumbrance on land constituted in favour of other land in that person's capacity as owner of that other land'[1]. The encumbered land is described as the 'burdened property' and the other land as the 'benefited property'. This makes it clear that the burden is enforceable by the owner of one property (the benefited property) against the owner of another property (the burdened property) and that the right to enforce and obligations to comply derive from land ownership[2].

1   Title Conditions (Scotland) Act 2003, s 1(1).
2   Though, as we will see below, enforcement rights as well as obligations to comply extend to certain others, such as tenants.

14.6   The 2003 Act then sets out various requirements for the existence of a valid real burden:
1   The primary requirement of any burden is that it must be either affirmative, negative or ancillary[1]. An affirmative burden requires something to be done (for example erection or maintenance of a building), a negative burden involves an obligation not to do something (eg a prohibition on the use of the property for business purposes) and an ancillary burden may involve either a right to enter or make use of property or may make provision for management or administration.

This last type of burden must be ancillary to one of the other burden types. For example, there may be an affirmative burden to keep the common parts of a building well maintained and an ancillary burden setting up a management structure to enable this.

2   The burden must relate to the burdened property, in other words it must be directed at the property itself and its use rather than simply being an obligation imposed on a particular owner of the property[2]. This will often be a question of the correct interpretation of the deed imposing the burden.

3   Except in the case of a community burden or a personal real burden (see below), the burden must confer some benefit on the benefited property. A community burden must confer a benefit on all or part of the community which it covers[3].

4   The burden must not be illegal, contrary to public policy or repugnant with ownership[4]. This requirement reflects the pre-2004 rules for the constitution of a real burden and specifically instances the restraint of trade as being contrary to public policy. An example of this is found in *Aberdeen Varieties Ltd v James F Donald (Aberdeen Cinemas) Ltd* [5] where there was a burden which prohibited the performance of plays in the property subject to the burden. This was held to be contrary to public policy as being in restraint of trade[6]. A restriction on what can be sold or done in commercial premises will not always be regarded as being in restraint of trade and therefore incapable of being a real burden. In *CWS v Ushers Brewery*[7] the view was taken that a restriction on the sale of alcohol for the benefit of a pub was not invalid as it was concerned with the protection of the property interest of the pub proprietor and also because it had been imposed as part of a scheme for a small shopping development[8]. An illustration of repugnancy with ownership right can be drawn from the case law related to the former requirement that a real burden should not be inconsistent with the nature of property. In *Beckett v Bissett* [9] it was claimed that an exclusive right of shooting over the defender's land had been created by way of a real burden. Since, as noted in CHAPTER 9, shooting rights are a normal incident of ownership, it was held that this 'real burden' was inconsistent with the normal ownership rights held in land, and therefore was not valid.

5   The burden must not create a monopoly unless this is otherwise permitted by the 2003 Act. The example of monopoly given is providing for a particular person to be or to appoint a manager of the property[10].

As we will see a limited monopoly of this type is allowed in the form of manager burdens.

6 The 2003 Act makes it clear that it is acceptable to create a real burden requiring that the owner of the burdened property pay a share of maintenance or other costs without specifying the precise sums of money involved[11].

7 It is now also competent, in certain limited circumstances, for a real burden to refer to a public document outwith the titles to the burdened property[12]. The types of public document to which reference can be made are restricted to Acts of either Parliament[13] or records or rolls to which the public readily has access. Reference to such outside documentation is only permissible in relation to a burden specifying an obligation to pay some cost, the amount of which is not set out in the burden, or to contribute towards costs, for example maintenance costs for common property[14]. Aside from this slight relaxation the pre-November 2004 requirement that a burden had to be complete within the deeds to the property and not require reference to any extrinsic document remains. For example in *Aberdeen Varieties* the burden in dispute was considered invalid *inter alia* because it referred to an Act of Parliament. The consequence of this was that the owner of the land could only be clear about the scope of the restriction on use by referring to the Act, a source outwith the title deeds of the property.

8 Although not specifically dealt with in the legislation the former requirement that the burden must be clearly specified will continue. For example, a condition which required that the flow of water in a lade should be maintained at a level such as to provide an adequate flow to cleanse and drain the lade to the satisfaction of the disponers was held to be invalid because it was too vague[15].

---

1   Title Conditions (Scotland) Act 2003, s 2.
2   Title Conditions (Scotland) Act 2003, s 3(1). For example in *Marsden v Craighelen Lawn Tennis and Squash Club* 1999 GWD 37-1820 an obligation to use land as a tennis club was held to be expressed in such a way as to bind only the original purchasers of the land rather than burdening the land itself. See also *Kemp v Magistrates of Largs* 1939 SC (HL) 6.
3   Title Conditions (Scotland) Act 2003, s 3(3) and (4).
4   Title Conditions (Scotland) Act 2003, s 3(6).
5   1940 SLT 374.
6   See also *Phillips v Lavery* 1962 SLT (Sh Ct) 57; *Co-operative Wholesale Society Ltd v Ushers Brewery* 1975 SLT (Lands Tr) 9.
7   1975 SLT (Lands Tr) 9.
8   See the discussion in R Rennie, *Land Tenure in Scotland*, at para 5-12.
9   1921 2 SLT 33.

10 Title Conditions (Scotland) Act 2003, s 3(7).
11 Title Conditions (Scotland) Act 2003, s 5(1). Despite the concerns expressed in *David Watson Property Management v Woolwich Equitable Building Society* 1990 SLT 764, 1992 SLT 430, it was reasonably clear that such requirements were already valid real burdens; see *Wells v New House Purchasers* 1964 SLT (Sh Ct) 2; *Crampshie v North Lanarkshire Council* (20 February 2004, unreported), OH.
12 Title Conditions (Scotland) Act 2003, s 5(2).
13 Ie the UK and Scottish Parliaments.
14 In such cases the liability to pay might be related to the rateable value of the property which would require consultation of the valuation roll.
15 *Lothian Regional Council v Rennie* 1991 SLT 465. See also *Murray's Trustees v The Trustees for St Margaret's Convent (*1906) 8 F 1109; *Dumbarton District Council v McLaughlin* 2000 Hous LR 16. Contrast *Meriton Ltd v Winning* 1995 SLT 76.

CREATION AND TYPES OF NEW REAL BURDEN

Creation

14.7 New real burdens must be created in a deed (the constitutive deed). Except where a specific type of burden is created, for example, a community burden, the constitutive deed must use the term 'real burden' in describing the burden(s) which it seeks to create[1]. Where a specific type of burden is being created the deed may instead use the term 'community burden', 'facility burden', etc as appropriate. This is in contrast to the previous position where no special form of words was required. Instead of setting out the burdens at length in the constitutive deed they may be imported from another deed, eg by referring to a deed of conditions[2].

1 Title Conditions (Scotland) Act 2003, s 4(2)(a); see also CHAPTER **19**.
2 Title Conditions (Scotland) Act 2003, s 6.

14.8 Both the land to be affected by the burden and the land benefited must be clearly identified[1]. Where a community burden is being created the community which is to benefit must be identified. The deed must be granted by the owner of the land burdened, for example the selling owner of a piece of land could impose burdens in the document transferring ownership of the land. In order to effectively create the burden the constitutive deed must be registered against *both* the burdened *and* the benefited properties. For new burdens this means that there will be clarity as to who is entitled to enforce the burdens.

1   Title Conditions (Scotland) Act 2003, s 4(2)(c). See *Anderson v Dickie* 1915 1 SLT 393.

14.9   Any real burden created after 28 November 2004 must be created expressly in a constitutive deed; it will no longer be possible to create rights to enforce real burdens by implication after that date[1].

1   Title Conditions (Scotland) Act 2003, s 49(1); see below for continuation of pre-existing implied enforcement rights.

Community burdens

14.10   These are burdens which apply to two or more properties where each property is not only bound by the burden but also enjoys enforcement rights against all the other properties in the community[1]. Examples would be burdens imposed by a deed of conditions on flats in a tenement building or new houses in a new housing development. In such cases all owners enjoy mutual enforcement rights against each other.

1   Title Conditions (Scotland) Act 2003, s 25.

14.11   The burdens are still community burdens even if all of the separate properties are owned by the same person. As well as newly created burdens being community burdens, existing burdens which are effectively continued in force, as discussed below, will also fall into the category of community burdens. There are special rules, also discussed below, for the variation and discharge of community burdens and a variety of special rules, not considered fully here, applying to sheltered and retirement housing[1].

1   Title Conditions (Scotland) Act 2003, ss 35(1)(a), 54, 55 and 97(2)(c).

Facility burdens

14.12   A facility burden is a burden which provides for the maintenance, management, reinstatement or use of a facility, for example a tenement close or a recreational area, which is shared by a number of properties[1].

1   Title Conditions (Scotland) Act 2003, s 122(1) and (3).

Service burdens

14.13 A service burden is a burden which relates to the provision of services to land other than the burdened property[1].

[1]   Title Conditions (Scotland) Act 2003, s 122(1).

Manager burdens

14.14 Manager burdens[1] can exist where there is a group of related properties. Whether a group of properties is related will, for this purpose, depend on all the circumstances, but indicators will include the convenience of managing all of the properties together and shared ownership of common property. The manager burden can confer on the owner of one of the related properties either the power to act as manager or the power to appoint and dismiss a manager. This might arise, for example, where a public sector housing landlord was selling off flats in a tenement building to tenants exercising their right to buy. The landlord might retain the power to act as manager of the tenement by creating a manager burden.

[1]   Title Conditions (Scotland) Act 2003, s 63.

14.15 Despite the existence of a manager burden, the manager appointed under it can be dismissed by two thirds of the owners of the related properties acting together, and this proportion can appoint a replacement manager. Where such a dismissal takes place the manager burden will be extinguished. It will also be extinguished:
1   By the ending of any time period specified for it in the deed creating it.
2   If 90 days passes during which the person entitled to exercise the burden does not own one of the related properties.
3   30 years from the date of registration of the deed creating the burden in cases where the burden is imposed by a seller on sale to a secure tenant.
4   Three years from the date of registration of the deed creating the burden in cases where the related properties are part of a sheltered or retirement housing development.

14.16 Manager burdens created in favour of superiors (for example those created in favour of public sector landlords) before 28 November 2003 are not extinguished by the 2000 Act, but continue in force subject to the extinction provisions considered above. So, for example, if in a sale to a sitting tenant in 1990 Glasgow District Council feued the land to the buyer and incorporated a manager burden created in a deed registered in 1990, that burden will, subject to extinction in other ways, continue until 2020[1].

[1]   Contrast the unlimited terms of the burden in *Dumbarton District Council v McLaughlin* 2000 Hous LR 16: the revised form of burden described there will now be subject to this limiting provision.

Personal real burdens

14.17   The 2003 Act creates a new category of personal real burdens. These are real burdens which are binding on particular properties, but where there is no benefited property, rather the rights to enforce are conferred on organisations. There is a variety of different types of personal real burden. In all cases, however, the interest of the organisation to enforce is presumed[1] and the burden can be discharged by registration of a discharge against the burdened property[2].

[1]   Title Conditions (Scotland) Act 2003, s 47.
[2]   Title Conditions (Scotland) Act 2003, s 48.

Conservation burdens[1]

14.18   These are burdens designed to protect or preserve the architectural, historical or any other special characteristics (such as appearance, flora or fauna) of land. Such burdens are created in favour of either the Scottish Executive or conservation bodies prescribed by the Scottish Ministers[2]. Anyone intending to create a conservation burden must first obtain the agreement of the organisation which is going to have the ability to enforce it. This type of burden will be extinguished if the organisation entitled to enforce it ceases to be a conservation body, for example by being removed from the list approved by the Scottish Ministers.

[1]   Title Conditions (Scotland) Act 2003, ss 38–42.
[2]   Title Conditions (Scotland) Act 2003 (Conservation Bodies) Order 2003 (SSI 2003/453) as amended by the Title Conditions (Scotland) Act 2003 (Conservation Bodies) Amendment Order 2004 (SSI 2004/400).

Rural housing burdens[1]

14.19 These are conditions drawn in favour of a rural housing body[2], for example a local authority or a housing association, and take the form of a right of pre-emption in favour of the body. The effect of this is that if someone who has bought a house from a rural housing body wishes to sell it he/she must give the body the opportunity to buy it back. Given that one of the intentions behind this provision is that the rural housing body will be able to buy back properties to keep them available for rent to local residents it is perhaps curious that a burden of this type cannot be created in cases where a Scottish secure tenant is exercising their right to buy.

[1]   Title Conditions (Scotland) Act 2003, s 43.
[2]   Title Conditions (Scotland) Act 2003 (Rural Housing Bodies) Order 2004 (SSI 2004/477) lists the rural housing bodies entitled to impose this type of burden.

Maritime burdens[1]

14.20 These are burdens over the seabed or foreshore for the benefit of the public. They are created in favour of the Crown.

[1]   Title Conditions (Scotland) Act 2003, s 44.

Economic development burdens[1]

14.21 These are designed to promote economic development and are created in favour of either the Scottish Executive or a local authority.

[1]   Title Conditions (Scotland) Act 2003, s 45.

Health care burdens[1]

14.22 These are burdens, enforceable by the Scottish Ministers or by a NHS Trust, which are intended to promote the provision of facilities for healthcare.

[1]   Title Conditions (Scotland) Act 2003, s 46.

WHAT HAPPENS TO EXISTING BURDENS?

14.23   As well as catering for the creation of new burdens the 2000 Act and the 2003 Act provide for the continuation of some existing burdens.

Feudal burdens previously enforceable by the superior

14.24   With the abolition of feudal tenure the right of the superior to enforce real burdens disappeared unless he/she took active steps to continue the burden in existence. These steps in essence involve realloting the burden to specific property owned by the superior[1] and then registering the burden against both the benefited and the burdened property before 28 November 2004. In this context the burdened property is the property which is subject to the burden and the benefited property is the property which carries with it the right to enforce the burden.

[1]   Ie allotting it to a piece of land or other property interest rather than the superior's *dominium directum* interest in the burdened property.

14.25   Consideration will first be given to the ways in which a superior could achieve this registration to allow them a continuing right to enforce. There are three methods by which this could be done:
1   In certain circumstances the superior could proceed to register a notice realloting the burden without reference to the vassal(s)[1]. This could be done, firstly, if the superior owned land containing a building used either as a place of human habitation or human resort and this building was within 100 metres of the burdened property. Secondly, a notice could be registered if the burden was in the form of a right to enter or use the servient property, a right of pre-emption or a right of redemption. Third, where the land which would become the benefited property consisted of minerals or salmon fishings or some other form of incorporeal property a notice could be registered, provided that the burden was created originally for the benefit of one of these property interests[2]. The effect of registration was to reallot the benefit of the burden away from the superior's *dominium directum* interest in land and allot or attach it to the land or, in the case of the last option, the other property interest. Such a reallotment would only successfully create a real burden surviving the abolition of feudal tenure if the burden was enforceable immediately before 28 November 2004.
2   Where the burden could not be realloted in this way the superior could seek to reach an agreement with the vassal(s) to reallot the

burden. If agreement was reached it had to be registered against both properties[3].

3   If the superior had tried to reach an agreement to reallot the burden, but this had been unsuccessful, he/she could apply to the Lands Tribunal for Scotland seeking an order realloting the burden. The Tribunal can make such an order only if it is satisfied that loss of the burden would result in material detriment to the value or enjoyment of the superior's ownership of their property[4].

1   Abolition of Feudal Tenure etc (Scotland) Act 2000, s 18.
2   For example, a burden allowing access to the surface of land in connection with the extraction of minerals.
3   Abolition of Feudal Tenure etc (Scotland) Act 2000, s 19.
4   Abolition of Feudal Tenure etc (Scotland) Act 2000, s 20.

14.26   Pre-existing burdens which fell within the definition of either an economic development burden[1] or a health care burden[2] could be converted into these types of burden and continued by registration of a notice. Similarly, existing burdens related to preservation of the character of land and buildings could be preserved as conservation burdens[3]. Finally, rights to fishing or game enjoyed by a superior because of their ownership of the superiority could be continued by registration of a notice against the land affected[4]. Such rights would only have been considered to be valid real burdens and therefore capable of continuation if they gave the superior non-exclusive rights to fishing or game[5].

1   Abolition of Feudal Tenure etc (Scotland) Act 2000, s 18B.
2   Abolition of Feudal Tenure etc (Scotland) Act 2000, s 18C.
3   Abolition of Feudal Tenure etc (Scotland) Act 2000, ss 27–28A.
4   Abolition of Feudal Tenure etc (Scotland) Act 2000, s 65A.
5   *Beckett v Bissett* 1921 2 SLT 33.

14.27   The final type of burden for which continuation is provided by the 2000 Act is a burden which is designed to allow the superior to share in any increased value of the land as a result of development. Such a burden may make direct provision for this or the benefit to the superior may be provided indirectly. Indirect provision will occur where the uses to which the property can be put are limited by the burden, for example a limitation to use as a police office and related residential accommodation. The ability to claim compensation under such a burden would arise from the superior's ability to charge a fee for a discharge or variation of the burden to allow other development. Where there is such a burden and where a reduced (or zero) price was paid for the property because of the burden, the superior can reserve the right to claim compensation by registration of a notice[1]. Once a notice is registered the former superior will be able to claim compensation if there is (or has been) any breach of the burden (or something equivalent to breach of the burden[2]) between 28 November 1999 and 28 November 2024[3]. The amount of compensation is, however, limited to a sum not exceeding the reduction in the price (or feuduty) paid for the land because of the existence of the condition (or the development value released by breach of the condition in the unlikely event that this is less)[4].

1   Abolition of Feudal Tenure etc (Scotland) Act 2000, s 33.
2   This involves the landowner doing something which, but for the burden being extinguished or made unenforceable by the 2000 Act, would have been in breach of the burden.
3   Abolition of Feudal Tenure etc (Scotland) Act 2000, s 35.
4   Abolition of Feudal Tenure etc (Scotland) Act 2000, s 37.

Other enforcement rights[1]

14.28   Prior to the abolition of the feudal system it was possible to create enforceable real burdens in a straightforward disposition of property, in other words in cases where the property was transferred by outright sale rather than being feued with the attendant creation of a new relationship of superior and vassal. These burdens might affect a single property, eg where part of a large garden was sold off subject to a requirement that only one house should be built there, or they might impose restrictions on a wider area. Where the deed creating the burdens nominates the benefited property or properties the changes introduced by the 2003 Act will have no effect on the validity of such burdens. It is more likely that the deed creating the burdens would have been silent both as to the identity of the benefited property and as to what happened to enforcement rights if the property was sold by the original disponer. For instance, A sells of part of her land to B for building (area 1) retaining the rest (area 2) and imposes restrictions on what can be built on area 1. She later sells area 2 to C, who sells off part of it to D. In such a case it is generally accepted that the right to enforce the conditions passed on to C and D without any specific reference to this either in the titles of B or of C and D. Since there was no express right to enforce mentioned in the titles to the property the right was implied[2]. Such implied enforcement rights will lapse on 28 November

2014 unless the owner of the property benefiting from the enforcement right registers a notice preserving the right before that date[3].

1   See generally R Rennie, *Land Tenure in Scotland*, paras. 6-10 to 6-12.
2   The views expressed in *J & A Mactaggart & Co v Harrower* (1906) 14 SLT 277 seem to be generally preferred to the outcome (reached without explicit discussion of this point) in *The Botanic Gardens Picture House Ltd v Adamson* 1924 SLT 418. See *Stair Memorial Encyclopaedia*, vol 18, paras 403–404.
3   Title Conditions (Scotland) Act 2003, ss 49 & 50.

14.29   A second category of implied enforcement rights are those rights which existed by implication prior to 28 November 2004 and involved reference to a common scheme of development.

14.30   Under the previous law, co-feuars[1] who held their land from the same superior could have rights to enforce burdens *inter se*. This was usually referred to a *ius quaesitum tertio*. The leading case in this area is *Hislop v MacRitchies Trustees*[2] which set out guidelines for establishing when a right to enforce on behalf of co-feuars arose. It was said there that the right could only arise if there was a mutuality and community of interest between the co-feuars. It was further suggested that such mutuality could arise in three ways:

1   There might be an express grant by the superior to the co-feuars of the right to enforce *inter se*.
2   There might be an agreement between the co-feuars that they would be able to enforce the burdens against each other. This of course is not truly a case of *ius quaesitum tertio* since the right to enforce arises directly from the contract of the co-feuars.
3   The right to enforce might arise by implication from a reference to a common plan or scheme of building in the title of the co-feuars.

Subsequent case law suggested that the reference to a common building plan must be conceived for the benefit of the co-feuars and not the superior, in other words that the building plan had to be capable of being regarded as providing for the amenity of the co-feuars[3]. In addition it was clear that the reference to a common plan of building must be for a purpose other than simply indicating the location of the property[4].

1   That is, vassals who held their land from the same superior; see CHAPTER 1.
2   (1881) 8 R (HL) 95.
3   *Johnstone v The Walker Trustees* (1897) 24 R 1061.
4   *Murray's Trustees v The Trustees for the Convent of St Margaret* (1906) 8 F 1109.

14.31   *Hislop* also suggested that the right might arise in two sets of circumstances:

1   Where the superior feud out[1] plots for building on a uniform plan (or sold off individual properties in a development). In this category the conditions in the respective titles must be similar, though not necessarily identical[2] It has also been held that an undertaking by a superior to insert the same condition in subsequent transfer of land is indicative of an intention to create a *ius quaesitum,* though no such right will be created if the superior fails to honour this undertaking[3].

2   Where the superior feued out a considerable area with a view to its being subdivided and built on. Here there might be no definite plan but certain general restrictions which must be included in subsequent transfers of the property. It is generally easier to establish a community of interest in this type of case[4]. Unlike the first category there may be reciprocal rights to enforce different conditions applying to different parts of the large area originally feued out[5].

[1]   That is, transferred them retaining a legal interest in the property; see CHAPTER 1.
[2]   *Botanic Garden Picture House Ltd v Adamson* 1924 SLT 418.
[3]   *Johnstone v The Walker Trustees* (1897) 24 R 1061.
[4]   *Hill v Millar* (1900) F 799.
[5]   *Lees v North East Fife DC* 1987 SC 265, 1987 SLT 769.

14.32   In general terms if the superior expressly reserved the right to waive/vary/discharge burdens this was fatal to the creation of a *ius quaesitum tertio*[1], though not where an enforcement right was expressly conferred on co-feuars by the superior[2]. Co-disponees were in a similar disposition to co-feuars.

[1]   *Gray v Macleod* 1979 SLT (Sh Ct) 17.
[2]   *Lawrence v Scott* 1965 SLT 390.

14.33   The 2003 Act abolishes this type of implied right of enforcement, but creates a statutory implied right to replace it. Aside from special rules relating to sheltered and retirement housing[1], there are two provisions, ss 52 and 53, setting out implied rights of enforcement.

[1]   Title Conditions (Scotland) Act 2003, s 54.

Section 52 implied rights

14.34 According to section 52 an implied right to enforce will be created provided that four conditions are met[1]:

1 The burdens must be imposed under a common scheme.
2 The deed imposing the burden must either expressly refer to the common scheme or be worded in such a way that the existence of a common scheme can be implied. In assessing these two requirements the pre-2004 law discussed above will continue to be relevant.
3 There is nothing in the deed imposing the condition expressly or impliedly contradicting the creation of an implied enforcement right; an example would be an express reservation to the former superior of a right to waive or discharge a burden.
4 Any proprietor seeking to claim an implied right had not lost or waived the right to enforce prior to 28 November 2004. This means, for example, that where an owner had, before that date, granted a discharge of the condition to allow a neighbour to build on his or her property, the 2003 Act would not revive that owner's implied right of enforcement.

[1]   Title Conditions (Scotland) Act 2003, s 52.

Section 53 implied rights

14.35 Section 53 contains a different set of rules for establishing the existence of implied enforcement rights where the properties concerned are related properties[1]. There is no clear definition of related properties in the legislation; whether properties are related is to be inferred from all the circumstances. Circumstances supporting a finding that properties are related include the convenience of managing properties together, shared ownership of common property, a shared obligation of maintenance, being subject to a common scheme by virtue of a deed of conditions and being flats in the same tenement. Pending clarification in future judicial decision, it is not clear how far beyond these (non-exhaustive) identifying criteria the courts will extend the concept of related properties. For example in a housing development where the same burdens were not imposed by a deed of conditions but by incorporation of the same burdens in each individual transfer a common sense view would suggest that the houses were related properties, particularly since the burdens would be imposed to achieve a common benefit to all of the houses in maintaining amenity. It would be difficult to justify differentiating between developments covered by identical, amenity-directed conditions purely on the basis of whether these were created by reference in individual transfers of property or whether they were contained in a deed of conditions.

1   Title Conditions (Scotland) Act 2003, s 53.

14.36   If it is established that a group of properties are related properties implied enforcement rights will arise under section 53 where:
(a)   real burdens are imposed on all the related properties under a common scheme. This common scheme may be expressly set out (for example in a deed of conditions), or it may arise by implication as discussed above; and
(b)   any proprietor seeking to claim an implied right had not lost or waived the right to enforce prior to 28 November 2004.

14.37   Where related properties are concerned it does not seem to be a barrier to the creation of a new statutory right to enforce that there is a provision in the deed imposing the condition expressly or impliedly contradicting the creation of an implied enforcement right. The effect of this is that some owners who would previously not have had a right to enforce will now enjoy such a right. For example, in *Turner v Hamilton*[1] burdens were imposed on an area of land requiring that most of it be used for housing with a small section to be used for shops. This is the type of situation which falls within the second set of circumstances explained in *Hislop v MacRitchie's Trustees* and, therefore, where mutual rights of enforcement would arise. In this case, though, there was provision for the superior to consent to departures from these restrictions, and the reservation of this power to consent was held to negate the creation of mutuality between owners of properties divided off from the initial area of land[2]. The result was, therefore, that there were no mutual rights of enforcement. Under section 53, however, it is sufficient for the properties to be related, which they were here, and for there to be reference to a common scheme. Therefore, applying section 53, the owners in *Turner* would have mutual rights of enforcement notwithstanding the superior's previous unilateral right to consent to departures from the burdens. It should also be noted that the proviso found in section 57 of the 2003 Act, to the effect that section 53 does not operate to revive a right of enforcement waived or otherwise lost as at 27 November 2004 is not relevant here. As the neighbours could have had no right at all on 27 November for the reasons explained above and therefore could not have lost or waived such a right, section 57 does not affect the operation of section 53.

1   (1890) 17 R 494.
2   See, eg per Lord President (Inglis) at 499.

14.38   As well as conferring implied enforcement rights on related properties already in existence on 28 November, section 53 may also extend implied enforcement rights to new properties built after this date. This will happen where such properties are related, either to each other or to properties existing before that date, and there is a common scheme covering all of them in a deed registered before 28 November 2004. For example, if a deed of conditions was registered in 2003 and a number of houses in a development were built and sold before 28 November 2004, then any houses built after that which qualified as related properties would also be covered by the implied rights of enforcement.

14.39   Although section 52 precedes section 53 in the 2003 Act, therefore suggesting that it is the more widely applicable provision, in fact section 53 is likely to be the most common source of implied enforcement rights because its terms are broader[1]. Regardless of which of the provisions relating to common schemes applies, the burdens concerned will normally apply to two units or more and therefore will be governed by the rules for community burdens. As we shall see, one aspect of these is that proprietors can create new community burdens.

1   KG C Reid, *The Abolition of Feudal Tenure in Scotland* (2003) 5.5.

ENFORCEMENT OF BURDENS

14.40   In order to enforce a real burden it is necessary to demonstrate both title and interest. The owner of any benefited property will have title to enforce. A number of other, non-owning, individuals now also have title to enforce. One group is, of course, those who are entitled to enforce personal real burdens. A second group consists of those who, although they do not own the benefited property, have a direct interest in enforcement because of their day-to-day use of this property. This group comprises tenants having a real right, non-entitled spouses with occupancy rights and liferenters[1]. In addition to extending the categories of those entitled to enforce, the 2003 Act also changes and clarifies the law about the parties against whom enforcement action can be taken. It is now possible to enforce a negative or ancillary burden against not only the owner of the burdened property, but also against a tenant or any other person having use of the property[2]. Affirmative burdens can be enforced not only against the current owner, but also against a previous owner who has breached the burden. The liability of new and previous owner is several. The new owner can also recover from the previous owner any costs of performing the obligation not performed by the previous owner[3].

[1]   Title Conditions (Scotland) Act 2003, s 8(2).
[2]   Title Conditions (Scotland) Act 2003, s 9. Previously the law on enforcement against tenants was not clear: *Colquhoun's Curator v Glen's Trustees* 1920 2 SLT 197; *Eagle Lodge Ltd v Keir and Cawdor Estates* 1964 SC 30.
[3]   Title Conditions (Scotland) Act 2003, s 10.

14.41   A person seeking to enforce a burden will have interest to enforce either[1]:
(a)   if breach of the burden is resulting, or will result, in material detriment to the value or enjoyment of the person's ownership of or right in the benefited property; or
(b)   if the burden imposes an obligation to pay a contribution to costs and the person is seeking to enforce this.

[1]   Title Conditions (Scotland) Act 2003, s 8(3).

14.42   Interest to enforce may be lost in the following ways[1]:
(a)   bad faith on the part of the person entitled to enforce the real burden, for example, demanding an excessive consideration for variation or discharge;
(b)   change in circumstances. The possibility of loss of interest through change of circumstances was mentioned in *Earl of Zetland v Hislop*[2]. It is clear that the change in circumstances must be dramatic and be such as to render the enforcement of the condition relatively pointless.

[1]   Both of these grounds for loss of interest are discussed at length in *Howard De Walden Estates Ltd v Bowmaker Ltd* 1965 SLT 254.
[2]   (1882) 9 R (HL) 40.

14.43   Real burdens will be enforced by personal action. For example where the burden involves making of a payment it can be enforced by an action for payment; where the burden requires that the person bound does not act in a certain way breach can be enjoined by interdict; and where the burden requires some specific action on the part of the person bound by the burden this can be enforced by an action for specific implement[1].

1   For an example of enforcement by way of interdict see *Mannofield Residents Property Co Ltd v Thomson* 1983 SLT (Sh Ct) 71.

TERMINATION AND EXTINCTION OF BURDENS

14.44   Burdens can be varied, terminated or extinguished in a variety of ways. A later section of this chapter considers achieving this by application to the Lands Tribunal for Scotland. This section will consider other methods of termination etc and the following section will consider the special provisions which apply to community burdens.

Discharge

14.45   A burden can be discharged by the owner of a benefited property[1]. Where there is more than one benefited property more than one discharge may be required, and there arc special rules for the discharge of community burdens which are considered in the next section. Discharge will normally be by way of a minute of waiver. This is simply a document granted by the person entitled to enforce the condition waiving the application of the condition to the land. The minute is effective against the person granting it without registration or recording, but registration or recording is necessary in order to make it effective against successors in title to the person who granted it[2].

1   Title Conditions (Scotland) Act 2003 S 15.
2   Land Registration (Scotland) Act 1979, s 18.

Acquiescence

14.46   Acquiescence is a form of personal bar. The previous law regarded acquiescence as a form of implied consent to the breach of the condition[1]. The 2003 Act provides that the effect of acquiescence is to extinguish the burden, at least to the extent that it has been breached. Acquiescence occurs where there is express consent to a breach of a real burden which fulfils the conditions (a) and (b) below[2]. In addition, and not applying to conservation, economic development or health care burdens, acquiescence will arise by implied consent where[3]:

(a) There has been a breach of the burden involving substantial expenditure on the part of the person responsible for the breach.
(b) The benefit of this expenditure would be substantially lost if the burden was enforced.
(c) The owner of the benefited property, is, or ought to be, aware of the breach of the burden, and fails to object within a reasonable time. The assessment of a reasonable time depends on the circumstances of the breach. No objection made more than 12 weeks after substantial completion of the work amounting to the breach can be regarded as having been made within a reasonable time.

[1]   In *North British Railway Company v Clark* 1913 1 SLT 207 it was stated that consent by a superior to changes was not to be regarded as evidence of acquiescence; rather it was to be treated as evidence of an active interest in the management of the estate.
[2]   Title Conditions (Scotland) Act 2003, s 16.
[3]   For the previous common law rules see *Ben Challum Ltd v Buchanan* 1955 SLT 294.

14.47   After the 12-week period has elapsed there will also be a rebuttable presumption that the benefited owner was or ought to have been aware of the breach. Acquiescence in the breach of a particular condition does not negate rights to enforce other conditions; it only affects the condition breached and conditions of the same type[1].

[1]   *Johnstone v The Walker Trustees* (1897) 24 R 1061.

Negative prescription

14.48   Breach of a burden followed by the passing of five years without any attempt to enforce the burden by court action or any acknowledgement by the person subject to the burden will extinguish the burden[1]. The acknowledgement can either be a written acknowledgement of the burden or it can be deduced from the actions of the person bound.

[1]   Title Conditions (Scotland) Act 2003, s 8; Prescription and Limitation (Scotland) Act 1973, ss 9 and 10.

The sunset rule[1]

14.49 One of the motives behind reform of the law relating to real burdens was a desire to remove outdated burdens, and initially the proposal was that burdens over a certain age would simply, like the Norwegian Blue, cease to exist. One difficulty with this, of course, was that many elderly burdens are still of value in protecting amenity. One example is a restriction on the use of property to prevent non-residential use; another is the management burdens often found in the titles to tenement properties. The final provision in the 2003 Act therefore does not provide for automatic extinction. Instead it provides a procedure by which burdens that are 100 years old or older can be extinguished. Anyone against whom such a burden can be enforced can serve a notice of termination to extinguish the burden as it affects their property (the burdened property). In recognition of the value of some older burdens, however, facility and service burdens cannot be terminated by this means and neither can conservation or maritime burdens and certain other burdens mainly linked to minerals and agricultural land[2].

[1]   Title Conditions (Scotland) Act 2003, ss 20–24.
[2]   This last group is listed in Title Conditions (Scotland) Act 2003 Sch 11.

14.50 The notice of termination will specify a renewal date, which must be more than eight weeks from the date of intimation of the notice. It must be served in writing on the owner of the burdened property (if, for example, the notice is being served by a tenant), the holder of a personal real burden if it is proposed to terminate such a burden, and on any benefited proprietors having a property within four metres of the property owned or occupied by the person serving the notice. Aside from cases where written notice is required, notice must be given by affixing a notice to a lamp post or lamp posts or, if this is not possible, by advertisement in a local newspaper.

14.51 If the owner of a benefited property wishes to continue the burden in force he/she must apply to the Lands Tribunal for Scotland for renewal of the burden before the renewal date[1]. If such an application is refused the Tribunal can award compensation to a benefited proprietor or to the holder of a personal real condition where either the termination of the condition causes substantial loss or inconvenience or where a reduced consideration was paid for the property because of the condition being terminated[2]. As an alternative to granting the renewal or refusing it outright the Tribunal can either vary the burden or impose a fresh burden[3].

208   *Real burdens*

Title Conditions (Scotland) Act 2003, s 90(1)(b).
2   Title Conditions (Scotland) Act 2003, s 90(6) and (7).
3   Title Conditions (Scotland) Act 2003, s 90(8).

14.52   If there is no application for renewal or the application is refused, the notice of termination must be registered and the effect is that the burdened property is no longer bound by the burden.

Compulsory purchase

14.53   In general burdens will be extinguished when the land affected by them is compulsorily purchased[1].

1   Title Conditions (Scotland) Act 2003, ss 106 and 107.

SPECIAL PROVISIONS APPLYING TO COMMUNITY BURDENS

14.54   The deed creating a community burden may provide a mechanism for variation and discharge of the burdens which it creates. Alternatively, the 2003 Act contains special provisions for the variation and discharge of community burdens. A significant point in this context is that variation includes the imposition or creation of a new burden. These provisions are important because implied rights to enforce created by ss 52 and 53 of the 2003 Act will, in most cases, involve community burdens.

14.55   In the terminology of the 2003 Act, the properties in respect of which a burden is to be varied or discharged is described as an 'affected unit' and an 'adjacent unit' is a unit within four metres of an affected unit.

14.56   The first method of securing discharge or variation is by registering against each affected unit a deed of variation or discharge granted by the owners of a majority of units in the community to which the burdens apply, or, where this is permitted in the titles to community properties, by the manager of the community[1]. Owners of properties who have not been involved in granting the deed must be informed in writing of the proposal to register this deed. On receipt of this notice they can apply to the Lands Tribunal to preserve the burden and if the Tribunal grants the application its effect will be to continue the burden as it exists both in favour of and against those who have not signed the deed of variation or discharge[2]. For example, 60 per cent of the owners grant a deed discharging a condition.

One of the 40 per cent who did not sign the deed can apply to preserve the burden. If his/her application is granted not only will the burden still affect the 40 per cent, but any one of the 40 per cent will still have title to enforce the burden against any one of the 60 per cent (though, of course, they may not have interest to do so depending on the respective positions of the properties and the nature of the burden).

1   Title Conditions (Scotland) Act 2003, s 33.
2   Title Conditions (Scotland) Act 2003, s 34.

14.57   An alternative method of seeking discharge or variation is for the owner of the affected property to obtain a deed of variation or discharge signed by the owners of all adjacent properties. This method cannot be used to vary or discharge a facility or service burden or where the community consists of sheltered or retirement housing[1].

1   Title Conditions (Scotland) Act 2003, s 35.

14.58   Once the deed has been granted owners of units who have not been involved in granting the deed must be notified. The notification requirements are not as strict as in cases where the deed is granted by the majority in the community and there is no requirement for individual notification of these owners. Instead notification can be by notice affixed to each affected unit and to a lamp post or lamp posts, or where this cannot be done, by advertising in a local newspaper[1].

1   Title Conditions (Scotland) Act 2003, s 36.

14.59   As with discharge by a majority, owners who have not signed the deed can apply to the Tribunal for preservation of the burden. In both cases if the application for preservation is refused the Tribunal can award compensation where either the termination of the condition causes substantial loss or inconvenience or where a reduced consideration was paid for the property because of the condition being terminated[1].

1   Title Conditions (Scotland) Act 2003, s 90(6) and (7).

VARIATION OR DISCHARGE BY THE LANDS TRIBUNAL

14.60   Because of difficulties in getting agreement from superiors to vary burdens to permit new uses, and because of the suspicion that in some cases superiors were charging excessive sums of money to allow such variation or discharge, the Conveyancing and Feudal Reform (Scotland) Act 1970 introduced a new method for having real burdens varied or discharged. This procedure, by way of application to the Lands Tribunal for Scotland, is continued and substantially amended by the 2003 Act.

Jurisdiction

14.61   The Lands Tribunal for Scotland is permitted to vary or discharge title conditions. The term 'title condition'[1] includes not only real burdens, but also servitude rights and conditions in registrable leases[2].

[1]   Title Conditions (Scotland) Act 2003, s 122
[2]   *McQuiban v Eagle Star Insurance* 1972 SLT (Lands Tr) 39.

14.62   There are, however, certain statutory exclusions from the jurisdiction of the Tribunal:
(a)   The constitutive deed creating the condition may provide that no application for variation or discharge is to be made before a specified date (which cannot be more than five years after the creation of the title condition)[1]. If no such provision is contained in the constitutive deed there will be no time restriction on applications for variation or discharge.
(b)   Certain conditions conceived in favour of the Crown, conditions relating to mineral working, and conditions applying to agricultural holdings cannot be varied[2].
(c)   The Tribunal will not vary or discharge a condition if the result of this would be to impose an additional burden on other land not owned by the applicant[3].

[1]   Title Conditions (Scotland) Act 2003, s 92. This replaces the provision (originally in Conveyancing and Feudal Reform (Scotland) Act 1970 s 2(5)) that the Tribunal could not vary any condition which is less than two years old; see *Watters v Motherwell District Council* 1991 SLT (Lands Tr) 2.
[2]   Title Conditions (Scotland) Act 2003, Sch 11.
[3]   See *Murrayfield Ice Rink Ltd v Scottish Rugby Union* 1973 SLT 99.

14.63   The Tribunal now has the power to decide on the validity, applicability, enforceability or interpretation of real burdens[1]. This allows the Tribunal to determine such issues whilst examining an application for variation or discharge of a burden, but it also means that applicants may make a free-standing application to the Tribunal to ask it to decide on one of these issues.

1 Title Conditions (Scotland) Act 2003, s 90(1)(a)(ii); in contrast to their former jurisdiction, see, for example, *McCarthy & Stone (Developments) Ltd v Smith* 1995 SLT (Lands Tr) 19 at 26.

14.64 An application for variation (including imposition of a new burden) or discharge of a community burden can be made by owners of one quarter of the units in the community. The application can seek variation or discharge either in respect of some of the units in the community or the community as a whole[1].

1 Title Conditions (Scotland) Act 2003, s 91.

Notice and representations

14.65 Notice of an application to vary or discharge must be given to any owner of benefited property (benefited proprietor), or, where the burden is a personal real burden, to the holder of the burden, or to the holder of the title condition, for example, the landlord if the variation is in respect of a condition in a registrable lease.

14.66 Representations in writing on the application can be made by anyone who has title to enforce the burden and anyone against whom the condition can be enforced[1].

1 Title Conditions (Scotland) Act 2003, ss 95 & 96.

Unopposed applications

14.67 Aside from cases where the burden is a facility or services burden or a burden in sheltered or retirement housing, an unopposed application for variation or discharge must be granted as of right[1]. The fact that representations have been received does not mean that the application is opposed. Although they do not have to be notified of an application for variation or discharge, tenants and other non-owners who have title to enforce a real burden can make representations regarding an application to vary or discharge[2]. However, an application is to be treated as unopposed unless there is a representation opposing it either from an owner of the benefited property or, if relevant, the holder of a personal real burden[3].

Therefore an application will still be granted as of right as an unopposed application even if, for example, a tenant makes a representation opposing the application.

¹   Title Conditions (Scotland) Act 2003, s 97.
²   Title Conditions (Scotland) Act 2003, s 95(a).
³   Title Conditions (Scotland) Act 2003, s 97(3)(a).

Imposition of new burdens

14.68   The Lands Tribunal may, when making an order of variation or discharge, impose a new burden on the burdened property or vary another existing burden. This can be done only when the owner of the burdened property agrees. This might be done, for example, to minimise the impact of the changes in the amenity of the area which are likely to follow on the Tribunal's order[1].

[1]   See, for example *Leney v Craig* 1982 SLT (Lands Tr) 9.

Compensation

14.69   Proprietors of benefited properties may be awarded compensation by the Tribunal in two circumstances[1]:
1   Where the order granted by the Tribunal causes substantial loss or disadvantage to the proprietor of benefited property in his/her capacity as owner[2]. An example of this might be a reduction in the value of the property caused by the changes resulting from the variation of discharge of the condition[3]. Compensation will be assessed as the difference between the 'before' and 'after' values of the property[4]. In the *CWS* case, however, the Tribunal also stated that, 'following English authority, we leave for consideration in a future case whether compensation can ever be claimed... in respect of personal loss or disturbance unrelated to heritage'[5].
2   Where a reduced consideration (for example a lower price or feuduty) was accepted because of the existence of the condition which is varied or discharged[6]. An example of this might be the situation where a restrictive condition resulted in a lower price being fixed for the property compared to that which would have been fixed on the same property without the application of the restrictive condition.

Compensation was awarded on this ground in *Cumbernauld Development Corporation v County Properties and Development Ltd*[7], and the method of calculation was considered in *Gorrie and Banks Ltd v Musselburgh Town Council*[8].

[1]   Title Conditions (Scotland) Act 2003, s 90(6).
[2]   Title Conditions (Scotland) Act 2003, s 90(7)(a).
[3]   For example *Leney v Craig* 1982 SLT (Lands Tr) 9.
[4]   *Cooperative Wholesale Society Ltd v Ushers Brewery* 1975 SLT (Lands Tr) 9.
[5]   1975 SLT (Lands Tr) 9 at 14.
[6]   Title Conditions (Scotland) Act 2003, s 90(7)(b).
[7]   1996 SLT 1106.
[8]   1974 SLT (Lands Tr) 5.

14.70   Compensation is not payable for loss of the benefited proprietor's opportunity to charge a burdened proprietor a fee for voluntary variation or discharge[1], nor is compensation payable to allow the benefited proprietor to capture the development value released by the variation or discharge[2].

[1]   For a discussion of the compatibility of this view with Article 1 of Protocol 1 to the European Convention on Human Rights, see *Strathclyde Joint Police Board v The Elderslie Estates Ltd* 2002 SLT (Lands Tr) 2.
[2]   *Robertson v Church of Scotland General Trustees* 1976 SLT (Lands Tr) 11.

14.71   Where compensation is payable the Tribunal may fix a time limit for its payment and the order for variation or discharge will be void if the compensation is not paid within that period[1]. Where no period is specified the variation or discharge will not take effect until either the compensation is paid or those entitled to payment agree that it can take effect[2].

[1]   Lands Tribunal for Scotland Rules 2003 (SSI 2003/452), r 6(3).
[2]   Lands Tribunal for Scotland Rules 2003 (SSI 2003/452), r 6(2).

The order of the Tribunal becomes effective on recording/registration

14.72   The order varying or discharging a land obligation will become effective when it is registered in the Land Register or recorded in the Register of Sasines as appropriate. This is subject to suspension of the effectiveness of the order where compensation is payable to benefited proprietors as described above[1].

[1]   Title Conditions (Scotland) Act 2003, s 104(2).

FACTORS TO BE CONSIDERED BY THE LANDS TRIBUNAL

14.73 The Lands Tribunal can only grant an opposed application for variation or discharge if they consider it is reasonable to do so. Any application will need to be specific enough as to the proposed use as a result of the variation or discharge to allow the Tribunal to make this judgement[1]. In taking this decision they are directed to take into account the factors considered below. As well as applying to variation and discharge these factors are also to be considered in deciding whether it is reasonable to grant an application to renew or, with two exceptions, preserve a burden. The exceptions are cases where the application is made to preserve burdens in the face of a document varying or discharging community burdens granted by a majority of the community or by the adjacent proprietors[2].

[1]   *Itelsor Ltd v Smith* 2001 Hous LR 120.
[2]   Title Conditions (Scotland) Act 2003, s 100.

14.74 The factors listed in the 2003 Act are less prescriptive than the grounds which were set out in the Conveyancing and Feudal Reform (Scotland) Act 1970 ('the 1970 Act'), and arguably tilted more towards grant of variation and discharge than was the case under the 1970 Act. Although there is no specific instruction to do so, it is clear that the Tribunal will have to balance or weigh the different factors against each other and the way in which this will be done in practice remains to be seen.

Change in circumstances

14.75 The first ground is that there has been a change in circumstances since the title condition was created. This is specifically stated to include any change in the character of the benefited or burdened properties or the neighbourhood of the properties. This has strong similarities to some of the factors in the first ground for variation or discharge which was found in the 1970 Act. This ground was that 'by reason of changes in the character of the land affected by the obligation or of the neighbourhood thereof or other circumstances which the Tribunal may deem material, the obligation is or has become unreasonable or inappropriate'[1]. Clearly case law on the first three elements is likely to be relevant to applications under the 2003 Act and this is now considered.

1   Conveyancing and Feudal Reform (Scotland) Act 1970, s 1(3)(a). See Agnew of
    Lochaw, *Variation and Discharge of Land Obligations*, 6-02 to 6-11.

14.76   In looking at whether there has been a change in circumstances
the Tribunal will discount any changes brought about by the applicant in
breach of burden which the application seeks to vary or discharge. In
Solway Cedar Ltd v Hendry[1] the applicants were restricted to a certain
number of houses to be built on a piece of land. The applicants had, by
breaching the condition, managed to fit more houses in, and sought
variation of the condition affecting the land to allow what they had done.
The Tribunal took the view that the applicants could not found on this
change, which had been brought about in breach of the condition, as a
ground for application for variation of discharge.

1   1972 SLT (Lands Tr) 42; see also *Bruce v Modern Homes Investment Co Ltd*
    1978 SLT (Lands Tr) 34.

Changes in the character of the land

14.77   There are very few cases reported on this ground. A reduction in
profitability of the current use enjoined by the condition was held not to
fall into this category[1].

1   See *Bolton v Aberdeen Corporation* 1972 SLT (Lands Tr) 26.

Changes in the neighbourhood

14.78   What is regarded as the relevant neighbourhood for these
purposes depends on the circumstances of each individual case and one
case was restricted to a group of six houses[1]. In another the relevant
neighbourhood was considered to be the whole of Perth[2]. It has been held
that the Tribunal is entitled to consider the group of properties covered by
a single set of burdens as the relevant neighbourhood and that it is not
necessary for the neighbourhood to be centred on the property in respect
of which variation or discharge is sought[3]. Examples of changes which
have been considered by the Tribunal have been a growth of tourism[4],
additional housing developments[5], and a decline in the number of
schoolchildren in the area[6]. Minor changes, for example erection of dormer
windows or car ports, which do not affect the character of the area, have
been considered to be irrelevant[7].

1   *Mercer v Macleod* 1977 SLT (Lands Tr) 14.
2   *Manz v Butters Trustees* 1973 SLT (Lands Tr) 2.
3   *Anderson v Trotter* 1999 SLT 442.
4   See *Manz v Butters Trustees* 1973 SLT (Lands Tr) 2. In at least one case the Tribunal has taken the view that the area was the opposite of a tourist attraction: *Cooperative Wholesale Society Ltd v Ushers Brewery* 1975 SLT (Lands Tr) 9.
5   *Leney v Craig* 1982 SLT (Lands Tr) 9.
6   *Highland Regional Council v Macdonald-Buchanan* 1977 SLT (Lands Tr) 37.
7   See *Stoddart v Glendinning* 1993 SLT (Lands Tr) 12.

Changes in other circumstances

14.79   Examples of other changes which the Tribunal has considered to be material have been: changes in attitudes to alcohol[1], the decline in demand for industrial buildings[2], local demand for nursery places[3], and the decline in domestic service where there was a large property with servants' rooms[4].

1   *Owen v McKenzie* 1974 SLT (Lands Tr) 11.
2   *British Bakeries (Scotland) plc v City of Edinburgh District Council* 1990 SLT (Lands Tr) 33.
3   *Anderson v Trotter* 1999 SLT 442.
4   *Morris v Feuars of Waverley Park* 1973 SLT (Lands Tr) 6.

The benefit resulting from the condition

14.80   More fully this ground is that 'the extent to which the condition (i) confers a benefit on the benefited property or (ii) where there is no benefited property, confers a benefit to the public'[1]. In some respects this is a disaggregation of the second ground that existed prior to the 2003 Act which was that 'the obligation is unduly burdensome compared to any benefit resulting or which would result from its performance'[2]. It was suggested that to succeed on this ground the applicant had to prove that the condition had become relatively pointless and giving no real benefit[3]. Application of this ground involved the Tribunal in weighing up the benefits to the benefited proprietor against the burden imposed on the burden proprietor. Since the new factor does not involve such an explicit balancing exercise it can be suggested that the comparatively slight benefit which might under this test have justified keeping a condition in place may no longer be enough to justify refusal of an application. Of course, under the old regime the different grounds for variation were considered separately and a refusal to vary on this ground because of a slight benefit might be rendered moot because the variation was granted on one of the other grounds (as was often the case).

1   Title Conditions (Scotland) Act 2003, s 100(b).
2   Conveyancing and Feudal Reform (Scotland) Act 1970, s 1(3)(b). See Agnew of
     Lochaw, *Variation and Discharge of Land Obligations*, 6-12 to 6-17.
3   *Lothian Regional Council v George Wimpey* 1985 SLT (Lands Tr) 2.

14.81   Given that one of the purposes of real burdens is the preservation of amenity, the amenity benefits of continuing the condition will be an important consideration. It may be that the Tribunal will continue to have regard to whether the development which will follow from the variation or discharge is the thin end of the wedge[1].

1   See *Mercer v Macleod* 1977 SLT (Lands Tr) 14.

14.82   It is likely to continue to be the case that any benefit must accrue from continued compliance with the condition rather than from the ability of the person entitled to enforce the condition to charge a fee for voluntary discharge or variation[1].

1   *West Lothian Cooperative Society Ltd v Ashdale Land & Property Co* 1972 SLT
     (Lands Tr) 30.

The extent to which the condition impedes enjoyment of the burdened property

14.83   Because title conditions are conditions affecting property, any impediment to enjoyment suffered by the burdened proprietor must be one which would affect any proprietor of the subjects and not one which is merely personal to the applicant or the applicant's family. For example, in *Stoddart v Glendinning*[1] an applicant applied for variation of a real burden to allow an extension to be built on to a house to accommodate his wife's disability. It was held that the burden imposed by the real burden was purely personal, arising from the disability of the applicant's wife, and therefore not a relevant consideration[2].

1   1993 SLT (Lands Tr) 12.
2   See also *Millar Group Ltd v Gardiner's Executors* 1992 SLT (Lands Tr) 62.

14.84 One question might arise as to the extent of enjoyment by the applicant which is relevant here, and whether this level of enjoyment is subject to limits. For example, under the 1970 Act it was considered not to be a substantial burden on the applicant that, although he could make a profitable use of the land, he could not make the *most* profitable use of his property[1].

1   *Smith v Taylor* 1972 SLT (Lands Tr) 34.

Practicality and cost of compliance

14.85 This factor is concerned with how costly or practicable it is for the applicant to comply with or continue to comply with the condition. This brings into play a factor which the Tribunal had previously refused to consider, at least in considering whether or not it amounted to a change in circumstances. It may be that this new factor would lead the Tribunal to a different decision from the one reached in *James Millar and Partners v Hunt*[1] where it was held that the fact that complying with the condition was more difficult or expensive than originally thought did not amount to a change in circumstances.

1   1974 SLT (Lands Tr) 9.

The length of time which has elapsed since the condition was created

14.86 This is in line with the sunset rule and with the view that with the passing of time conditions become irrelevant or redundant. As has been argued, this may be true of some conditions, but not of others, so that this should not always be an important factor in the overall decision of the Tribunal.

The purpose of the title condition

14.87 This factor might operate in conjunction with other factors. For example, if the condition had been imposed for essentially planning reasons in order to control development the grant of planning permission (see para **14.88**) would then become very significant and deserve more weight[1].

¹   *British Bakeries (Scotland) plc v City of Edinburgh District Council* 1990 SLT (Lands Tr) 33.

Grant of planning or other permissions

14.88   In order for a development to take place a variety of different consents may be required. The most obvious of these are planning and building control. The Tribunal has always considered the grant of planning or other consent. The grant of planning or other consent will not be a conclusive indicator that it is reasonable to grant the application as the concerns of the planning system and the rights protected by real burdens and other title conditions are entirely separate¹. These differences are explained in detail *British Bakeries (Scotland) plc v City of Edinburgh District Council* as follows²:

'The considerations to which a planning authority give weight may be very different to those which the tribunal must have in mind, and while there may be no justification on planning grounds for prohibiting a particular use of land, the person in right of the [title condition] may have a strong, continuing interest to enforce it, so that it may be entirely reasonable and appropriate that it should stay unchanged.'

As is suggested in this extract, the Tribunal has viewed planning decisions as being concerned with questions of public right, whereas it is concerned with questions of safeguarding private rights³. In addition it has been pointed out that planning procedures do not necessarily provide for the canvassing of the opinions of all those likely to be affected by a proposed development before permission is granted⁴.

¹   *Solway Cedar Ltd v Hendry* 1972 SLT (Lands Tr) 42 and *Tully v Armstrong* 1990 SLT (Lands Tr) 42 are examples of refusal of an application to vary or discharge despite the grant of planning permission for the proposed development.
²   1990 SLT (Lands Tr) 33 at 34, HL; other cases discussing the issue of planning permission include *Cameron v Stirling* 1988 SLT (Lands Tr) 18 and *Millar Group Ltd v Gardiner's Executors* 1992 SLT (Lands Tr) 62.
³   *Main v Lord Doune* 1972 SLT (Lands Tr) 14 at 17.
⁴   *Ross & Cromarty District Council v Ullapool Property Company Co Ltd* 1983 SLT(LandsTr) 9 at 13.

14.89   In *Stoddart v Glendinning*¹ the fact that the proposed development was exempted from the requirement to obtain planning permission was regarded as having no bearing on the reasonableness of the proposed use.

1   1993 SLT (Lands Tr) 12.

14.90   It may be that the phrasing of this factor might encourage the Tribunal to give greater weight to the grant of permissions than it has in some cases in the past. Absence of detailed planning permission may make it difficult to decide whether granting the application is reasonable[1].

1   Itelsor Ltd v Smith 2001 Hous LR 120.

Whether the owner of the burdened property is prepared to pay compensation

14.91   This will involve consideration of whether the person seeking the change is prepared to pay compensation for the effect on the amenity, etc of the benefited proprietors. Compensation can, of course, be ordered by the Tribunal as a condition of granting variation or discharge and it may be that this ground will allow them to consider any offers to compensate in cases where they have no power to make such an order.

Any other factor which the Tribunal consider to be material

14.92   One example of this type of factor from pre-2003 Act cases is the unwillingness of women to enter public houses[1].

1   See *Owen v Mackenzie* 1974 SLT (Lands Tr) 11; *Co-operative Wholesale Society Ltd v Ushers Brewery* 1975 SLT (Lands Tr) 9.

Maintenance of community burdens

14.93   Where the Tribunal is considering an application to preserve community burdens following a deed of variation or discharge signed either by a majority in the community or by adjacent proprietors they must grant the order for preservation if the proposed variation or discharge is either:
(a)   not in the best interests of the owners of all the units in the community; or

(b)   unfairly prejudicial to one or more of these owners.

OCCUPANCY RIGHTS

14.94   These are not strictly speaking real burdens affecting property, but since they confer rights over property which can limit the proprietor's dealings with that property they are dealt with here.

14.95   Prior to the coming into effect of the Matrimonial Homes (Family Protection) (Scotland) Act 1981 ('the 1981 Act') the position of a spouse who was not the owner or tenant of the family home was a precarious one. It was well established that she had no legal right to occupy the home and could be removed at the will of the other spouse[1]. The situation where one spouse alone, usually the husband, owned or was the tenant of the family home was common. One of the purposes of the 1981 Act was to provide some protection to the other spouse, usually the wife.

[1]   *MacLure v MacLure* (1911) 1 SLT 6; *Millar v Millar* 1940 SLT 72.

14.96   The legislation is designed to provide this protection in relation to what it describes as 'matrimonial homes'. A matrimonial home means any home[1] provided or made available by one or both spouses as, or which has become, a family residence[2]. The definition also includes gardens attached to the home but specifically does not include a home provided by one spouse for the other spouse to live in separately.

[1]   Including houses, caravans, houseboats and 'other structures'.
[2]   Matrimonial Homes (Family Protection) (Scotland) Act 1981, s 22.

14.97   Spouses are divided into entitled and non-entitled spouses, the entitled spouse being the one who is owner or tenant of the matrimonial home. Occupancy rights in the matrimonial home are then conferred on the non-entitled spouse. The nature of the rights depends on whether or not the non-entitled spouse is in occupation of the matrimonial home. If so, the right is to continue in occupation; if not, the right is to be allowed to enter and occupy the home[1]. Application must be made to court for the exercise of the right in the latter case, and the courts also have the power to make orders regulating, declaring and restricting occupancy rights[2]. In certain circumstances the court may also make an order excluding the entitled, or indeed the non-entitled, spouse from the matrimonial home[3].

[1]   Matrimonial Homes (Family Protection) (Scotland) Act 1981, s 1(1).

²   Matrimonial Homes (Family Protection) (Scotland) Act 1981, s 3.
³   Matrimonial Homes (Family Protection) (Scotland) Act 1981, s 4.

14.98   The significance of occupancy rights for property law is that the occupancy rights of non-entitled spouses are, subject to the exceptions noted below, preferable to those obtained by a third party (eg a purchaser of the property) in a voluntary dealing with the entitled spouse. The consequence of this is that any such third party will not be entitled to occupy the matrimonial home or any part of it if there is a non-entitled spouse with occupancy rights[1]. 'Dealing' is not very clearly defined in the legislation, but it certainly includes sale and the granting of a security over the property.

¹   Matrimonial Homes (Family Protection) (Scotland) Act 1981, s 6(1).

14.99   The occupancy rights of a non-entitled spouse are not protected against a third party acquiring rights in a dealing with the entitled spouse where the non-entitled spouse has consented to the dealing: where the non-entitled spouse has renounced her occupancy rights; where a court order has been made dispensing with the consent of the non-entitled spouse[1]; and where the special provisions concerning sale and granting of securities apply[2]. In each of these cases, therefore, the third party dealing with the entitled spouse will be protected from claims to exercise occupancy rights by a non-entitled spouse.

¹   This can be done if she is unable to consent or is withholding consent unreasonably.
     Matrimonial Homes (Family Protection) (Scotland) Act 1981, s 7.
²   Matrimonial Homes (Family Protection) (Scotland) Act 1981, s 6(3).

14.100   Occupancy rights may be terminated in the following ways: the ending of the marriage; passing of the long negative prescription period of 20 years without exercise of the rights; cessation of the entitled spouse's entitlement to occupy the matrimonial home; non-exercise of the rights for a period of five years following a disposal by the entitled spouse; destruction of the matrimonial homes; and, renunciation of rights by the non-entitled spouse.

COMMUNITY MANAGEMENT

14.101   Although not strictly the imposition of a real burden, the 2003 Act also makes some provision for management of communities[1], as these are defined for the purposes of community burdens. There are two aspects to this provision. The first allows the owners of a majority of units in the community to appoint a manager (and dismiss him/her) and to confer appropriate powers on the manager[2]. These powers can include the power to instruct maintenance of the property and to enforce, vary or discharge community burdens and are subject to any specific manager burden, the provisions of the community burdens and special provision in the case of sheltered housing. The second aspect is the conferring on the owners of a majority of units of the power to take decisions that will ensure that maintenance work is carried out. This power can only be exercised where the community burdens include either an obligation to maintain certain property (eg the roof of a tenement building) or to contribute towards the cost of such maintenance[3]. Maintenance is defined as including repair or replacement and any demolition, alteration and improvement which is reasonably incidental to maintenance[4].

[1] See also the discussion in CHAPTER 11 of the management scheme introduced by the Tenements (Scotland) Act 2004.
[2] Title Conditions (Scotland) Act 2003, s 28.
[3] Title Conditions (Scotland) Act 2003, s 29.
[4] Title Conditions (Scotland) Act 2003, s 122.

DEVELOPMENT MANAGEMENT SCHEMES

14.102 The owner of land which is to be developed can apply to this land a development management scheme. Amongst other things the scheme will provide for the creation of an owners' association, to be made up of the purchasers of properties in the development, and the appointment of a manager of this association[1]. Restrictions imposed in the scheme can be disapplied or replaced by the owners' association or replaced by real burdens[2]. Any proposal to disapply must be notified to other owners who can apply to the Lands Tribunal for preservation of the restriction[3]. Such an application must be granted as of right if it is unopposed. If there is opposition to such an application an order of preservation is to be granted if the disapplication is not in the best interests of the owners or unfairly prejudices one or more of the owners in the development[4].

[1] Title Conditions (Scotland) Act 2003, ss 71 & 72.
[2] Title Conditions (Scotland) Act 2003, s 73.
[3] Title Conditions (Scotland) Act 2003, s 74.
[4] Title Conditions (Scotland) Act 2003, s 99.

FEUDUTY

14.103   As we saw in CHAPTER 1, the system of land tenure in Scotland prior to 28 November 2004 involved a relationship between superior and vassal[1]. As we noted the return given by the vassal in exchange for the grant of land was originally military service. Soon after the introduction of the feudal system, however, the return in most cases came to be the payment of money in the form of feuduty[2]. In many cases this return made the superior's interest in land a valuable investment and many superiorities came to be held by insurance companies and others for investment purposes. In 1974 it was made impossible to create new feuduties or to increase the value of existing feuduty[3]. In addition, mechanisms were introduced to provide for redemption of feuduties on payment of compensation to the superior[4]. As a result, feuduties died out to a large extent except in cases where a number of properties contributed to a single feuduty (as usually was the case in tenement closes). The 2000 Act abolishes all remaining feuduties, subject to compensation being paid to the superior[5].

[1]   Subject to a very limited number of exceptions: see Gordon ch 3.
[2]   Military service as a return being abolished after the Jacobite uprisings.
[3]   Land Tenure Reform (Scotland) Act 1974.
[4]   Land Tenure Reform (Scotland) Act 1974, s 5.
[5]   Abolition of Feudal Tenure (Scotland) Act 2000, Pt 3.

CHAPTER 15

Heritable securities

INTRODUCTION

15.1 Heritable securities are grants of security over heritable property which, in case of default by the debtor, will generally allow the creditor to recover the amount owed by sale of the property. Because the security relates to an interest in land it must be in writing, and for the creditor to have a real right it must be recorded in the Register of Sasines[1] or registered in the Land Register. The most common situation in which a heritable security will be granted is where property is purchased with the assistance of a loan and the lender takes a security over the property purchased.

[1] This will continue to be the case where the title to the property is recorded in the Register of Sasines.

15.2 The precise form of the security will depend when it was granted. The only means of creating a heritable security since 1970 has been by way of a standard security[1]. However, as will be discussed in CHAPTER 18 relating to examination of title, it is important when property is being bought to ensure that any previous securities over property have been discharged properly. For this reason we will consider briefly the main forms of pre-1970 security[2]. In addition, companies may also create floating charges, which are general securities over all of their property, heritable and moveable. These will be considered at the end of the chapter.

[1] Conveyancing and Feudal Reform (Scotland) Act 1970, s 1.
[2] For a brief discussion of other forms see Halliday ch 47.

PRE-1970 SECURITIES

15.3   Only two of the pre-1970 securities are discussed here. As from 28 November 2004, assignation, discharge, variation, redemption and remedies on default are the same for these types of security as for a standard security[1].

[1]   Abolition of Feudal Tenure (Scotland) Act 2000, s 69; for the law that applied prior to that date see the references in the following two paragraphs.

Bond and disposition in security

15.4   The bond and disposition in security[1] was a deed containing two parts[2]. First was a personal undertaking by the debtor to repay the loan or perform any other obligation for which the security was granted. Second was a conveyance of heritable property belonging to the debtor in security of performance of his obligations. This was expressed to be 'redeemably as aftermentioned yet irredeemably in the event of sale by virtue hereof'. In other words it was a conveyance which only became effective as a transfer of the property to the creditor if the debtor defaulted and the creditor exercised his right of sale, and which expressly recognised the debtor's right to redeem the security.

[1]   Halliday ch 48; Gordon 20-04 to 20-83.
[2]   A statutory form is provided in the Titles to Land Consolidation (Scotland) Act 1868, Sch FF.

Ex facie absolute disposition

15.5   The *ex facie* absolute disposition[1] took the form of an unqualified and absolute conveyance of the security subjects granted by the debtor to the creditor and recorded in the Register of Sasines. There was no indication in the deed that the transfer of the property was a grant in security. In other words, the deed, apart from the specification of the consideration which was usually expressed to be for 'certain good and onerous causes', was identical to a disposition on sale. Because of this it could be used to secure future advances or fluctuating amounts.

[1]   Halliday ch 49; Gordon 20-86 to 20-102.

15.6 In addition to the disposition there was a collateral agreement between the debtor and creditor which was not normally recorded and which disclosed the true nature of the transaction and contained a considerable number of provisions regarding the loan and the security subjects. This agreement normally contained, amongst other things, the following: an acknowledgement of the true nature of the transaction, ie that the conveyance was truly in security for a loan and not absolute or irrevocable; a personal undertaking by the debtor to repay the loan according to the terms of the agreement; details regarding the size of the loan, instalments and interest rates; provision for the debtor to redeem the loan and a procedure for doing this; obligations on the debtor in connection with the upkeep and maintenance of the security subjects; and specification of the powers of the creditor on default either in respect of repayment or other terms or conditions.

STANDARD SECURITIES[1]

Introduction

15.7 As a result of the defects and difficulties affecting the existing forms of security, and following the publication of the Report on *Conveyancing Legislation and Practice*[2], these earlier forms of security were effectively abolished from 29 November 1970[3]. This was achieved by a provision in s 9 of the Conveyancing and Feudal Reform (Scotland) Act 1970 to the effect that after that date any attempt to create a heritable security in a form other than a standard security would be void.

[1]   Halliday chs 51-55, Cusine and Rennie *Standard Securities* (2nd edn), *passim*, McDonald ch 22, Gordon 20-119 to 20-204, Halliday *The Conveyancing and Feudal Reform (Scotland) Act 1970* (2nd Ed) chs 6–10.
[2]   (1966) Cmnd 3118, paras 102–106.
[3]   Conveyancing and Feudal Reform (Scotland) Act 1970, ss 9(4) and 54(2).

15.8 A standard security can be granted over any land or real right in land. Real rights in land are rights other than ownership or real burdens capable of being owned or held separately and to which title can be recorded in the Register of Sasines or registered in the Land Register[1]. This is wide enough to include not only ownership of land but also registrable leases and even other heritable securities since these are also real rights in land title to which can be recorded or registered.

1   Conveyancing and Feudal Reform (Scotland) Act 1970, s 9(8)(b); Land
    Registration (Scotland) Act 1979, s 29(1).

15.9   The debt secured by the standard security can be any obligation to
pay money or an obligation *ad factum praestandum*[1]. Thus as well as
being used to secure a loan or an overdraft a standard security might also
secure the performance of some other non-monetary obligation (eg
completion of a building) by the debtor.

1   Conveyancing and Feudal Reform (Scotland) Act 1970, s 9(8)(c).

15.10   A standard security may be granted by someone other than the
debtor and the person granting need not have completed title to the land
or real right in land and may deduce title in the security deed[1]. Deduction
of title involves the proprietor who has not completed title either by
recording in the Register of Sasines or registration in the Land Register
linking their ownership of the land, via a series of deeds and documents,
back to the last recording of the interest. Deduction of title in the standard
security is not necessary where title has been registered in the Land
Register[2].

1   Conveyancing and Feudal Reform (Scotland) Act 1970, s 12.
2   Land Registration (Scotland) Act 1979, s 15(3).

Forms

15.11   Two forms of standard security are provided for, imaginatively
entitled Form A and Form B[1], and actual security deeds must conform to
these 'as closely as may be'[2]. In Form A the security is achieved in one
deed which contains a brief personal obligation which is given statutory
meaning[3] and a grant of security over the land or real right in land. Form B
consists of two separate deeds, the grant of security and a separate
agreement which will be referred to in the security and which will contain
details of the personal obligation secured. This separate agreement will
not usually be recorded in the Register of Sasines or registered in the Land
Register.

1   Conveyancing and Feudal Reform (Scotland) Act 1970, Sch 2.
2   Conveyancing and Feudal Reform (Scotland) Act 1970, s 53(1); for styles see
    Halliday 52-32 to 52-72.
3   Conveyancing & Feudal Reform (Scotland) Act 1970, s 10(1).

15.12 Regardless of the form used the security deed will contain certain common clauses. First of these is a description of the land or real right in land. In all cases this should take the form of a description which is sufficient to identify the land or the right in land[1]. In securities over an interest already registered in the Land Register all that is necessary to achieve this is reference to the title number of the property[2]. In any event it is unnecessary to refer to burdens affecting the property in the description[3].

[1] Conveyancing and Feudal Reform (Scotland) Act 1970, Sch 2, Note 1, as amended by the Abolition of Feudal Tenure etc (Scotland) Act 2000, Sch 15, para 23(a).
[2] Land Registration (Scotland) Act 1979, s 15(1).
[3] Conveyancing (Scotland) Act 1924, s 9(1).

15.13 Secondly there will be an importation of the standard conditions (see below) and any variation thereof and finally there will be a grant of warrandice[1]. Because Form A contains a personal obligation it also contains a clause of consent to registration for execution; this will normally be found in the separate agreement in Form B.

[1] See CHAPTER **19**.

Standard conditions[1]

15.14 The standard conditions set out in Sch 3 to the Conveyancing and Feudal Reform (Scotland) Act 1970 apply to all standard securities, either in the form in which they appear in the schedule or as varied. Variation is very common in practice and will be considered in the next section. The effect of the unvaried conditions is as follows.

[1] Halliday ch 53, Cusine & Rennie *Standard Securities* (2nd edn), ch 4.

Standard condition 1

15.15 This obliges the debtor to maintain the security subjects in a good state of repair to the reasonable satisfaction of the creditor; permits the creditor, on giving notice, to inspect the premises; and requires the debtor to remedy any defects or disrepair within a reasonable time fixed by the creditor.

Standard condition 2

15.16   The debtor must complete any unfinished building or works forming part of or affecting the security subjects to the reasonable satisfaction of the creditor. Demolition or alteration of, or addition to, any part of the security subjects requires the consent of the creditor and must also comply with the terms of any consent or approval required by law.

Standard condition 3

15.17   The debtor must:
(a)   observe all of the title and other conditions affecting the property;
(b)   make prompt payment of all monetary burdens payable in respect of the property (eg council tax);
(c)   comply with any statutory requirements affecting the property.

Standard condition 4

15.18   Within 14 days of receipt by the debtor the creditor must be given notice of any planning or other notice or order affecting or likely to affect the security subjects. The debtor must comply with the terms of any such notice or order and if required by the creditor object to, or join with the creditor in objecting to or making representations regarding the notice or order.

Standard condition 5

15.19   The debtor must insure, or permit the creditor to insure, the security subjects to the extent of their market value and pay the premiums on such a policy as they fall due. Any possible claims under the policy must be notified to the creditor within 14 days.

Standard condition 6

15.20   The debtor must not let or sub-let the security subjects without the prior written consent of the creditor[1]. In the case of residential tenancies the creditor will only be able to evict a tenant if the tenant has been given notice of this possibility prior to the commencement of the tenancy[2].

1   As to the consequences for the lessee of a letting without the creditor's consent
see *Trade Development Bank v Warriner & Mason* 1980 SLT 223; *Trade
Development Bank v David W Haig (Bellshill) Ltd* 1983 SLT 510.

2   See CHAPTER 12; *Tamroui v Clydesdale Bank plc* 1997 SLT (Sh Ct) 20.

Standard condition 7

15.21   The creditor may perform any obligation imposed on the debtor
by the standard conditions where the debtor fails to, and may recover any
reasonable expenses so incurred from the debtor. Where the creditor has
to enter on to the security subjects to implement this condition he may do
so on giving seven days' notice.

Standard condition 8

15.22   The creditor is entitled, subject to any provision in the security, to
call up the standard security in the manner prescribed by s 19 of the
Conveyancing and Feudal Reform (Scotland) Act 1970 (see below, PARAS
15.39–15.41).

Standard condition 9

15.23   The debtor shall be held to be in default:
(a) where a calling-up notice in respect of the security has been served
and has not been complied with;
(b) where there has been a failure to comply with any other requirement
arising out of the security;
(c) where the proprietor of the security subjects has become insolvent.

Paragraph 2 of the condition details what is to be considered as insolvency
and includes someone who is notour bankrupt and a company in respect
of which a receiver has been appointed.

Standard condition 10

15.24   Where the debtor is in default the creditor has the following
remedies, which must be exercised in accordance with the provisions of
Part II of the Conveyancing and Feudal Reform (Scotland) Act 1970, in

addition to any others arising from the contract to which the standard security relates:

(a) sale of the security subjects;
(b) entering into possession of the security subjects and receiving any monetary payment due from them;
(c) where the creditor enters into possession he/she may let them;
(d) where the creditor enters into possession all rights relating to the granting of leases and management and maintenance of the property pass to him or her;
(e) effecting repairs to the property and carrying out such reconstruction, alteration and improvement of the subjects as would be expected of a prudent proprietor to maintain the market value of the subjects. In exercise of this power the creditor may enter the subjects at any reasonable time;
(f) application may be made for a decree of foreclosure.

Standard condition 11

15.25   This condition details the procedure for the exercise of the debtor's right of redemption.

Standard condition 12

15.26   The debtor is personally liable for all of the creditor's legal and other expenses arising out of the constitution and enforcement of the standard security.

15.27   Where the standard security is granted by someone other than the proprietor of the security subjects the obligations imposed in standard conditions 1–7 are imposed on the proprietor. In such cases both the proprietor and the debtor may exercise the right of redemption.

Variation of standard conditions

15.28   As noted above there is provision for variation of the standard conditions by agreement between the parties[1]. There are three exceptions to this ability to vary. The provisions relating to the power of sale and to foreclosure cannot be varied, for example by substituting another procedure for that set out in the Conveyancing and Feudal Reform (Scotland) Act

1970; and although the right of redemption can be denied the debtor, if it exists, the procedure for it's exercise set out in standard condition 11 cannot be varied[2].

[1]   Conveyancing and Feudal Reform (Scotland) Act 1970, s 11(3).
[2]   Conveyancing and Feudal Reform (Scotland) Act 1970, s 11(3).

15.29   Variation of standard conditions is very common in practice and can be effected either in a separate deed (which need not be recorded in the Register of Sasines or registered in the Land Register) or by provision in the standard security itself [1]. Building societies and some other institutional lenders favour a deed of variation registered in the Books of Council and Session.

[1]   Conveyancing and Feudal Reform (Scotland) Act 1970, Sch 2, Note 4.

15.30   Common variations include an obligation to insure for reinstatement rather than market value, a prohibition against parting with possession of the security subjects rather than letting or sub-letting, and a provision permitting the creditor to deal with the debtor's moveable property in the event of them taking possession of the security subjects[1].

[1]   See Cusine & Rennie, *Standard Securities* (2nd edn), 4.18–4.56 for a fuller discussion of common variations.

Ranking[1]

15.31   Where there are two or more standard securities over the same property the question of ranking may arise. Ranking is concerned with the relative position of the securities and is a particular concern when the security subjects are sold and do not raise enough to pay off all of the securities in full. In such a situation the ranking of the securities will determine the order in which they are paid off. As between two securities the ranking may be prior and postponed, in which case the prior security would be paid first, with the postponed taking whatever was left; or the two may rank *pari passu*, ie equally, with the proceeds going equally to the creditors in both securities.

[1]   Cusine & Rennie, *Standard Securities* (2nd edn), ch 7.

15.32   As illustration take the position where the Priory Local building society and the Bank of Paisley each hold standard securities for £25,000 over Greene's house, the securities being registered respectively on 21 January 1990 and 2 February 1991. The house is sold for £40,000. In this case the building society's security ranks prior to the bank's and so they would be paid off in full leaving the bank with £15,000. If both securities had been registered on the first date the two would have ranked *pari passu* and bank and building society would each receive £20,000.

15.33 In general the ranking of securities is determined by the date of recording or registration, so that a security recorded or registered earlier will rank prior to one recorded or registered later. Where securities are recorded or registered on the same day they will rank *pari passu*. This order of ranking can be changed by express agreement, in the form of a ranking clause in the securities, a separate ranking agreement, or by the holder of an earlier security consenting to a change in the normal order in the body of the later security. There are two situations where such changes will need to be made. The first is where two securities will be recorded on the same day and one is to be postponed to the other; and the second is where a later security is to rank prior to or *pari passu* with an earlier security.

15.34 Where the creditor in a recorded or registered standard security receives notice of the creation of a subsequent security the preference in ranking of that creditor is restricted as regards the creditor in the new security. The preference is restricted to the amount advanced at the time of the notice, any future advances the creditor is bound by contract to make, interest and any expenses of the creditor in connection with the security[1]. There has been some dispute about the effect of this provision. One view was that the earlier creditor had no security for any sums advanced after the date of notice of the second security[2]. On the other view all that was restricted was the first creditor's preference in ranking, so that the effect of the provision was that security still existed for future advances, but this was postponed to the security of the second creditor[3]. The latter view appears preferable, although Cusine and Rennie point out that further advances are rarely, if ever, made in these circumstances[4].

---

[1] Conveyancing and Feudal Reform (Scotland) Act 1970, s 13(1).
[2] G Gretton, 'Ranking of Heritable Creditors', (1980) 25 JLSS 275, (1981) 26 JLSS 280.
[3] J Halliday, 'Ranking of Heritable Creditors', (1981) 26 JLSS 26, Halliday 36-20.
[4] *Standard Securities* (2nd edn), 7.12; see also Gordon 20-132 where this view is stated without comment.

Creditor's remedies 1: remedies provided for in the standard conditions[1]

15.35 As noted above, standard condition 10 confers a variety of rights on the creditor in the event of default by the debtor. The remedies specified in that standard condition and the statutory provisions regarding their exercise are the subject of this section. The following section will consider other remedies available to the creditor. The principal remedies provided for by standard condition 10 are the power of sale; entry into possession and letting; repair, reconstruction and improvement; and foreclosure.

1   Halliday ch 54, Cusine & Rennie, *Standard Securities* (2nd edn) ch 8.

15.36 The creditor acquires the right to exercise these remedies in one of three ways: service of a calling-up notice; service of a notice of default; or application to the sheriff court under s 24 of the Conveyancing and Feudal Reform (Scotland) Act 1970

Restrictions on creditor's remedies

15.37 The creditor does not have completely unfettered power to exercise the remedies provided for in the standard security. One restriction is the right of the debtor (or, in some cases, someone else living with the debtor) to make an application under the Mortgage Rights (Scotland) Act 2001, which is considered more fully below. A second is the requirement that in exercising the right of sale the creditor realises the best price that can reasonably be obtained. The implications of this are considered under the heading 'sale' below. There is, however, an unreported case referred to in *Armstrong, Petitioner*[1] of a judicial factor on the estates of a bankrupt partnership being granted interdict against a creditor to prevent him exercising any of his standard condition 10 remedies. There is also, in *Armstrong, Petitioner*, an *obiter dictum* to the effect that 'A heritable creditor cannot use his powers for the primary purpose of advancing his own interests at the expense of the debtor when he has the alternative of proceeding in a more equitable manner'[2]. As we will see below, it is unlikely that any court would make use of this *dictum* to restrict the exercise of the power of sale by the creditor. However, there is no reason in principle why it might not apply in other cases. For example, if the value of the security subjects exceeds the outstanding loan it would seem to be in the interests of both debtor and creditor to sell these. Suppose, however, that the creditor instead decided to exercise their power of entry into possession. In those circumstances the creditor would not seem to be acting in the interests of the debtor (or their own) and there seems to be no reason why the court should not prevent the creditor from acting in this way[3].

1   1988 SLT 255.
2   1988 SLT 255 at 258C, quoted with approval in *G Dunlop & Sons' Judicial Factor v Armstrong* 1995 SLT 645, at 648 H–J.
3   T Guthrie, 'Controlling Creditors' Remedies under Standard Securities', 1994 SLT (News) 93; M Higgins, *Scottish Repossessions*, 7.6.1; though see *Halifax Building Society v Gupta* 1994 SLT 339.

15.38   A final possible response to the creditor seeking to enforce a standard security is a claim that they have acted in bad faith. This type of case usually concerns a standard security granted by a wife in respect of her share of the family home which secures debts incurred by a business run by the husband[1]. The argument is that the wife in such a case is a gratuitous cautioner[2], though this may be difficult to establish in two types of cases. First, where the security is an all sums security (ie a security securing any and all sums due to the creditor) the view has been taken that the wife does obtain a potential benefit in that the husband incurs a potential liability for his wife's debts[3]. In the second place the security may be signed by the wife for the purchase of the family home and only subsequently come to support an agreement between the creditor and the husband's business; in this case doubt has been cast on whether, when the security is signed, the wife is acting as a cautioner[4]. If it can be established that the wife is a gratuitous cautioner then two requirements have to be present to justify a claim for bad faith which would lead to the security being set aside:

1   The signature of the cautioner must have been obtained by misrepresentation[5], undue influence or other wrongful act. The mere existence of a relationship between the cautioner and the beneficiary does not mean that there is undue influence[6].

2   The creditor has not acted in good faith. The specific requirement here arises where the circumstances are such as to lead a reasonable person to believe that because of the personal relationship between the principal debtor and the cautioner the consent of the latter may not be fully informed or freely given. In these circumstances the creditor has to take steps to warn the potential cautioner of the possible consequences of granting the security and to advise them to take independent advice[7]. There will be no need to give this advice where

the creditor is aware that the wife has a solicitor, even though this solicitor is shared with the husband, as, in the absence of knowledge to the contrary, they are entitled to assume that proper advice is being given by the solicitor[8].

[1] Though it can potentially cover other family relationships: *Wright v Cotias Investments Inc* 2001 SLT 353.
[2] In other words she is guaranteeing the husband's debts without getting any benefit in return.
[3] *Royal Bank of Scotland plc v Wilson* 2003 SLT 910 at 914, per Lord Justice Clerk Gill.
[4] Royal Bank of Scotland plc v Wilson 2003 SLT 910 at 922, per Lord Osborne; though it does seem unfortunate that security ends up being used for a purpose not contemplated by the granter at the time of signature.
[5] A positive misrepresentation rather than mere silence is required.
[6] See the discussion in *Thomson v Royal Bank of Scotland plc* (28 October 2003, unreported), OH at [51].
[7] *Smith v Bank of Scotland* 1997 SLT 1061.
[8] *Forsyth v Royal Bank of Scotland plc* 2000 SLT 1295; *Royal Bank of Scotland plc v Wilson* 2003 SLT 910.

Calling-up notice

15.39 In terms of standard condition 8 the creditor has the right to serve a calling-up notice, subject to the terms of the security and any rule of law. Thus, for example, the security may provide for payment by instalments and preclude the creditor from requiring full repayment so long as these are being paid. The calling-up notice requires repayment of the loan in full within two months of the date of service of the notice[1]. The sum stated in the notice should be correct at the date of service. If the sum is stated in the notice as being subject to adjustment the person on whom the notice is served may require the creditor to supply the debtor with a statement of the final amount within one month of the date of service of the notice. If this is not done the notice is deemed to be of no effect[2].

[1] Conveyancing and Feudal Reform (Scotland) Act 1970, Sch 6, Form A.
[2] Conveyancing and Feudal Reform (Scotland) Act 1970, s 19(9).

15.40 The notice is served on the proprietor of the security subjects rather than on the debtor; these, as we have noted, may not be the same[1]. However, if the creditor wishes to preserve a right of action against the debtor under the latter's personal obligation a copy of the calling-up notice must be served on him[2]. The statutory requirements as to service must be

238 *Heritable securities*

strictly adhered to. In *Hill Samuel & Co v Haas*[3] a notice addressed to Mr and Mrs Haas was held to be invalid when Mrs Haas alone was the proprietor[4]. Although there is no statutory right of objection to a calling-up notice as there is to a notice of default it is possible to apply to court for a calling-up notice to be reduced or for an order suspending the operation of the notice[5].

1   Conveyancing and Feudal Reform (Scotland) Act 1970, s 19(2).
2   Conveyancing and Feudal Reform (Scotland) Act 1970, s 19(5).
3   1989 SLT (Sh Ct) 69.
4   1989 SLT (Sh Ct) 69 at 70G–I.
5   *Gardiner v Jacques Vert plc* 2002 SLT 928.

15.41   The period of notice may be shortened or dispensed with by the person(s) on whom the notice is served, though the agreement of any creditors holding securities postponed to or *pari passu* with that of the serving creditor and of any non-entitled spouse must be obtained to this[1]. Failure to comply with a calling-up notice entitles the creditor to exercise any of the rights in standard condition 10, though further court action may be required before some remedies can be exercised, for example, an action to recover possession of the property to allow sale. In response to this further court action the debtor may state a defence, eg that no debt is due[2]. After service of a calling-up notice the debtor may still redeem the loan and this right lasts up until a binding contract for the sale of the property has been concluded by the creditor[3].

1   Conveyancing and Feudal Reform (Scotland) Act 1970, s 19(10).
2   *J Sykes & Sons (Fish Merchants) Ltd v Grieve* 2002 SLT (Sh Ct) 15.
3   *Forbes v Armstrong* 1993 SCLR 204.

Notice of default

15.42   A notice of default can be served where there has been a failure to comply with any requirement arising out of the security (other than failure to comply with a calling-up notice) and the failure is remediable[1]. Halliday suggests that

'[d]efault in payment of interest or of a periodic instalment of capital and interest, or breach of an obligation under standard condition 1, 2, 3 or 5, or failure to implement an obligation undertaken in the personal obligation or in a variation of the standard conditions, are obvious examples'[2].

It is clear that a notice of default can also be served where the creditor intends to require repayment of the whole loan[3], and there is no reason why a notice of default and a calling-up notice cannot both be served at the same time.

1   Conveyancing and Feudal Reform (Scotland) Act 1970, s 21(1), standard condition 9(1)(b); see also *United Dominions Trust Ltd v Site Preparations Ltd (No 2)* 1978 SLT (Sh Ct) 21 at 23.
2   Halliday 54-21; see also Cusine & Rennie, *Standard Securities* (2nd edn), 8.14.
3   *Bank of Scotland v Millward* 1999 SLT 901.

15.43   The other requirement, apart from default, is that it should be remediable. Thus a failure to comply with standard condition 4 which meant that, for example, the time for appealing against a closing order had passed, might not be remediable, and therefore a notice of default would not be appropriate.

15.44   The notice of default is served on the debtor 'and, as the case may be, on the proprietor' and must be in conformity with the statutory form[1]. It gives one month's notice to remedy the default, subject to the same provisions as to shortening of notice as apply to calling-up notices[2]. Anyone served with a notice of default can object to it by application to the sheriff court within 14 days[3], but if this is done the creditor may make a counter-application seeking leave to exercise any of the remedies available to them[4].

1   Conveyancing and Feudal Reform (Scotland) Act 1970, s 21(2), Sch 6, Form B.
2   Conveyancing and Feudal Reform (Scotland) Act 1970, s 21(3).
3   Conveyancing and Feudal Reform (Scotland) Act 1970, s 22(1).
4   Conveyancing and Feudal Reform (Scotland) Act 1970, s 22(3).

15.45   If the notice of default is not complied with the creditor can immediately exercise the powers of sale, repair, reconstruction and improvement, and foreclosure[1]. Should the creditor wish to make use of any of the other remedies provided for in standard condition 10 (ie those involving entering into possession of the security subjects) application must be made to the sheriff court for the appropriate warrant[2] at which time the debtors, even if they have made no previous objection, can state a defence, eg that there is in fact no default[3]. The exercise of these remedies is subject to the proviso that, after the expiry of the period of notice in the notice of default, the debtor or proprietor may redeem the security without notice, provided that this is done before conclusion of an enforceable contract to sell the security subjects[4].

240   *Heritable securities*

1   Conveyancing and Feudal Reform (Scotland) Act 1970, s 23(2).
2   Conveyancing and Feudal Reform (Scotland) Act 1970, s 24; *Bank of Scotland v Fernand* 1997 SLT (Sh Ct) 78.
3   *J Sykes & Sons (Fish Merchants) Ltd v Grieve* 2002 SLT (Sh Ct) 15.
4   Conveyancing and Feudal Reform (Scotland) Act 1970, s 23(3).

Application under section 24

15.46   An application under the Conveyancing and Feudal Reform (Scotland) Act 1970, s 24 may be made where the debtor is in default in the sense explained above in relation to the notice of default, and is also the appropriate means of proceeding where the proprietor is insolvent. Where the debtor is in default there is no need to precede the application by service of a notice of default[1]. The application is for warrant to exercise any of the standard condition 10 remedies and any other remedies which may be provided for in the security.

1   Although Halliday (54-37) suggests that this is the preferable course.

Sale

15.47   Once the creditor has obtained the right to exercise the power of sale this may be done either by public roup or by private bargain[1]. The only statutory requirements imposed on the creditor are that there must be advertisement of the property and that reasonable steps should be taken to ensure that the price is the best that can reasonably be obtained[2]. There is no further specification of the nature of advertising needed, but clearly the advertising would have to be extensive enough to ensure that this price was obtained[3]. The onus of establishing that the best price was not obtained rests on the debtor. It has been suggested that all the creditor has to do to comply with their statutory obligation is either to take and act on appropriate professional advice[4] or to employ competent agents to market the property[5]. However, it is not clear that simply appointing reputedly competent professional advisers will always be enough for creditors to meet their obligations[6]. There will also be a breach of duty where the particular choice of a mode of sale is so bizarre as to be outwith the power conferred on the creditor[7]. In addition to the statutory provision there is also a common law requirement that the seller '... must pay due regard to the interests of the debtor when he comes to sell the security subjects'[8].

1   Conveyancing and Feudal Reform (Scotland) Act 1970, s 25.
2   Conveyancing and Feudal Reform (Scotland) Act 1970, s 25.
3   *Dick v Clydesdale Bank plc* 1991 SLT 678; in *Davidson v Clydesdale Bank plc* 2002 SLT 1088 criticism was made of the advertising undertaken by the creditor's agent; see also Cusine & Rennie *Standard Securities* (2nd edn) 8.36–8.41; M Higgins *Scottish Repossessions*, 8.9.
4   *Dick v Clydesdale Bank plc* 1991 SLT 678 at 681E–F, per Lord President Hope.
5   1991 SLT 678 at 682H–I, per Lord Cowie, subject to the qualification that this will not suffice if the creditor is aware that the agents have made a serious blunder.
6   *Bisset v Standard Property Investment plc* (8 July 1999, unreported), OH.
7   *Bisset v Standard Property Investment plc* (8 July 1999, unreported), OH: an example might be a raffle sale conducted over the internet.
8   *Dick v Clydesdale Bank plc* 1991 SLT 678 at 681A, per Lord President Hope, who also approved Halliday's statement (now at 44-15) that the creditor is in a position of quasi-trustee for the debtor.

15.48   A selling creditor does not require consent from any other creditor to proceed with the sale. The timing of the sale is at the discretion of the creditor and the debtor cannot take any steps to prevent an exercise of the power of sale on the grounds that the best price will not be obtained. The remedy for the debtor is to seek damages after the sale has taken place if they can establish a breach of duty by the creditor[1]. It is not clear that an absolute refusal to control the exercise by the creditor of their right to sale is consistent with authority[2].

1   For example, *Associated Displays Ltd (in liquidation) v Turnbeam Ltd* 1988 SCLR 220; *Thomson v Yorkshire Building Society* 1994 SCLR 1014.
2   T Guthrie, 'Controlling Creditors' Remedies under Standard Securities', 1994 SLT (News) 93; though see M Higgins, *Scottish Repossessions*, 8.11.

15.49   Once the security subjects are sold the proceeds are applied firstly in payment of the selling creditor's expenses; secondly in payment of any prior security where the property is not being sold subject to it; thirdly in payment of the selling creditor's security and any others ranking *pari passu* with it; fourthly in payment of any postponed securities; and finally any surplus is payable to the debtor[1]. If the proceeds of sale are insufficient to repay all of the debtor's securities he will remain liable for the outstanding amount under the personal obligation.

1   Conveyancing and Feudal Reform (Scotland) Act 1970, s 27(1).

15.50   The disposition by the selling creditor disburdens the property of their security and any securities ranking *pari passu* with or postponed to it[1]. Separate discharges of prior securities must be obtained if the property is to be sold free of all securities. If the debt has ceased to exist prior to the sale or if there is any irregularity in the sale procedure or its preliminaries the title of a purchaser who receives a disposition bearing to be granted by a selling creditor will be protected from challenge provided that he has purchased in good faith and for value and on the face of it the seller's exercise of their power of sale was regular[2]. If, however, the right to sell has been lost before a sale is agreed, for example by a last minute redemption of the security, the purchaser's title will be open to challenge.

[1]   Including inhibitions lodged against the debtor after the date of infeftment of the creditor under the standard security: *Newcastle Building Society v White* 1987 SLT (Sh Ct) 81.

[2]   Conveyancing (Scotland) Act 1924, s 41(2); Conveyancing and Feudal Reform (Scotland) Act 1970, s 32.

Entering into possession

15.51   On entering into possession of the security subjects the creditor is entitled to receive any rents payable to the proprietor[1] and may also let the subjects for up to seven years, or longer with the consent of the sheriff court[2]. The creditor also has assigned to them all the rights and obligations of the proprietor relating to the management and maintenance of the subjects[3]. A creditor in possession is not liable for arrears of common charges arising before their entry into possession, but would be liable for those arising after this[4]. They may also, in the case of non-domestic properties, be liable to be entered on the valuation roll and so liable for rates if they are receiving the rents and profits of the security subjects[5]. Where a creditor has entered into possession of a domestic property, that property will be exempt from the council tax[6].

[1]   The entitlement is only to those rents payable after the creditor enters into possession: *UCB Bank plc v Hire Foulis Ltd (in liquidation)* 1999 SLT 950.

[2]   Conveyancing and Feudal Reform (Scotland) Act 1970, s 20(3).

[3]   Conveyancing and Feudal Reform (Scotland) Act 1970, s 20(5).

[4]   *David Watson Property Management v Woolwich Equitable Building Society* 1990 SLT 764.

[5]   *Armour on Valuation for Rating* (5th edn) 12-05.

[6]   Council Tax (Exempt Dwellings) (Scotland) Order 1997 (SI 1997/728), Sch 1.

Repair, reconstruction and improvement

15.52 Under standard condition 1 the creditor has power to require the debtor or proprietor to carry out repairs in the absence of default. The additional powers obtained on default are that the creditor may enter the property to carry out work at all reasonable times and may effect such reconstruction, alteration and improvement as would be expected of a prudent proprietor to maintain the market value of the subjects.

Foreclosure

15.53 Where the security subjects have been exposed for sale by public roup[1] at a price not exceeding the amount due under the selling creditor's security and any securities ranking prior to or *pari passu* with it, and no purchaser has been found, the creditor may, after two months, apply to the court for decree of foreclosure[2]. The court may grant the debtor or proprietor three months to pay the amount due under the security, order re-exposure or grant a decree of foreclosure. The effect of a decree of foreclosure, once an extract has been recorded or registered, is to transfer the subjects irredeemably to the creditor with effect from the date of recording or registration and to disburden the property of any securities postponed to that held by the foreclosing creditor[3]. The title obtained by the creditor is not open to challenge on the ground of any irregularity of the foreclosure proceedings or any prior notices[4].

[1]   See CHAPTER 17.
[2]   Conveyancing and Feudal Reform (Scotland) Act 1970, s 28(1).
[3]   Conveyancing and Feudal Reform (Scotland) Act 1970, s 28(6).
[4]   Conveyancing and Feudal Reform (Scotland) Act 1970, s 28(8).

15.54 The value of the property to the creditor will be the price at which it was last exposed for sale, which must not exceed the amount due under the foreclosing creditor's security and any prior or *pari passu* security. The debtor will remain personally liable for any amount by which this price is less than the sum required to repay the outstanding debt to the foreclosing creditor[1].

[1]   Conveyancing and Feudal Reform (Scotland) Act 1970, s 28(5) and (7).

Conclusion

15.55   Of these remedies sale is the one which will be used most often in practice. The advantage of this from the creditor's point of view is that, in normal market conditions, it enables them to recover the debt which they are owed. The remedies involving entry onto the property and carrying out of repairs are unlikely to be commonly used because of administrative inconvenience. Foreclosure will generally only be used where the security is worth less than the debt owed.

Creditor's remedies 2: other remedies

15.56   The remedies provided in standard condition 10 are stated to be without prejudice to any other remedy arising out of the contract to which the standard security relates. The contract, then, may provide additional remedies for the creditor. As well as these there are two other remedies generally available to the creditor. These are enforcement of the personal obligation and adjudication.

Personal obligation

15.57   The personal obligation may be enforced by court action, either an action for debt or, where the security has been granted to secure an obligation *ad factum praestandum*, an action for implement. In addition where there is a clause of consent to registration for execution (as there will be in a Form A security and will usually occur in the agreement ancillary to a Form B security) the creditor may proceed by way of summary diligence.

Adjudication

15.58   Adjudication involves a judicial transfer of the security subjects to the creditor in satisfaction of the loan. Application is made to the Court of Session for decree of adjudication. The drawback of the remedy is that the transfer does not become final until the passing of a ten-year period, known as the 'legal', after the recording or registration of the extract decree[1].

---

[1]   Adjudication will be replaced by a new diligence of land attachment if the proposals contained in the draft Diligence Reform Bill proposed by the Scottish Executive are implemented.

Conclusion

15.59   These remedies are rarely used. In the case of the first the reason is that any amount raised would probably be quite inadequate to repay the debt outstanding.

Mortgage Rights (Scotland) Act 2001 [1]

15.60   This allows an application to be made either to suspend the creditor's exercise of their rights under a notice of default or calling-up notice or to have an application under the Conveyancing and Feudal Reform (Scotland) Act 1970, s 24 continued. The court can grant such an application if it considers that it is reasonable in all the circumstances to do so and in taking this decision and in deciding on the terms of any order it is directed to have regard to:

1   The nature of and reasons for the default.
2   The applicant's ability to fulfil their obligations under the security in respect of which the debtor is in default within a reasonable time.
3   Any action taking by the creditor to assist the debtor to comply with their obligations.
4   The ability of the applicant to secure reasonable alternative accommodation.

[1]   M Higgins, *Scottish Repossessions*, ch 4; M Dailly, 'The Mortgage Rights Act in practice', SCOLAG, January 2004, 6.

15.61   It will be seen that these factors refer to the applicant rather than simply to the debtor. This is because an application can not only be made by the debtor, but also by others related to the debtor. These include a non-entitled spouse (in cases involving the matrimonial home) and anyone living as the spouse of the debtor (regardless of sex). The Act indicates that there are time limits within which an application must be made. These are stated to be either:

(a)   before the expiry of the period of notice under a calling-up notice;
(b)   not later than one month after the date stated in the notice by which the default is to be remedied; and
(c)   before the conclusion of s 24 proceedings.

In respect of the last of these it is now clear that it is possible to have a decree in absence recalled[1] or to appeal against a decree in default[2] and then proceed to lodge an application.

1   *GMAC-RFA Ltd v Murray* 2003 Hous LR 50.
2   *Bradford & Bingley plc v Bayley* 2003 Hous LR 53.

Variation, assignation and restriction[1]

15.62 It is possible to vary the provisions of a recorded or registered standard security by means of a variation endorsed on the security or by a separate deed of variation. In either case the variation must be duly recorded or registered[2]. Variation would be appropriate, for example, when the amount of the loan was being increased. The only restriction on variation is that it cannot be used when the same end could be achieved by an assignation, discharge or variation of the security.

1   Halliday 55-01 to 55-37, 55-47 to 55-53; Cusine & Rennie *Standard Securities* (2nd edn) 5.09–5.13 and 6.01–6.07.
2   Conveyancing and Feudal Reform (Scotland) Act 1970, s 16 and Sch 4, Form E.

15.63 Standard securities can be assigned by the creditor, and a statutory form is provided[1]. Where the standard security is in Form B an assignation of the security will not, unless it is specifically mentioned in the assignation, operate to transfer the personal obligation[2].

1   Conveyancing and Feudal Reform (Scotland) Act 1970, s 14 and Sch 4, Forms A and B.
2   *Watson v Bogue (No 1)* 2000 SLT (Sh Ct) 125.

15.64 It is also possible to restrict the scope of a standard security, in other words to disburden part of the security subjects. This can be done either in the form of a deed of restriction[1] or by a partial discharge and deed of restriction when some of the outstanding loan is also repaid[2].

1   Conveyancing and Feudal Reform (Scotland) Act 1970, s 15(1) & Sch 4, Form C.
2   Conveyancing and Feudal Reform (Scotland) Act 1970, s 15(2) & Sch 4, Form D.

Discharge[1]

15.65 In most cases the standard security will be discharged by the execution of a discharge in the statutory form[2], followed by recording in the Register of Sasines or forwarding to the Land Register to be given effect to[3]. The standard security will also be extinguished by payment of the debt in full or performance of the other obligation secured; it is, however, desirable to get a formal discharge as evidence of payment or performance. Finally, the security may be discharged by confusion, where the same person acting in the same capacity becomes both debtor and creditor in the security.

1   Halliday 55-66 to 55-77; Cusine & Rennie, *Standard Securities* (2nd edn) 10.02–10.11.
2   Conveyancing and Feudal Reform (Scotland) Act 1970, s 17, Sch 4, Form F.
3   *Registration of Title Practice Book* 8.55.

Redemption[1]

15.66   The debtor's right of redemption can, as we noticed earlier, be dispensed with by variation of the standard conditions. However, even when that has happened a security over a private dwelling house can still be redeemed after 20 years[2]. The procedure for redemption is set out in standard condition 11. Where, despite repayment of the debt in full or performance of the other obligation, the debtor is unable to obtain a discharge there is provision for them to be released from the security[3].

1   Halliday 55-53 to 55-65; Cusine & Rennie, *Standard Securities* (2nd edn), 10.12–10.16.
2   Land Tenure Reform (Scotland) Act 1974, s 11.
3   Conveyancing and Feudal Reform (Scotland) Act 1970, s 18(2).

Matrimonial Homes (Family Protection) (Scotland) Act 1981

15.67   The full provisions of this Act are considered in CHAPTER 17. It should be noted here, however, that in order to protect the creditor in a standard security from the occupancy rights of any non-entitled spouse an affidavit to the effect that the security subjects are not a matrimonial home, a renunciation of occupancy rights by the non-entitled spouse or a consent to the dealing by the non-entitled spouse will have to be produced by the debtor. Previously the requirement was for this evidence to be produced prior to the granting of the security, but this is no longer the case[1].

Standard securities granted by companies

15.68   As noted in the introduction, the creditor's right in a standard security only becomes real on recording of the security in the Register of Sasines or registration in the Land Register. In addition to this securities granted by companies must also be registered in the Companies Register of Charges within 21 days of being granted[1]. Failure to register means that although the charge is valid against the company it is void against any liquidator or administrator in insolvency proceedings and against any other creditor having a security interest in the subject matter of the unregistered security[2]. Late registration may be allowed following application to court[3].

1   Though see the proposal in Scottish Law Commission Discussion Paper 121, *Registration of Rights in Security by Companies* (2002), 3.5–3.12.
2   Companies Act 1985, ss 410 & 415.
3   Companies Act 1985, s 420,

FLOATING CHARGES[1]

Introduction

15.69   Fixed charges, such as the standard security, attach to a specific piece of property which cannot be disposed of without either the charge continuing to affect it or, alternatively, being discharged on repayment of the loan or debt. A floating charge in contrast is a charge over part or all of a company's assets which allows the company to continue to deal with these assets and does not attach specifically to them until the charge crystallises. On crystallisation the charge fixes on the assets and becomes a fixed charge over them.

1   Halliday ch 56, McDonald ch 23.

15.70   The distinction has also been expressed as follows[1]:

'A specific [fixed] charge ... is one that without more fastens on ascertained and definite property or property capable of being ascertained or defined; a floating charge, on the other hand, is ambulatory and shifting in its nature, hovering over and so to speak floating with the property which it is intended to affect, until some event occurs or some act is done which causes it to settle and fasten on the subject of the charge within its reach and grasp.'

¹   *Illingworth v Houldsworth* [1904] AC 355 at 358, per Lord Macnaghten.

15.71   The significance of the floating charge is that it allows the company to grant a security over its assets and at the same time deal with them without the consent of the creditor being necessary for each transaction as it would be with a strict security. It would clearly be impracticable to grant a fixed security over the stock in trade of a company; however, a floating charge would not affect the company's ability to deal.

Constitution and registration

15.72   Floating charges can be created over any assets of a company including heritable property. Although this is the case they need not be recorded in the Register of Sasines or registered in the Land Register. The same requirements as to registration in the Register of Charges applies to them as applies to standard securities. There is no specific form of floating charge. A style is given in Halliday¹.

¹   Halliday 56-05.

Crystallisation

15.73   Crystallisation occurs on the happening of one of three events: if an event specified in the instrument of charge occurs (eg if the assets of the company fall below a certain level); on the appointment of a receiver; or on the commencement of winding up.

Ranking¹

15.74   Floating charges commonly contain ranking clauses which specifically prohibit the subsequent creation of fixed or floating charges ranking prior to or *pari passu* with them. Where such a clause exists any subsequent charge, fixed or floating, will be postponed to the earlier floating charge. In the absence of express provision, fixed charges granted before the crystallisation of a floating charge will rank before that charge, even if granted subsequently. As between floating charges the order of ranking is determined by the order of registration.

1   See also G Gretton, 'Searches', (1989) 34 JLSS 50 at 51.

CHAPTER 16

Public law restrictions on land use

16.1 In modern times the most comprehensive restrictions on an owner's rights are imposed by the state (by means of legislation) and implemented (usually) by local authorities. There are good reasons, of course, for this official intervention. While the law is prepared to allow a property owner the maximum freedom to use his/her property as he/she wants, it is desirable in the public interest that he/she should conform to some systematic policy for land use so that (say) a factory emitting noxious fumes is not placed in the middle of a residential area. It is also desirable that any new buildings conform to acceptable standards of construction, and that its inhabitants are not endangered by inadequate fire precautions. The main concerns in this chapter will be the legislation on town and country planning, the regulations regarding building control and local authority housing controls. However, we will finish with a brief indication of various other statutory provisions of which property owners and would-be developers should be aware and, if necessary, investigate further.

PLANNING CONTROL

Administrative structure

16.2 Following the passing of the Local Government (Scotland) Act 1994, Scotland was divided into 32 unitary authorities. These unitary authorities have responsibility for development control, that is, the granting of planning permission, enforcement in cases where the planning rules are contravened, and the formulation of local plans. Some also have the responsibility for producing structure plans, though in many cases there are special arrangements combining a number of authorities for the preparation of such plans, for example the eight local authorities involved in preparation of the Glasgow and Clyde Valley structure plan. A structure plan is an overall strategic plan for the area and sets the context for the local plans prepared by local authorities. In the process of preparation of the structure plan there will be consultation in the area concerned and the final structure plan has to be approved by the Scottish Ministers. A local plan sets out detailed policies for development and land use within the local authority. The significance of these plans is that when a local authority takes decisions on planning applications it has to take these in accordance with the development plan unless material considerations indicate otherwise[1]. The development plan is the local and structure plans taken together.

[1]   Town and Country Planning (Scotland) Act 1997, s 25.

Development control

16.3   Subject to a number of exceptions, some of which are considered below, any development requires the consent of the relevant local authority in the form of planning permission. For these purposes, 'development' is defined as either:

(a)   the carrying out of any building, engineering, mining or other operations in, over, or under land; or

(b)   the making of any material change in the use of any building or other land[1]. (The key word here is 'use'; a development for these purposes need not involve any physical change to the property.)

Some further guidance on what is included in the term development is provided in the Town and Country Planning (Scotland) Act 1997. Excluded from the term are any works affecting only the interior of a building or which do not materially affect the external appearance of a building[2], certain work undertaken by local authorities or statutory undertakers or use of land for agricultural (excluding irrigation or drainage works) or forestry purposes. On the other hand, subdividing a house to produce more than one dwelling is specifically included within the term development[3].

[1]   Town and Country Planning (Scotland) Act 1997, s 26.

²   Though these may require a building warrant: see PARA **16.21**.
³   Town and Country Planning (Scotland) Act 1997, s 26.

16.4   As well as the statutory provisions there are two pieces of delegated legislation that are important in determining whether planning permission is required. The first of these is the Town and Country Planning (Use Classes) (Scotland) Order 1997[1]. This sets out 11 use classes, though it does not cover all of the possible uses of premises. Examples are class 1 (shops)[2]; class 3 (food and drink)[3]; class 9 (houses)[4]; and class 11 (leisure)[5]. The significance of these is that there will be no development where a building which was used for one purpose in a particular class is used for another purpose within the same class. If, for example, as happened in the 1970s, there was a change in use from a cinema to a bingo hall this would not be a development and would therefore not require planning permission.

¹   SI 1997/3061.
²   Which includes use for retail sale of goods, as a post office, as a travel agency, and for the sale of cold food for consumption off the premises.
³   Use for the sale of food or drink for consumption on the premises.
⁴   Use as a house, other than a flat, or as a bed and breakfast establishment or guesthouse with a maximum of two bedrooms.
⁵   Use as a cinema, concert hall, bingo hall or casino, dance hall or discotheque, or swimming bath, skating rink, gymnasium or area for other indoor or outdoor sports or recreation, not involving motorised vehicles or firearms.

16.5   The second piece of delegated legislation sets out a number of cases where a development is deemed to have planning permission[1]. Examples of development falling within the realm of permitted development are:

1   Enlargement, improvement or other alteration of a dwelling house, though there are restrictions on how much floor area can be added both in absolute terms and in relation to the existing floor area and further restrictions if the development is near a property boundary. It is important to note that the definition of dwelling house excludes flats so that any work of this type to be carried out on a flat would require planning permission.

2   Provision of new buildings, including swimming pools, for purposes incidental to the enjoyment of a dwelling house. Again this is subject to size and location constraints. This would permit, for example, the erection of a garden shed without planning permission.

3   Installation of a satellite dish, subject to some constraints, eg if the
     house is in a conservation area or the dish will be above the highest
     point of the house.
4   Certain changes to one use class from another, eg to class 1 from
     either class 2, class 3, from use as a hot food takeaway or from use as
     a car showroom.

The Scottish Ministers have the power to issue directions which effectively
remove the permitted development status of some or all of the activities
covered by the order in a particular area[2].

1   Town and Country Planning (General Permitted Development) (Scotland) Order
     1992 (SI 1992/223).
2   SI 1992/223, art 4.

Applying for planning permission

16.6   Where planning permission is required an application is made to
the appropriate local authority. The application can be either for outline
planning permission or for full permission. In applying for outline planning
permission it is not necessary to include with the application detailed
plans of the proposed development, but it is enough to describe it in
general terms and identify the location where it will take place. If full
permission is being applied for then detailed plans will be required. If
outline planning permission is granted the details of the development,
known in the legislation as reserved matters, will be the subject of later
application for approval. An example of this process would be an application
for outline permission for a housing development; the detailed plans for
the development could then be dealt with as a reserved matter. The benefit
of outline permission is that it allows a developer to get an indication of
the views of the local authority on the proposed development without
incurring the expense of preparing and lodging detailed plans.

16.7   Regardless of the type of permission or approval sought, the
applicant must, when lodging the application, certify that certain
notification requirements have been complied with. The first of these
requires that if the applicant is not the owner of the land the owner is
notified. This reflects the fact that it is not necessary to own land to make
a planning application in respect of it[1]. In addition any agricultural tenant
of the land must be notified as well as the owners, lessees or occupiers of
neighbouring land.

1   As we will see in CHAPTER 17 it is common for a purchaser to undertake in missives
    to apply for permission and for the grant of permission to be a suspensive
    condition.

16.8   Once the application is lodged with the local authority it is entered
in a register of planning applications. In some cases the local authority will
have to include details of the application in a notice published in a local
newspaper[1]. This must be done where the proposed development qualifies
as a bad neighbour development, essentially a development which may
have an adverse effect beyond neighbouring land (including bingo halls,
hot food shops, public conveniences, sewage works, licensed premises
and developments involving the use of land for plucking poultry[2]), or
where the proposed development is contrary to the development plan.
Other cases in which publication of a notice in this way is required include
cases where there are problems notifying those with an interest in
neighbouring land. Community councils will be notified of any planning
applications in their area and there is an extensive list of bodies which
have to be consulted in relation to particular types of proposed
development; for example where a proposed development is likely to result
in loss of a playing field the Scottish Sports Council must be consulted[3].

1   Though generally the applicant will have to cover the cost of this.
2   Town and Country Planning (General Development Procedure) (Scotland) Order
    1992 (SI 1992/224), Sch 7.
3   SI 1992/224, art 15.

16.9   Decisions on applications must, in general, be notified to the
applicant within two months. In taking the decision the authority must, as
noted above, generally decide in accordance with the development plan,
though they can diverge from it if this is supported by material
considerations[1]. They must also take account of any representations
received as a result of notification procedures[2]. In some cases the Scottish
Ministers will call in the application and where this happens the decision
on planning permission will be made by them and not by the local authority[3].

1   See A McAllister and R McMaster, *Scottish Planning Law* (2nd edn), 6.51–6.76
    for a discussion of this term.
2   Town and Country Planning (Scotland) Act 1997, s 36(1).
3   Town and Country Planning (Scotland) Act 1997, s 46.

16.10   A grant of planning permission can be made subject to conditions.
National guidance indicates that planning conditions should only be

imposed where they are necessary, relevant to planning, relevant to the development to be permitted, enforceable, precise, and reasonable[1].

1   SEDD Circular 4/1998, 'The Use of Conditions in Planning Permissions'.

16.11   Once full planning permission is granted the development involved must begin within five years. Where outline permission has been granted application for approval of reserved matters must be made within three years and the development must begin within five years of the original grant or two years of approval of the reserved matters, whichever is later. Planning permission can be revoked if the local authority changes its views on the development. This can only be done before any building or other operations are completed or before a change of use has started. Compensation may be payable if permission is revoked.

16.12   If planning permission or an application for approval of reserved matters is refused the local authority must give reasons for its decision and the applicant has a right of appeal to the Scottish Ministers against the decision. There is also a right of appeal if the authority does not notify the applicant of its decision within the statutory time limit and against conditions attached to a grant of planning permission. The appeal will normally be considered and decided on a by a reporter from the Scottish Executive Inquiry Reporters Unit on behalf of the Scottish Ministers. An appeal can be dealt with either by written submissions or a public hearing; the decision as to which procedure is used is for the applicant. There is the possibility of further appeal to the Court of Session against the resulting decision either by way of the statutory appeals process or by way of judicial review.

16.13   The fact that UK Ministers and their Scottish counterparts are involved in both formulating planning policy and in deciding on appeals[1] involving the application of that policy gave rise to challenges to the system under Article 6 of the European Convention on Human Rights. Essentially this article gives the right to a fair trial, including the essential element of an independent decision maker. It has been decided, however, that the system as a whole does comply with the requirements of Article 6 because of the procedures to be followed, the requirement to give reasons for decisions and the extensive powers of the courts to review decisions made by or on behalf of the Scottish Ministers[2].

1   And on called in planning applications.

2   *R (on the application of Alconbury Developments Ltd) v Secretary of State for the Environment, Transport and the Regions* [2001] 2 All ER 929; *County Properties Ltd v The Scottish Ministers* 2001 SLT 1125.

Planning agreements

16.14   Before submitting a planning application a developer may seek to reach an agreement with the local authority as to the terms on which a proposed development would be acceptable to them. This can then be recorded in the form of a planning agreement which, as well as binding the authority and developer as a contract, can be registered in the Land Register and will then bind successive owners of the land. The advantage for the developer is that an agreement will normally ease the granting of planning permission for the development. From the point of view of the authority an agreement allows them to impose conditions on the development which could not be justified as planning conditions. In some cases the authority will seek to gain some community benefit or facilities from the developer in exchange for allowing the development and this would be unlikely to be acceptable if imposed as a condition of planning permission.

Enforcement of planning control

16.15   Where the local authority suspects that there has been a breach of planning control it can serve a planning contravention notice This is designed to obtain information about the use and planning status of the land and to encourage an offer from the person on whom the notice is served to remedy any breach[1]. The local authority may also serve a planning enforcement notice where it appears to them that there has been a breach of planning control and that it is expedient to issue the notice[2]. This notice will identify the breach of planning control, the steps needed to remedy this, a date (the effective date) when the notice will take effect and the time period within which the remedial work is to be carried out. In the case of failure to comply with the notice the local authority has the power to undertake the remedial work itself and recover their expenses. The person on whom the notice is served can appeal against it before the effective date. If this happens the operation of the notice is suspended. In order to prevent any activities in breach of planning control in the meantime, however, the authority can serve a stop notice[3]. There is no right of appeal against a stop notice. Where there has been breach of a condition attached to planning permission a breach of condition notice can be served[4]. Finally a local authority may seek to restrain or prevent any actual or apprehended breach of planning controls by way of interdict[5]. Failure to comply with a planning enforcement notice, a stop notice or a breach of condition notice is a criminal offence.

1   Town and Country Planning (Scotland) Act 1997, s 126.
2   Town and Country Planning (Scotland) Act 1997, s 127.
3   Town and Country Planning (Scotland) Act 1997, s 140.
4   Town and Country Planning (Scotland) Act 1997, s 145.
5   Town and Country Planning (Scotland) Act 1997, s 146.

16.16   The passing of time affords some immunity to enforcement. In the case of development involving the carrying out of any building, engineering, mining or other operations in, over, or under land and in the case of a change of use to a single dwelling house the immunity arises after four years; in other cases the period before immunity is ten years[1].

1   Town and Country Planning (Scotland) Act 1997, s 124.

Certificate of lawful use or development[1]

16.17   If someone wants confirmation that an existing or proposed use or development is lawful (eg if it was originally unauthorised, but may now be immune, or if there is some doubt as to whether permission is or was legally required) they can apply to the local authority for a certificate of lawful use or development. The issue of such a certificate in respect of a current use gives rise to a conclusive presumption that the use, operations or other matter covered by the certificate are lawful. Where the certificate covers a proposed use it gives rise to an irrefutable presumption as to the lawfulness of anything covered by the certificate, unless there is a material change in circumstances before the proposed use or operations are started.

1   Town and Country Planning (Scotland) Act 1997, ss 151 and 152.

Special controls

16.18   There are certain special matters with regard to which it is felt that restrictions beyond the normal development control system should be imposed. These include controls relating to listed buildings, conservation areas, tree preservation and reclamation of waste land among others[1]. Here we will give a brief account of the first three of these:

1   *Listed buildings*. The Scottish Ministers maintain a list of buildings which are considered to be of special architectural or historical interest. In such cases a special consent (known as listed building consent) is required; the application is made to the planning authority, but the Scottish Ministers must be notified and may call in the application. Listed building consent is required for changes which in relation to other buildings would be permitted development (eg small extensions or dormer windows) or not even development at all (eg internal alterations). An owner has no right to contest the fact that his building has been listed in the first place; however if he is refused listed building consent, or granted a conditional consent, he is entitled to appeal to the Scottish Ministers in the normal way, and one of his possible grounds of appeal is to challenge the merits of the listing. Planning authorities have the discretion to award grants to owners of listed buildings in order to help with their maintenance. An owner who allows a listed building to fall into disrepair may be served by the planning authority with a repairs notice, and this may be followed up by a compulsory acquisition if necessary.

2   *Conservation areas*. A local planning authority can declare a whole area to be of special architectural or historical interest. All buildings in the area are given special protection, and trees are also protected. The Scottish Ministers may declare certain conservation areas to be of outstanding merit, which makes them eligible for grants towards their enhancement.

3   *Tree protection*[2]. Planning consent is not normally required to fell or otherwise damage trees. However, there are three exceptions to this general rule:

   (a)   The planning authority may impose a *tree preservation order* upon any tree or group of trees, which makes it an offence to fell or otherwise harm them without the planning authority's consent.

   (b)   A local authority has to ensure, whenever it is appropriate, that in granting planning permission for any development adequate provision is made, by the imposition of conditions, for the preservation or planting of trees[3].

   (c)   If trees are located within a conservation area, they may not be felled or otherwise harmed unless the planning authority have first been given notice. If the authority do not impose a tree preservation order within six weeks of such notice, the applicant may proceed.

1   For a full treatment of all of these see McAllister & McMaster, *Scottish Planning Law* (2nd edn), chs 12–14.
2   Town and Country Planning (Scotland) Act 1997, Pt VII, Ch I.
3   Town and Country Planning (Scotland) Act 1997, s 159.

BUILDING CONTROL

16.19   There are two aspects to building control. The first of these is a set of regulations governing buildings. These regulations, known as the building standards regulations, are designed to ensure the health, safety, welfare and convenience of people making use of buildings. The second aspect is the control of new building works by local authorities. The system is currently in the process of change with new legislation due to come into effect on 1 May 2005. We will first of all consider the current system and then the new system.

Building standards regulations

16.20   The current building standards regulations are the Building Standards (Scotland) Regulations 1990[1]. These take the form of a series of very general statements of requirements to be met by new buildings and are supplemented by more detailed technical standards which are published as a separate volume. Certain classes of buildings are exempted from the building regulations. The principal exceptions include: agricultural buildings, caravans, most garages and garden huts, greenhouses and nuclear shelters[2]. The exceptions for garages, huts and greenhouses do not apply if they are very large (exceeding 30 m²), or, in the case of garages or huts, if they are close to a dwelling house or a property boundary. It is also possible to apply to the Scottish Ministers, and in some cases the local authority, for relaxation of or dispensation with the building regulations. This may be done in respect of a particular building, or, more unusually, in respect of a class of buildings. The effect of a relaxation is that the application of particular building standards requirements is relaxed for the building or buildings, but there are still some requirements to be met. A dispensation simply dispenses with particular requirements for the building or buildings[3].

¹   SI 1990/2179.
²   SI 1990/2179, Sch 1.
³   Building (Scotland) Act 1959, ss 4 and 4A.

Building control

16.21   Subject to the exceptions below, application must be made to the local authority for a building warrant before the commencement of any building operations. The term 'building operations' includes works of construction, demolition or change of use. In this context change of use means either a change in use of a building bringing it within the scope of the building regulations for the first time, or a change which will result in more onerous requirements of the regulations applying to the building. Certain types of work do not need a building warrant, these include: replacement of a fixture by another of the same general type (fixtures include windows, roof coverings and sanitary appliances); replacement of a window by another not of the same general type (eg replacement of single by double glazing); installation of gas or solid fuel central heating; and insulation, including cavity wall insulation¹. It should be noted that although these works do not require a building warrant they must, when completed, meet any relevant requirements of the building regulations. These exceptions do not cover one common type of situation, namely the conversion of attic space from storage space to accommodation, such work requires a building warrant. If the authority is satisfied that the proposed works will comply with the building standards regulations they must grant the warrant. The works must then be completed in accordance with that warrant².

¹   Building Standards (Scotland) Regulations 1990 (SI 1990/2179), Sch. 2.
²   Building (Scotland) Act 1959, s 6.

16.22   Once the works are complete it is an offence to occupy the property unless a completion certificate or certificate of temporary occupation has been granted. A completion certificate will be granted if the works have been carried out in accordance with the building warrant¹.

¹   Building (Scotland) Act 1959, s 9.

16.23   The local authority has enforcement powers in respect of buildings constructed without a building warrant or in breach of the terms of a warrant. Ultimately they can require the owner to undertake works to remedy the situation and if he does not do so they are empowered to do the work themselves and charge him[1]. Authorities also have power to require works to existing buildings to make them comply with the building standards regulations[2]. In some cases where work has been undertaken in breach of the building control legislation the local authority will be prepared to issue what is sometimes described as a letter of comfort. This indicates that they will not take enforcement action in respect of the breach.

1   Building (Scotland) Act 1959, s 10.
2   Building (Scotland) Act 1959, s 11.

16.24   Local authorities also have powers to secure the evacuation and demolition of dangerous buildings[1].

1   From 1 May 2005 these will be in the Building (Scotland) Act 2003, ss 29 and 42.

Building (Scotland) Act 2003

16.25   This will make a number of changes to the current system, some more substantial than others. There will continue to be building standards regulations[1] in a similar form to those which currently exist and these will be supplemented by technical handbooks which will give guidance on ways of meeting these standards. As at present, there are certain buildings which are exempted from the regulations. Some of these exemptions are slightly different, for example, there is no mention of nuclear shelters and the floor area qualification for greenhouses, carports and single storey buildings ancillary to houses is reduced from 30m^2 to 8m^2. Most agricultural buildings are still exempted, as are caravans. It will still be possible to apply for relaxation of or dispensation with building regulations and relaxations and dispensations will have the same effect as at present.

1   Building (Scotland) Regulations 2004 (SSI 2004/406).

16.26   It is in the context of applications for building warrants that the biggest changes take place. The Building (Scotland) Act 2003 introduces verifiers and certifiers. Verifiers will be responsible for issuing building warrants and accepting completion certificates. At present the only verifiers are local authorities, but the legislation envisages that this role could be fulfilled by others. Certifiers will be approved either as certifiers of design or certifiers of construction and entered in a register kept by the Scottish Building Standards Agency. The different roles played by each of these will be seen below. A building warrant will be required for any work for the construction or demolition of, or the provision of services, fittings or equipment in or in connection with, a building to which building regulations apply, or any conversion of a building[1]. Certain types of work will not require a building warrant; these are divided into two categories. The first category includes certain types of building work to a house, single storey buildings with a floor area between 8m² and 30m² ancillary to a flat or house, installation of decking, and window replacement. Work in this category, although it does not need a warrant, must comply with the building regulations on completion and if it does not enforcement action can be taken. The second category of work mainly involves replacement and repair of existing equipment and fixtures, such as sanitary appliances, guttering and broken glass. The exemption here is subject to the qualification that the standard of the replacement or repaired article is no worse than it was before the replacement or repair.

[1]   Building (Scotland) Act 2003, s 8.

16.27   Where a building warrant is required the application is made to a verifier. Certain aspects of the design of the proposed works (or all of it) may be certified by a registered certifier of design as compliant with the regulations and the verifier cannot question this.

16.28   On completion of the work a completion certificate must be submitted to the verifier who then has to decide whether to accept or refuse the certificate. This will certify that the work has been carried out in accordance with the warrant and that it complies with the building regulations. The completion certificate may be supported by a certificate from a certifier of construction and the verifier has to accept that certificate at face value. The verifier then has to accept or reject the certificate and their decision is then recorded in the building standards register maintained by the local authority. The certificate will be accepted where the verifier is satisfied, after reasonable inquiry, as to the matters certified in the certificate. If the completion certificate is rejected further work will be required followed by resubmission.

16.29   The enforcement powers under the Building (Scotland) Act 2003 are similar to those already in existence. In the course of time letters of comfort will be replaced by building standards assessments under s 6 of the Building (Scotland) Act 2003.

LOCAL AUTHORITY HOUSING CONTROLS[1]

16.30 The Housing (Scotland) Act 1987 brought together most of the powers that local authorities have to take action against houses in the private sector. The nature of the action that can be taken depends on whether or not the house falls below the tolerable standard. A house will be below the tolerable standard if it fails to meet one or more of a series of criteria. These include the house being substantially free from damp, having a water closet for the exclusive use of the occupants of the house and having an adequate supply of hot and cold water[2]. If a house is below the tolerable standard the authority has a number of options. If the house is part of a larger building (eg in a tenement) they can serve a closing order. The effect of this is that the property can no longer be used for human habitation[3]. Alternatively they can serve a demolition order where the whole building is below the standard. This requires demolition of the property[4]. In both cases the owners have a right of appeal and may also seek suspension orders, suspending the operation of the closing or demolition order for a period. The normal reason for granting a suspension order is to allow the owner to bring the property up to a tolerable standard[5]. More positively an improvement order can be served on a sub-tolerable house which requires its improvement. There is a right of appeal to the sheriff against this, and if the owner does not undertake this the authority may, in order to carry out the required work themselves, acquire the house by agreement or compulsorily[6].

[1] McDonald 20.27–20.29; C Himsworth *Public Sector Housing Law in Scotland* (4th edn) chs 11 & 12. See also the Scottish Executive Consultation Paper, *Maintaining Houses-Preserving Homes* (July 2004).
[2] Housing (Scotland) Act 1987, s 86.
[3] Housing (Scotland) Act 1987, s 114.
[4] Housing (Scotland) Act 1987, s 115.
[5] Housing (Scotland) Act 1987, s 117.
[6] Housing (Scotland) Act 1987, s 88.

16.31 Where an authority is faced with an area of housing which falls below the tolerable standard they may decide to declare a Housing Action Area. This may require the improvement and/or demolition of housing in the area. Declaration of a Housing Action Area gives an authority considerable compulsory purchase powers[1].

[1] Housing (Scotland) Act 1987, ss 89–104.

16.32 In the case of a house not falling below the tolerable standard a repairs notice can be served if it is in a state of serious disrepair. This notice requires specified repairs to be made to the property[1]. Where the disrepair is not serious the authority has power under the Civic Government (Scotland) Act 1982 to require repairs to be carried out[2]. In the event of failure to act by the owners the authority is empowered, in both cases, to carry out the necessary work and charge the owner.

[1] Housing (Scotland) Act 1987, s 108.
[2] Civic Government (Scotland) Act 1982, s 87; this will be replaced to some extent by the Building (Scotland) Act 2003, s 28.

16.33 There are two further points which should be noted in relation to repairs notices and notices under the Civic Government (Scotland) Act 1982[1]. Firstly, there is a right of appeal to the sheriff. Secondly, in cases where the authority carry out the work and charge the owners, the owners who are charged and responsible for payment are those at the time the demand is made, not those at the time the notice was served or the work carried out[2].

[1] And those under the Building (Scotland) Act 2003, s 28.
[2] *Howard v Hamilton District Council* 1985 SLT (Sh Ct) 42; *Purves v City of Edinburgh District Council* 1987 SLT 366; though see *Smith v Renfrew District Council* 1997 SCLR 354.

16.34 The counterpoint of the enforcement powers of local authorities is the grant system which they administer and which makes grants available for repairs to and improvement of properties[1].

[1] Housing (Scotland) Act 1987, Pt XIII; Housing (Scotland) Act 2001, Pt VI.

OTHER STATUTORY CONTROLS

16.35 There is a wide variety of other statutory provisions which affect, directly or indirectly, heritable property or the uses which are made of it. Examples include the Control of Pollution Act 1974 relating to noise; Sewerage (Scotland) Act 1968 dealing with the maintenance of drains and sewers and the control of discharges into them; Fire Precautions Act 1971 requiring certain premises to have specified means of fire escape, fire certificates etc; Health and Safety at Work Act 1974; Offices, Shops and Railway Premises Act 1963; and the Weeds Act 1959.

16.36 In addition there are a number of statutes requiring the licensing of properties for certain uses. Examples are the sale of alcohol[1], residential and nursing homes[2], amusement arcades[3], rented accommodation, and the provisions of the Civic Government (Scotland) Act 1982 which allow local authorities to introduce schemes for the licensing of, for example, sex shops[4] and places of public entertainment[5].

[1] Licensing (Scotland) Act 1976.
[2] Regulation of Care (Scotland) Act 2001.
[3] Lotteries and Amusements Act 1976.
[4] Civic Government (Scotland) Act 1982, s 45 & Sch 2.
[5] Civic Government (Scotland) Act 1982, s 41.

16.37 Control of rented accommodation takes two forms. Only one of these, that is the compulsory licensing of houses in multiple occupation, is currently in force[1]. A house in multiple occupation is house occupied by three or more people who are not members of the same family or of one or other of two families. This means that a flat let to three students who were unrelated would qualify, but the same flat let to a family of 19 would not[2]. All houses in multiple occupation must be licensed and certain standards as regards structure and safety have to be met in order for a licence to be granted. If a property is let in such a way that it qualifies as an HMO without a licence then a criminal offence is committed, though there is no effect on the tenancy agreement. The second form of licensing is that provided for in the Antisocial Behaviour etc (Scotland) Act 2004[3]. This will require all private sector landlords to register with the local authority. The authority will have to be satisfied that the applicant is a fit and proper person to act as a landlord, which will involve considering matters such as any offences involving fraud, violence or drugs committed by the prospective landlord, any history of unlawful discrimination and any breaches of housing or landlord and tenant law. A person can be removed from the register if they no longer fulfil the conditions for registration. It will be an offence to enter into a lease or other occupancy arrangement without being entered on the register and where this happens the local authority will have power to serve a notice to the effect that no rent will be payable. In addition to licensing it will be possible for the local authority to serve an anti-social behaviour notice on a landlord[4]. This is directed at anti-social tenants and requires the landlord to take specified action to deal with the tenant's anti-social behaviour. The end result of this may be that the local authority will apply to court to take over the management of the flat involved.

1   Civic Government (Scotland) Act 1982, Pt I; Civic Government (Scotland) Act 1982 (Licensing of Houses in Multiple Occupation) Order 2000 (SSI 2000/177) as amended.
2   Though it might be the subject of action by the local authority because of overcrowding.
3   Antisocial Behaviour etc (Scotland) Act 2004, Pt 8.
4   Antisocial Behaviour etc (Scotland) Act 2004, s 68.

CHAPTER 17

Voluntary transfer of heritable property 1: conclusion of the contract of sale

17.1   Ownership rights in heritable property can be transferred in three ways:
1   By voluntary transfer.
2   By compulsory transfer, eg following compulsory purchase or bankruptcy.
3   By transmission to heirs on the death of the proprietor.

17.2   Here we will be concerned only with the first situation, that of voluntary transfer of ownership in a piece of land. In such a transfer the initial contract can be the result either of a sale by private bargain, which is by far the most common method, or by means of a public sale at auction. We will concentrate first on the conclusion of a contract and what follows from that in a sale by private bargain before considering public sale and the initiation of purchase in exercise of various statutory rights to buy.

17.3   In such a sale there are, after the pre-contract activities discussed briefly below, three main stages:
1   Conclusion of a contract for the sale and purchase of the property. This stage, referred to as the missives stage, usually involves the exchange of letters between the solicitors acting for the purchaser and seller, though in some cases involving a purchase from housebuilders the offer to purchase may be a standard form signed by the prospective purchasers. Once the contract has been concluded the purchaser has a personal right to require the transfer of the

property, always provided, of course, that he/she meets his/her side of the bargain.

2   Delivery by the seller of a conveyance of the property in favour of the purchaser in exchange for payment of the price or other consideration. At this stage, as will be discussed more fully below, the purchaser still only has a personal right in the property. Prior to this settlement stage, and after conclusion of the contract, the purchaser's solicitor will be involved in examining the title to the property to ensure that the seller can pass on a good title. This process is less important where the property being sold has already been registered in the Land Register. The process and the reasons for the differences are considered more fully in **CHAPTER 18**, as are the respective obligations imposed by law on the seller and purchaser.

3   Completion of the purchaser's title by registration in the Land Register. It is this registration which finally confers a real right on the purchaser.

17.4   Each of these stages will now be considered in more detail. This chapter will consider the process up to conclusion of missives; **CHAPTER 18** will consider what happens after that.

PRE-CONTRACT STAGE

17.5   The initial step might be considered to be the putting of a property up for sale by the present owner. This will trigger certain practical activity by the seller's solicitor, which will not be considered here[1], as well as the advertising of the property either by the solicitor or by an estate agent. The main issue which will be considered here is the step that the intending purchaser takes in order to satisfy themselves that the property is in good condition and that it is worth what they are prepared to pay for it, in other words obtaining a survey of the property. In reality the purchaser often relies on a survey undertaken by the bank or building society to satisfy them that they will obtain a good security for their loan.

[1]   See Sinclair, ch 2; McDonald, 33.2–33.11

Types of survey

Mortgage valuations

17.6   The most basic type of survey is the mortgage valuation, and this is the type which is most commonly encountered in relation to the purchase of houses. It is estimated that 90 per cent of purchasers rely on this type of survey. The mortgage valuation involves a reasonably careful visual inspection of the property lasting about thirty minutes which should draw attention to any obvious features likely to affect the value of the property. It will not usually involve lifting carpets, moving furniture or the inspection of roof and sub-floor spaces. However, where the valuer sees some signs of possible trouble they are required to 'follow the trail of suspicion' behind furniture and under carpets[1]. The very basic nature of this survey and the extent of reliance on it by purchasers who are making a substantial financial commitment are amongst the reasons for introducing the single survey discussed below.

1   *Roberts v J Hampson & Co* [1989] 2 All ER 504 at 510, quoted with approval in *Smith v Eric S Bush* [1989] 2 All ER 514 at 525.

17.7   Some consternation was caused when it was suggested in *Martin v Bell-Ingram*[1] that the valuer carrying out this sort of survey had two duties. The first was to the lender to draw attention to any matter which might affect the value of the property; the second was to the prospective purchaser to draw to their attention any matter which might influence their decision as to whether or not to buy the property. Clearly this second responsibility is potentially far more extensive than the first. This potential, however, is limited by the fact that the court could not actually instance any matter which fell under the second responsibility which would not already be covered by the first.

1   1986 SLT 575.

RICS Homebuyer Survey and Valuation

17.8   This is a more extensive survey and the report is presented on a pre-printed form. The areas covered are clearly explained before the survey is undertaken, and the survey excludes certain things, eg, sub-floor inspection and the testing of services. Most building societies and other lenders offer the option of this type of survey, but it is seldom taken up.

Full structural survey

17.9   This is the most extensive and expensive type of survey. The precise form of the survey will depend on the precise terms of engagement of the surveyor but could involve a full survey of all areas of the building and the testing of all services.

The single survey

17.10   In July 2004 a number of areas were identified for the pilot of a single survey scheme. Under this scheme a single survey, based on the Homebuyer Survey and Valuation, will be obtained by the seller. This survey will be provided to potential purchasers and the surveyor undertaking the survey also undertakes to provide a lender's report to any institution lending money to the purchaser. The pilot scheme will not be compulsory, ie sellers are not obliged to proceed using the single survey, and the pilot will be evaluated before any decision is made on extending the scheme[1].

[1]   For more detail on the background to this see L Crerar, 'Best foot forward?', (2004) 49 JLSS Mar/60; www.singlesurveypilot.co.uk.

Specialist reports

17.11   It is not uncommon to find in a mortgage valuation a requirement that a specialist report on some matter be obtained, particularly in relation to older properties. A common example is a report by timber specialists on the state of the woodwork. These reports are generally obtained from specialist contractors.

Liability of surveyors

To client

17.12   Surveyors are liable to their client, with whom they have a contract, for any loss which he/she suffers as a result of the surveyor's negligence. This liability arises from an implied term in the contract that the surveyor will display the level of ability expected of a reasonably competent member of the profession.

To third parties

17.13   As noted above the commonest type of survey encountered in practice is the mortgage valuation. In these cases the report is instructed by the lending institution, and their client (the purchaser), who will be relying on the report and may suffer loss if it is inaccurate, therefore has no contractual relationship with the surveyor. However, it is now clear, following the general principles of the law of delict, that such clients have a claim against the surveyor for any loss suffered as a result of relying on a negligent report[1]. The basic claim in such cases is for the difference between the lesser of the price paid or negligent valuation on the one hand, and the true value of the property on the other. In addition claims may be made for distress and disturbance, additional legal and other expenses, and even physical injury[2].

1   *Martin v Bell-Ingram* 1986 SLT 575; *Smith v Eric S Bush* [1989] 2 All ER 514.
2   *Martin v Bell-Ingram* 1986 SLT 575: *Hunter v J & E Shepherd* 1992 SLT 1095; *Fraser v D M Hall & Son* 1997 SLT 808.

Exclusion of liability

In contract

17.14   Any attempt to exclude liability for negligence is subject to the requirement imposed by the Unfair Contract Terms Act 1977 that it is fair and reasonable in the circumstances[1].

1   Unfair Contract Terms Act 1977, s 16.

Non-contractual

17.15 Where there is no contract between the surveyor and the person ultimately relying on their report, as in the case of mortgage valuations, liability can be excluded by a non-contractual disclaimer provided that it is fair and reasonable[1]. Non-contractual disclaimers will not be fair and reasonable where the survey is of a house in the medium price range. However, where the property is particularly expensive, or where the transaction is a commercial one, a different view may be taken[2].

[1]   Law Reform (Miscellaneous Provisions) (Scotland) Act 1990, s 68.
[2]   *Smith v Eric S Bush* [1989] 2 All ER 514 at 532c–e; *Bank of Scotland v Fuller Peiser* 2002 SCLR 255.

THE MISSIVES STAGE

Conclusion of the contract of sale[1]

17.16 The initial stage of the purchase/sale of heritable property usually involves the prospective purchaser making an offer to buy the property, followed by an acceptance of that offer by the seller. There is nothing to prevent this being done the other way round, with an offer to sell being accepted by the purchaser. As well as containing an agreement to sell/ purchase the property at an agreed price, the missives will also contain a number of terms and conditions relating to the agreement which are designed by the respective sets of solicitors to protect the interests of their client. Once missives have been concluded (ie an offer has been accepted) a legally binding contract exists between seller and purchaser and either can be compelled to perform their part of the bargain by legal action.

[1]   Cusine & Rennie, ch 3.

17.17 Before discussing the essential contents of missives, as well as considering some of the most commonly found terms found there, it should first be noted that since missives are simply a form of contract three basic contractual requirements must be fulfilled:
1   The parties must have contractual capacity. This means generally that the law must recognise them as having the power to make a legally binding agreement[1].

2   The offer and acceptance must be in writing[2]; it is sufficient that the written offer and acceptance are signed by the solicitors acting for the purchaser and seller. It has been held that a contract can be concluded provided that a signed offer and acceptance actually exist, even though the original of the signed document is not delivered to the offeror and instead a copy is faxed to them[3].

3   There must be *consensus in idem*, ie the offer and acceptance must meet each other's terms. In most cases the offer will take the form of a lengthy document containing a large number of conditions. Unless prior negotiations have taken place it is unlikely that this will meet with a simple acceptance; more usually the acceptance will attempt to modify the terms of the offer and add conditions designed to protect or benefit the seller. A very simple example might be that the date of entry originally offered does not suit the seller who then responds to the offer suggesting a different date. Such a qualified acceptance is legally regarded as a counter-offer which displaces the original offer and must be accepted by the prospective purchaser to complete the contract. This process of counter-offer is often repeated several times before a final offer is accepted and a contract concluded.

1   See PARA **4.35**.
2   Requirements of Writing (Scotland) Act 1995, s 1(2). This requirement may be displaced by the advent of e-conveyancing: see the discussion in P McKellar et al, 'The E-Conveyancing Matrix', (2003) 8 SLPQ 95.
3   *McIntosh v Alam* 1997 SCLR 1171; Gretton & Reid 3.04.

17.18   As a result of this view that a qualified acceptance is a counter-offer it is generally not open to either party to withdraw qualifications they have imposed in a qualified acceptance and accept an earlier offer; the earlier offer simply no longer exists for acceptance[1]. There are, however, some unusual cases where there are effectively two offers open for acceptance and one of the parties can withdraw their offer and accept the other[2]. It is possible to withdraw an offer orally as long as this is done before it is accepted[3] and an offer cannot be withdrawn early if it contains an undertaking to keep it open until a specified time[4].

1   *Rutterford Ltd v Allied Breweries Ltd* 1990 SLT 249.
2   *Findlater v Maan* 1990 SLT 465.
3   *McMillan v Caldwell* 1991 SLT 325 at 329J–L.
4   *Littlejohn v Hadwen* (1882) 20 SLR 5.

17.19   In addition to these general contractual requirements, there are some more specific requirements that must be fulfilled:

1   The parties and the subject matter of the contract (ie the property being sold) must be sufficiently described to allow them to be clearly identified[1]. This is usually done simply by reference to the postal address of the property, or in new houses by reference to the plot number. Where areas of land are involved in a transaction it is advisable to have a plan of the property attached and referred to in the missives. Where a flat is involved the floor and position must be clearly stated.

2   The price or other consideration, or a procedure for arriving at the price or consideration, must be specified in the missives[2]. In most cases the consideration will be the payment of money, or, occasionally, the transfer of another piece of property, with or without a balancing payment, but, in accordance with the general law of contract in Scotland, it is possible to enter a binding gratuitous contract for the transfer of heritage.

3   It used to be considered that it was essential to include in the missives a date of entry; that is, a date on which entry would be given which would normally also provide for contemporaneous payment of the price. It now seems clear that this is not required[3]. Prudence of course suggests that a date of entry is included in the missives in order to give certainty as to when the transaction is likely to be concluded[4].

[1]   *Grant v Peter G Gauld & Co* 1985 SLT 545 and *Bogie v The Forestry Commission* 2002 SCLR 278 are examples where the description of the property was too vague.

[2]   *MacLeod's Executor v Barr's Trustees* 1989 SC 72; 1989 SLT 392, *Miller Homes Ltd v Frame* 2001 SLT 459.

[3]   *Sloan's Dairies v Glasgow Corporation* 1976 SLT 147; *Gordon District Council v Wimpey Homes Holdings Ltd* 1988 SLT 481.

[4]   A date will be implied if there is no mention of it in the missives; Gretton & Reid 4.08.

Common conditions in missives[1]

17.20   A simple agreement containing details of the parties, property and price is, of course, sufficient to constitute a binding contract for the sale of heritage. Most missives, however, contain in addition a large[2] number of standard conditions. These conditions have been added (in so far as it is clear why they should exist) to make explicit or alter the common law obligations of the parties, to provide protection for one or other of the parties or to deal with a particular aspect of an individual transaction. What follows is a review of some of the common general conditions and other conditions applicable to particular types of property.

1   Halliday 30-25 to 30-138, Gretton & Reid ch 4; Sinclair chs 3–5, McDonald 28.20–28.60; Cusine & Rennie, ch 4.

2   In comparison, see the style of missive at p 173 in the 3rd edn of Burns *Conveyancing Practice* published in 1926.

Vacant possession

17.21   Missives will normally specify a date of entry either by stating a date or tying the date of entry to another event, eg by providing that it will occur a specified period after the granting of planning permission or a completion certificate for the property. The missives will also provide for vacant possession to be given at the date of entry. If this last provision is not included the seller's obligation is simply to give possession within a reasonable time. If the property being purchased is subject to a lease or leases this should be mentioned. In such cases there will be no vacant possession of the property, but the right to collect the rent will be transferred on the date of entry. In addition conditions will be included dealing with the terms of the leases[1].

1   Eg *Rockcliffe Estates plc v CWS Ltd* 1994 SLT 592, where the purchaser of a portfolio of properties was permitted not to proceed with the purchase of certain properties if the lease terms were not to their satisfaction.

Payment of price and interest

17.22   At common law the position is that in 'a contract for the sale of heritage, where it is stipulated that the price is to be paid on a particular date, payment of the price on the appointed date is not, in general, an essential condition of the contract and failure to pay on that date does not entitle the seller to rescind'[1]. All that is required is payment within a reasonable time of the date of entry. The exception to this general rule is where punctual payment is expressly provided for in the missives, and this is now done as a matter of course.

1   *Rodger (Builders) Ltd v Fawdry* 1950 SLT 345 at 350, per Lord Sorn.

17.23 It is now also common practice to include a condition requiring the payment of interest if payment of the price is not made on the date of entry. This alters the common law rule that interest is only payable if the purchaser takes entry without paying the price[1]. The rate of interest is usually fixed by reference to the prevailing mortgage or bank base rate, and the condition will normally not apply where the failure to pay arises as a result of the fault of the seller; for example if the seller cannot provide a marketable title on the date of entry[2]. In addition the condition should be phrased in such a way that it will allow interest to be claimed even if payment is never made by the seller (as, for example, in cases where the purchaser rescinds the contract on the grounds of non-payment)[3].

1 *Tiffney v Bachurzewski* 1985 SLT 165.
2 *Bowie v Semple's Exrs* 1978 SLT 9; see also PARAS **18.6–18.16**.
3 *Lloyds Bank v Bamberger* 1993 SC 570.

Marketable title and clear searches

17.24 This condition elucidates the seller's common law obligation to produce a marketable title to the property and will be considered more fully when that obligation is considered in CHAPTER **18**. The condition may add to the common law obligation, and the precise terms will depend on whether the transaction will result in a first registration of the title in the Land Register or registration of a property already registered there.

Rates and local taxes

17.25 In the case of non-domestic properties this condition will specify the rateable value of the property and provide for apportionment of rates around the date of entry. For domestic properties the provision will be for notification of the appropriate local authority to permit them to allocate the council tax as appropriate.

Minerals

17.26 It is normal to make some mention of minerals, if only to confirm that there are no mineral rights attaching to the property. This is because, as explained in CHAPTER **9**, it is assumed that a purchaser buying a piece of land purchases it *a coelo usque ad centrum*[1]. Therefore, if minerals are found to be excluded and this is not made known to the purchaser prior to the agreement to purchase he will be entitled to withdraw from the contract of purchase on the grounds that he will not get all that he agreed to buy. This condition may also contain provisions as to rights of entry to the surface, support and compensation, to guard against the rare situations where the owner of minerals is entitled to enter the surface to work them or where compensation for damage to the surface is excluded[2]. These provisions will be of greater significance when ownership of the surface and minerals are being separated for the first time. Where the property is situated in an area where there has been considerable coal mining it may be advisable to obtain a mineral report[3].

[1]   Literally from the heavens to the centre (of the earth).
[2]   See Rennie, *Minerals and the Law in Scotland*, ch 7, for a discussion of the marketability of title in cases where rights of entry and immunity from compensation are involved.
[3]   See Cusine & Rennie 4.73-4.75, Rennie, *Minerals and the Law in Scotland*, ch 8.

Moveables

17.27   It is not necessary to contract in writing for the purchase of moveables, but it is sometimes advisable to do so to avoid any disputes and doubt as to what is being transferred, eg the sort of disputes referred to in CHAPTER 6 as to whether or not an item is a fixture and is, therefore, transferred with the land. In some cases, for example where stock is being purchased along with a business, a list of moveable property being purchased will be particularly important, as will be a statement of the basis for valuing the stock if the value is not already agreed.

Implementation of notices

17.28   This condition is designed to protect the purchaser against the existence and effect of notices served by local authorities. Local authorities have the power under a variety of statutory provisions to serve notices requiring action by property owners, some of the most common being notices requiring repairs to be carried out, particularly affecting tenement properties[1]. The significance of such notices is twofold. First, the purchaser will be bound by them in so far as they have not been complied with. Secondly, if, as is common, repair works have been undertaken by the local authority following service of a notice on the property owner requiring repairs, the person liable to pay for these works is the owner at the time the demand is made, not the owner at the time the notice was served. The purchaser might, therefore, find himself having to pay for repairs carried out when the property was owned by the seller[2]. In order to ensure that there are no such notices the purchaser will normally require the seller to produce a Property Enquiry Certificate prepared by the relevant local authority. This Certificate will also contain information about any planning or other proposals likely to adversely affect the property[3].

[1]   For example, under the Housing (Scotland) Act 1987 s 108.
[2]   *Howard v Hamilton District Council* 1985 SLT (Sh Ct) 42; *Purves v City of Edinburgh District Council* 1987 SLT 366; though see *Smith v Renfrew District Council* and the comment thereon at 1997 SCLR 354.
[3]   On potential liability for negligence in the issue of these certificates see *MacGregor v City of Edinburgh Council* (20 January 2004, unreported), OH.

Damage to/destruction of property

17.29   Following the decision in *Sloans Dairies v Glasgow Corporation*[1] it is clear that the risk of damage to or destruction of the property not caused by the seller passes to the purchaser immediately on conclusion of the missives, even although the purchaser has no control over the premises until after the date of entry. The standard condition disapplies this rule of law and provides that the risk of accidental damage or destruction remains with the seller until the date of entry. Usually this will not impose too substantial a burden on the seller as he/she will have the property insured anyway, since a requirement to insure is one of the standard conditions affecting heritable securities[2]. In addition, many solicitors operate block policies which provide cover for their purchasing clients between conclusion of missives and date of entry. The Scottish Law Commission has made proposals for changes in the law in this area. The effect of these proposals, if implemented, would be that risk of damage would pass on what was the effective date of entry[3].

[1]   1976 SLT 147.
[2]   See PARA **15.14**FF.
[3]   *Report on the Passing of Risk in Contracts for the Sale of Heritable Property* HC 628 1989-90.

17.30   It is also normal to include, either in this condition or as a separate condition, an obligation for the seller to maintain the property in substantially the same condition between the date of the missives and the date of entry.

Repairs

17.31   This condition will simply repeat the common law rule that repairs instructed by the seller must be paid for by the seller[1].

1   See also PARA **11.14** relating to tenement properties.

Maintenance of roads and sewers

17.32   For older properties this condition will specify that the roads, footpaths and sewers *ex adverso* (ie opposite) the property have been taken over and are maintained by the local authority. In urban areas this will normally be the case and means that the cost of repair will be borne by the local authority.

17.33   In uncompleted houses where there is accompanying road building the condition should ensure that a sufficient guarantee has been lodged with the local authority to ensure completion of the roads to the standard required by the local authority. Lodging of such a guarantee is a statutory requirement and once the roads have been completed to the required standard they must be taken over by the authority[1]. If the local authority has not assumed responsibility for maintenance this could result in considerable expense for the purchaser.

1   Roads (Scotland) Act 1984, s 16(2).

Alterations to the property[1]

17.34   Any major and some minor alterations to a property will require some form of consent. The main consents likely to be required are planning consent and a building warrant and completion certificate[2]. The importance of these is that if work is done without consent there is the possibility of enforcement action being taken against the owner of the property for the time being. There are limits on the power of authorities to take action under the planning legislation. These include a four-year limitation on action against unauthorised building operations or change of use of a building to a single dwelling house and a ten-year limitation on enforcement of other breaches of planning control[3]. There is no such limitation on action under the Buildings (Scotland) Acts 1959, 1970 and 2003 against building works carried out without a building warrant or in breach of the terms of such a warrant, though in some cases local authorities will grant letters of comfort indicating that they will not take any action in respect of the breach.

[1] See Rennie, 'The Modern Missive', 2000 SLT (News) 65 at 69–70.
[2] See CHAPTER 16.
[3] Town and Country Planning (Scotland) Act 1997, s 124; on enforcement see A McAllister & R McMaster *Scottish Planning Law* (2nd edn, 1999), ch 9.

17.35   To protect the purchaser against the possibility of such action it is usual to include a condition requiring exhibition of any relevant consents and certificates, preferably before the date of entry. Where such a condition is included the purchaser is not obliged to accept an offer by the seller to produce a letter of comfort in place of one of the consents or certificates listed[1].

[1] *Hawke v Mathers* 1995 SCLR 1004.

17.36   Problems in this area are common in practice. It is almost universal practice for homeowners to alter their property with complete disregard for the need to obtain local authority or other consents. In light of this it may be tempting for the purchaser's solicitor not to insist on production of the relevant certificates and consents; this, however, could lead to problems when the purchaser tries to sell the property, and may also lead to problems with the fabric of a building as a result of failure to comply with statutory requirements.

Matrimonial Homes (Family Protection) (Scotland) Act 1981

17.37   The detail of this legislation is considered above in CHAPTER 14. The relevant point here is that, subject to the exceptions noted below, a non-entitled spouse has an occupancy right preferable to the rights of a purchaser purchasing from the entitled spouse. A purchaser is only protected against an occupancy right if he has acted in good faith and has had produced to him either: (1) an affidavit by the seller to the effect that the property is not a matrimonial home to which a spouse has occupancy rights; or, (2) a form of consent to the sale of the property; or, (3) renunciation of occupancy rights. The form of consent or the renunciation must bear to have been properly made or given by the non-entitled spouse[1]. Where the non-entitled spouse is unable or, without reasonable cause, unprepared to give consent, an application may be made to court for an order dispensing with her consent[2]. There is authority for the view that there must be a specific offer for the property before such an application can be made[3]. In other words, the entitled spouse cannot apply for what is effectively a blanket permission to sell on any terms if the non-entitled spouse is unwilling to consent.

[1]   Matrimonial Homes (Family Protection) (Scotland) Act 1981, s 6(3)(e).
[2]   Matrimonial Homes (Family Protection) (Scotland) Act 1981, s 7.
[3]   *Fyfe v Fyfe* 1987 SLT (Sh Ct) 38.

17.38   Missives will therefore contain a condition requiring production of one of the documents referred to in the last paragraph to ensure that the purchaser is protected against possible occupancy rights. Formerly in the case of a sale this had to be done before the delivery of the conveyance of the property to the purchaser; that restriction no longer applies[1].

[1]   Matrimonial Homes (Family Protection) (Scotland) Act 1981, s 6(3)(e) as amended by the Law Reform (Miscellaneous Provisions) (Scotland) Act 1990, s 74 and Sch 8.

Condition of services

17.39   Here provision is made that any central heating or other services (for example, lifts or swimming pools) will be in good working order at the date of entry. It is desirable to include this requirement as to the date of entry otherwise the condition may simply be regarded as a statement of the state of affairs at the date of the missives. Such conditions also commonly include a time limit within which notification of any defects must be made and an explicit undertaking by the seller to pay for repair works. Where notification is required it is enough that this indicates that, for example, the heating system is defective and there is no need to set out at length the specific repairs required[1].

[1]   *Williams v Mutter* 2002 SCLR 1127.

Specialist treatment

17.40 This condition will simply require that any guarantees obtained by the seller in relation to any specialist work carried out on the property will be transferred to the purchaser. The most common example relates to treatment of woodwork for rot.

Closing date

17.41 To avoid the offer lying open for an unlimited period it is usual to specify a closing date and time for acceptance of the offer. It is common in practice for the actual acceptance to arrive after this time and the offeror to waive the condition. It does, however, prevent the prospective purchaser from being in the position of having an offer lying open for an unspecified period of time with the possibility of it still being accepted. In order to avoid doubt the condition will normally provide for the acceptance to be received in the solicitor's hands by a certain time.

Supersession clause

17.42 The decision in *Winston v Patrick*[1] caused considerable doubt as to whether and if so, which, conditions in missives survived the transfer of the property to the purchaser. In turn this led to a variety of conditions designed to continue missive conditions in force and a considerable volume of (often contradictory) litigation[2]. This case law was swept away by s 2 of the Contract (Scotland) Act 1997 which provides that:

'Where a deed is executed in implement, or purportedly in implement, of a contract, an unimplemented, or otherwise unfulfilled, term of the contract shall not be taken to be superseded by virtue only of that execution or of the delivery and acceptance of the deed.'

The effect of this is that with limited exceptions the conditions in missives will survive the grant of a conveyance of the property to the purchaser and will be able to be relied on by them for the full prescriptive period. Sellers, however, are usually unwilling to accept a continuing liability for such a long period and this condition will normally limit the continuation of the missive conditions to a period of two years, though if such a condition is included the point at which the two-year period starts to run will need to be identified[3], and this will usually be the date of entry. Once missives have been brought to an end in this way no claim of any sort can be brought based on the missives[4].

1   1981 SLT 41.
2   Considered in the first edition of this text at pp 187–190.
3   *Lonergan v W&P Food Service Ltd* 2002 SCLR 681.
4   *Smith v Lindsay* 2000 SLT 287.

Other conditions

Buildmark

17.43   Most new houses will be built by builders who participate in the Buildmark scheme run by the National House Building Council, an organisation to which most builders belong, which provides insurance against certain defects affecting the property. The scheme was originally introduced in 1988, though the precise coverage has been varied since that date, most recently in January 2003. This insurance lasts for ten years, and any purchase of a property less than ten years old should include a condition that the property is covered by this type of insurance and for the transfer of the insurance to the purchaser[1]. The existence of this insurance cover is particularly important as otherwise the only recourse the owner will have is against the builder if a defect in construction causes death or personal injuries, but not for the cost of any repair work[2]; otherwise they may have a claim against the surveyor who surveyed the property prior to purchase[3].

1   For further details of the Buildmark scheme see the relevant section of the NHBC website at www.nhbc.co.uk.
2   *Murphy v Brentwood District Council* [1990] 2 All ER 908; see also *Forbes v City of Dundee District Council* 1997 SCLR 682.
3   See, for example, *Martin v Bell-Ingram* 1986 SLT 575.

Tenement properties

17.44   Offers to purchase flats in tenemental properties should include a condition to the effect that the costs of repair and maintenance are equally shared. This will be the default position in terms of the Tenements (Scotland) Act 2004[1]. However, the Act will not override express provisions in the tenement titles which may make different arrangements. Offers should also provide for apportionment of common charges at the date of entry.

1   See CHAPTER 11.

Apportionment of price

17.45   It is common to apportion the price paid between the heritage and any moveables also being purchased. In some cases this apportionment will reflect the fact that moveables of substantial value are being purchased, in others the apportionment will be made to reduce the amount of stamp duty payable. This is particularly relevant when the price paid is only slightly over the threshold for paying stamp duty land tax which is currently £60,000 for residential properties and £150,000 for non-residential properties[1]. There must be a real basis for any apportionment.

1   The £150,000 limit also applies to residential properties in disadvantaged areas: Finance Act 2001, s 99; Stamp Duty (Disadvantaged Areas) Regulations 2001 (SI 2001/3747).

Development

17.46   In cases where the purchaser intends to develop the property purchased this development will normally require some consents to allow it to proceed, the principal ones being planning consent and building warrant. In order to protect the purchaser and ensure that the planned development can take place a condition will usually be inserted in the missives to the effect that all necessary consents are to be obtained before entry and allowing the purchaser to withdraw if they are not forthcoming. Normally there will be a time limit requiring consents to be obtained within a specified time, this being necessary to protect the seller's interests; otherwise he/she could be bound by missives without limit of time while the purchaser unsuccessfully attempts to purify the condition relating to consents. Such conditions are often framed in terms that the consents obtained have to be to the satisfaction of the purchaser, and where this is the case he/she must generally act reasonably in deciding on the adequacy of the consents actually obtained[1].

1   *Gordon District Council v Wimpey Homes Holdings Ltd* 1989 SLT 141; *John H Wyllie v Ryan Industrial Fuels Ltd* 1989 SLT 302.

17.47   One question that has arisen in a number of cases is what happens if the consents are not obtained, or are not obtained by the specified date. Can the purchaser then waive the condition and proceed with the purchase? The answer to this depends on the precise terms of the condition and its relationship with the other terms of the missives. For the purchaser to be able to waive the condition it must have been conceived solely in his/her interest and be separable from the other conditions in the missives[1]. In one of the leading cases neither of these requirements was satisfied; both parties were given the right to withdraw from the bargain if the consents were not obtained and the last possible date of entry was fixed by reference to the date on which consent was obtained[2]. If it is desired to give the purchaser the right to waive this type of condition the missives must be carefully drawn to ensure that this can happen, perhaps with an express provision to this effect[3].

[1]   *Zebmoon Ltd v Akinbrook Investment Developments Ltd* 1988 SLT 146.
[2]   *Imry Property Holdings Ltd v Glasgow YMCA* 1979 SLT 261; see also *Manheath Ltd v H J Banks & Co Ltd* 1996 SLT 1006.
[3]   McDonald 28.18-28.19; Halliday 30.10; Gretton & Reid 3.20; Cusine & Rennie 3.20.

SALES OF PUBLIC SECTOR HOUSING[1]

17.48   Since 1980 tenants of certain public sector houses have had the right to buy their homes. The current provisions are contained in the Housing (Scotland) Act 1987 as amended by the Housing (Scotland) Act 2001. To be entitled to purchase the tenant must hold a Scottish secure tenancy from a public sector landlord; these are principally local authorities and registered social landlords. The Scottish secure tenancy was introduced on 30 September 2002, and registered social landlords are essentially those organisations which were housing associations before this date. The introduction of this new tenancy coincided with major changes in the right to buy and there are now two schemes in operation. Tenants who had the right to buy before 30 September 2002[2] enjoy what might be described as an 'old right to buy'. Tenants acquiring the right after that date as Scottish secure tenants come under what is known as the 'modernised right to buy'. The main differences are in the qualification period for the right and the discounts available.

[1]   McDonald 28.61-28.67, A McAllister *Scottish Law of Leases* (2nd edn) 484–502.

2   Mainly tenants of local authorities and Scottish Homes.

17.49   Under the old right to buy the purchaser must have been a public sector tenant for two years, either in their present house or in a house provided by another public landlord and they are entitled to a discount on the price of the house. For houses the minimum discount is 32 per cent after two years rising by 1 per cent for each additional year of tenancy up to a maximum of 60 per cent. For flats the minimum discount is 44 per cent rising by 2 per cent per year to a maximum of 70 per cent.

17.50   Under the modernised right to buy the qualification period is five years, except in the case of tenants of registered social landlords. There is an exemption from the right to buy applying to such landlords for ten years from 30 September 2002, though this exemption will not apply where the tenant already had a right to buy or where the house was transferred to a registered social landlord, for example the transfer by Glasgow City Council to Glasgow Housing Association. Discounts for all properties under the modernised right to buy start at 20 per cent and increase at 1 per cent a year up to a maximum of 35 per cent. In addition there is a maximum cash limit on the discount of £15,000.

17.51   In both cases there is a penalty if the house is disposed of within three years; this requires repayment of 100 per cent of the discount if the disposal takes place within one year, 66 per cent within two years and 33 per cent within three years. The penalty is secured by a standard security in favour of the landlord. Some disposals are exempt from this penalty, for example sales by the executor of the purchaser[1] and disposals as a result of compulsory purchase. The term disposal covers not only sales, but also, for example, the granting of a trust deed for the benefit of creditors[2].

1   *Clydebank District Council v Keeper of the Registers of Scotland* 1994 SLT (Lands Tr) 2.
2   *McDonald's Trustees v City of Aberdeen Council* 2000 SLT 985.

17.52   There are also some limitations on the right which apply in all cases. Some of these relate to the property or landlord, others to the conduct of the tenant. In the first category there will be no right to buy from a registered social landlord with charitable status, from housing co-operatives, from a registered social landlord which lets fewer than 101 houses and in respect of group housing for people with special needs, for example sheltered housing. In addition the Scottish Ministers can designate areas as pressured areas where demand for public sector housing substantially exceeds supply and where this imbalance will be exacerbated by sales under the right to buy. The designation can last for five years and during that period tenants whose tenancy began after the Scottish secure tenancy was introduced will not be able to exercise their right to buy unless they had a pre-existing right to buy. The second category of limitations includes cases where the tenant is in arrears of rent, council tax or water and sewerage charges and cases where eviction proceedings based on the tenant's conduct have been initiated.

17.53   The conditions which the landlord can attach to the sale are regulated by the legislation. They must include conditions which will, for example, ensure that the tenant obtains a marketable title and that the tenant will get as full enjoyment of the property as owner as they had as tenant. Retention by the seller of a right of pre-emption (ie an option to buy back the property on first sale by the new owner[1]) is excluded except in certain restricted circumstances. If the tenant objects to any conditions proposed by the landlord they may request a change in the terms within one month. If the landlord refuses the tenant may appeal to the Lands Tribunal.

[1]   See PARA **19.25**FF.

17.54   The procedure for exercise of the right to buy is that the tenant serves an application to purchase on the landlord. There is a statutory form for this. On receipt of the application the landlord may, within one month, issue a notice of refusal if the house falls into one of the categories excluded from sale or it disputes the tenant's right to buy. If the ground for refusal is that the information supplied by the tenant is incorrect the period for service of the notice of refusal is two months. If the landlord does not refuse to sell it must issue an offer to sell within two months. This offer will contain details of the market value of the house, the discount available and the price as well as the conditions attaching to the sale. A tenant who wishes to accept the offer to sell must do so within two months, and once the offer is accepted the sale will proceed in the same way as any other sale. Disputes arising during the sale process are generally to be resolved by application to the Lands Tribunal.

THE COMMUNITY RIGHT TO BUY

17.55 The community right to buy was introduced by the Land Reform (Scotland) Act 2003[1] and is designed to give rural communities the right to buy certain land (this includes salmon fishings and minerals) when the owner offers it for sale. As this purpose would suggest it can exist only in rural areas with land outwith these being defined as 'excluded land'[2]. The right to buy is triggered where the landowner proposes to transfer land against which a community interest has been registered by a community body[3].

[1] With effect from 14 June 2004.
[2] Land Reform (Scotland) Act 2003, s 33; Community Right to Buy (Definition of Excluded Land) (Scotland) Order 2004 (SSI 2004/296).
[3] See Scottish Executive, *Community Right to Buy: Guidance* (2004).

Community body[1]

17.56 A community body must be a company limited by guarantee. In addition, there is a list of other requirements that the body must fulfil in order for this status to be confirmed by the Scottish Ministers. These include a definition of the community to which the body relates, a requirement that a majority of members are resident in the community, and a requirement that any surplus made by the company is to be used for the benefit of the community.

[1] Land Reform (Scotland) Act 2003, s 34.

Registering an interest

17.57 The community body must, after advertising its intention, apply to the Scottish Ministers[1]. Once the application has been made the Ministers will ask the landowner and any holder of a heritable security for their comments as well as sending them a notice informing them that, pending determination of the application, they are prohibited from transferring, or taking any action with a view to transferring, the land. Any transfer in breach of this prohibition is of no effect. After receiving comments from the landowner and security holder the Ministers will seek comment on these from the community body before deciding on the application.

¹   Land Reform (Scotland) Act 2003, s 37. There are special procedures in s 39 for late registration once the process of sale of the land has started. See Community Right to Buy (Forms) (Scotland Regulations 2004 (SSI 2004/233).

17.58   Before an application can be granted the following criteria must be satisfied[1]:

1   Either a significant number of members of the community have a substantial connection with the land or the land is close enough to land with which such a connection exists to make acquisition of it compatible with fulfilling the achievement of sustainable development.
2   It is in the public interest.
3   There is a sufficient level of support in the community (normally at least 10 per cent of the community).

If the application is granted the interest will be registered in the Register of Community Interests in Land, as indeed will the original application and the prohibition notice sent to the landowner. The registration lasts for renewable periods of five years.

¹   Land Reform (Scotland) Act 2003, s 38: the criteria listed relate to land; there are slightly different criteria for salmon fishings and minerals in s 38(1)(d).

17.59   The effect of registration is that the landowner or heritable creditor must give notice of any proposed transfer to the community body or to the Scottish Ministers[1]. Any transfer which takes place without this notification is of no effect[2], and there are procedures which will allow the community body to activate the right to buy where a transfer has gone ahead without notification, which, in effect allows the right to buy to be exercised against the then owner of the property[3]. Not all transfers require notification: those which are exempt include gratuitous transfers, transfers implementing an agreement made before the community interest was registered, transfers between companies in the same group, and the vesting of property in a trustee in bankruptcy[4].

¹   Land Reform (Scotland) Act 2003, s 48.
²   Land Reform (Scotland) Act 2003, s 40(2).
³   Land Reform (Scotland) Act 2003, s 50; though it is not clear that this is consistent with the provision noted above that any transfer without notice is of no effect.
⁴   Land Reform (Scotland) Act 2003, s 40(4).

Exercising the right to buy

17.60   Once the right to buy has been activated by service of a notice of proposed transfer a notice is sent to the community body which then has 30 days to decide whether or not to exercise the right[1]. There then follows a process involving valuation, a community ballot (more than half the community must vote and a majority of those voting must be in favour) and consent from the Scottish Ministers. Consent to exercise of the right to buy is only to be given where the purchase is in the public interest and is compatible with furthering sustainable development. It is envisaged that the transaction will be completed within six months of the community body indicating its intention to exercise the right. Special procedures apply to the purchase of salmon fishings and minerals[2] and where the right to buy is being exercised following a transfer in breach of the Act[3].

[1]   Land Reform (Scotland) Act 2003, s 49. Note that more than one community body may register an interest against the same land; if more than one indicates a desire to exercise the right, the Scottish Ministers have to decide which one goes ahead.
[2]   Land Reform (Scotland) Act 2003, s 53.
[3]   Land Reform (Scotland) Act 2003, s 58.

CROFTING RIGHT TO BUY

17.61   The Land Reform (Scotland) Act 2003 also introduced a crofting right to buy[1]. Unlike the community right to buy, this is triggered by a request from a crofting community body (defined in a way similar to a community body except based on croft land), rather than a decision by a landowner to sell. The right is to buy croft land[2] though salmon fishings and minerals can also be bought along with the land[3]. To exercise the right the body must apply to the Scottish Ministers[4]. The Scottish Ministers will take account of the views of the landowner in deciding whether to grant the application, as well as considering other factors, such as the requirement for community support evidenced by a ballot, the public interest and the compatibility of the exercise with furthering the achievement of sustainable development[5]. The application for a right to buy and the decision of the Scottish Ministers must be registered in a register maintained by the Crofting Commission and any transfer to someone other than the crofting community body is to be of no effect once consent to the application to exercise the right to buy has been granted[6].

1   With effect from 14 June 2004.
2   Land Reform (Scotland) Act 2003, s 68.
3   Land Reform (Scotland) Act 2003, s 69.
4   Land Reform (Scotland) Act 2003, s 73.
5   Land Reform (Scotland) Act 2003, s 74.
6   Land Reform (Scotland) Act 2003, s 95.

AGRICULTURAL RIGHT TO BUY

17.62   The Agricultural Holdings (Scotland) Act 2003 confers a right on an agricultural tenant to register an interest in the land covered by his lease[1]. In order to register such an interest a notice must be sent to the Keeper of the Registers of Scotland who will then register the interest in the Register of Community Interests in Land. Once the notice is registered any proposal to transfer the land (subject to a list of exempted transfers similar to that for the community right to buy) must be notified to the tenant, who, if he/she wishes to exercise the right to buy, must give notice of this intention. If the tenant gives no notice or gives notice that they do not intend to exercise the right, the right is extinguished, but a new interest can subsequently be registered. The registration lasts for a renewable period of five years. The process of purchase must be completed in six months, and there is provision for the price to be fixed by a valuer in the absence of agreement on this. If the land is transferred without notice being given to the tenant he/she has a right to purchase the land from the person to whom it was transferred.

1   Agricultural Holdings (Scotland) Act 2003, Pt 2.

PUBLIC SALES[1]

17.63   Although it is now the case that virtually all sale transactions take the form of sales by private bargain, it is still possible to sell heritable property by auction at a public sale. This method of sale was formerly of importance in that heritable creditors under a bond and disposition in security or bond of cash credit selling security subjects had to proceed in this way. The rationale for this was that the creditor had a duty to obtain the highest possible price for the property, and a public sale was thought to be the best way of safeguarding this. However, the virtual disappearance of public sales in other contexts meant that this was no longer necessarily so, and this was recognised in the Conveyancing and Feudal Reform (Scotland) Act 1970 which allowed such creditors to exercise their power of sale by private bargain[2]. There are still some cases where a public sale is necessary, eg as a precursor to raising an action of foreclosure over security subjects[3], and it may occasionally be used in other circumstances.

1   Halliday 30-170 to 30-179.
2   See PARAS **15.47–15.50**.
3   Conveyancing and Feudal Reform (Scotland) Act 1970, s 28(1).

17.64   Public sales will generally proceed under articles of roup. This is a document which is in the form of an offer to sell by the seller. It will typically contain, among other things, the following:

1   A description of the property being offered for sale. This will normally be fuller than a description in missives. The exposer (seller) will also be identified.
2   An upset price.
3   A date of entry when possession will be given and the price will be payable.
4   An undertaking by the exposer to grant a valid conveyance of the property in exchange for payment of the agreed price.
5   A statement that the purchaser will be bound to take the title to the property as it stands. The effect of this is that the purchaser will be obliged to accept a title which is subject to minor deficiencies and to bear the cost of rectifying or curing these deficiencies. This is in contrast to the normal position in sales under missives where the seller is bound to produce a marketable title[1].
The obligation to accept the title as it stands only require the acceptance of minor deficiencies in title; the purchaser is not obliged to accept a title which is radically defective.
6   A requirement for the successful bidder to produce caution or a deposit within a short time of the sale, and provision for what is to happen if this is not done.
7   An arbitration clause referring disputes arising under the contract to arbitration.
8   A judge of roup will be appointed who will act as auctioneer and conduct the sale.
Once the articles of roup have been executed the sale will be held at the place and time advertised, with the property being sold to the highest bidder.

17.65   After the sale is completed a minute of enactment and preference will be endorsed on the articles of roup. This will identify the highest bidder and will be signed by him and the judge of roup. Once the minute of enactment and preference has been endorsed on the articles of roup, a binding contract of sale has been concluded. From this stage on the sale proceeds in the same way as a sale by private bargain.

CHAPTER 18

Voluntary transfer of heritable property 2: completion of title

18.1 In the previous chapter we considered the conclusion of a contract to buy and sell heritage and the possible contents of such an agreement. In this chapter we will consider the obligations of the purchaser and seller and the processes leading up to the purchaser obtaining a real right in the land by completing his title.

COMMON LAW OBLIGATIONS OF THE PARTIES TO THE CONTRACT

18.2 Following conclusion of missives the next stage of a conveyancing transaction is the examination of title[1]. The purposes of examination of title are to ensure that the seller has legal title to sell the property, that he/she is under no legal incapacity (eg bankruptcy) and that all of the conditions contained in the missives are complied with. Essentially, then, examination of title is a means of ensuring that the seller complies with his/her obligations under the contract of sale.

[1]   For a fuller discussion see McDonald ch 32; Halliday ch 36; Sinclair ch 7; Gretton & Reid chs 7 & 8.

18.3 The physical process of examination of title involves the inspection of relevant title deeds relating to the property. In first registration transactions the relevant deeds will be those needed to establish a marketable title and those deeds which contain burdens and conditions affecting the property. In the case of property which is already registered in the Land Register the relevant deeds will be the Land Certificate and any deeds affecting the property after the date of the certificate. As well as examining the deeds the purchaser's solicitor will also need to see searches affecting the property and other documents relevant to ensuring that the seller is fulfilling his obligations. Examples of this latter category would be planning and other consents and completion certificates for building work. At the stage of examination drafts of the various deeds needed to complete the transaction will be adjusted and finalised between the two solicitors.

18.4 The structure of the main types of title deed will be the subject matter of CHAPTER 19.

Obligations of the seller

18.5 At common law the obligations of the seller are to deliver or exhibit a marketable title, to deliver or exhibit clear searches, to deliver a valid conveyance of the property, to give possession and to comply with any other conditions of the contract. As we noted above these obligations are usually expressly stated, often with some modifications, in the missives.

Good and marketable title[1]

18.6 This is sometimes expressed as an obligation to deliver a good and marketable title. The basic obligation is that the seller should give the purchaser an unchallengeable right to the property which is not affected by any real conditions, servitudes or reservations which would materially diminish the value of that property. The precise content of the obligation will depend on whether the sale will induce first registration in the Land Register or involves a dealing in a property already registered, although some of the same principles apply in both cases. Regardless of the nature of the transaction the seller's obligation is to deliver or exhibit a marketable title within a reasonable time. In practice missives usually require this to be done before the date of entry.

[1]   See K Reid 'Good and Marketable Title' (1988) 33 JLSS 162, McDonald 28.32–28.37 and 32.101-32.102; Gretton & Reid ch 6.

18.7 Production of a marketable title in this context means essentially three things:

1 The seller must possess a title to the property which is sufficient to enable him to sell the property interest which he has undertaken to sell. This means, for example, that if he has undertaken to sell the ownership of the land, production of a title in the form of a lease, even for 999 years, will not be adequate[1]. He must also be in a position, if no qualification has been made in the missives regarding this, to convey the minerals lying under the property[2].

2 The seller must be able to produce a prescriptive or valid progress of title to the property.

3 Finally, the 'seller is bound to convey the subjects free from burdens that were unknown to the purchaser at the date of the missives if these burdens materially diminish the value of the subjects'[3].

[1]   *McConnell v Chassels* (1903) 10 SLT 790.
[2]   *Campbell v McCutcheon* 1963 SLT 290.
[3]   *Armia Ltd v Daejan Developments Ltd* 1979 SLT 147, per Lord Fraser at 161.

PRESCRIPTIVE PROGRESS

18.8 As has already been discussed[1], possession of property for the prescriptive period of ten years cures any latent defects (ie defects not apparent merely from perusal of the title deeds) in the title to that property and effectively gives the owner a guaranteed title which is not open to challenge by any third party. Prescription, however, will not cure patent defects in the foundation writ (see below). Patent defects are those which are obvious from looking at the title deeds. Examples of such defects would be the omission of necessary clauses from the deed, defects in signature by the parties or defects in witnessing. There is provision for rectification of deeds under the Law Reform (Miscellaneous Provisions) (Scotland) Act 1985, s 8(1). This allows rectification where the deed fails to reflect the intention of the parties as would arguably be the case if a necessary clause was left out of a deed rendering it ineffective contrary to the parties' intentions[2]. Defects which cannot be rectified or overlooked will vitiate a deed and hence the proprietor's title.

[1]   See CHAPTER 3.
[2]   See also CHAPTER 19.

18.9 To show that he/she has an unchallengeable title to pass on to the purchaser the seller must be able to demonstrate possession for the prescriptive period. In practice it is common for properties to change hands every few years so the title offered to the purchaser is unlikely to be a title possessed by the seller alone for ten years or more; more likely it will take the form of a number or progress of titles culminating in the deed in favour of the seller. In order to establish a good progress of title in such circumstances the seller must exhibit the first title deed outwith the ten-year period. This deed must be *ex facie* valid (ie free from patent defects) and sufficient in its terms to include the property being sold to the purchaser[1]. Following on this deed (referred to as the foundation writ) all of the transfers of the property must be in the form of deeds, each of which is *ex facie* valid and granted by someone having the legal capacity to do so. These deeds must be clearly linked together[2]. Linking may be evident from the grantor of one deed being the grantee of the previous deed, or it may be evidenced by some other document linking two recorded deeds together, or linking the right of the seller to sell back to a recorded deed. This linking (where it appears in a deed it is referred to as deduction of title[3]) is necessary where the granter of a deed has not recorded their title; his right to grant the deed is linked back to the recorded deed through a deed or document, for example a confirmation of an executor or an unrecorded disposition[4].

[1]   Prescription and Limitation (Scotland) Act 1973, s 1.
[2]   In *Sibbald's Heirs v Harris* 1947 SC 601 it was said that the obligation was to provide an *ex facie* valid progress of title and not to guarantee against every risk of subsequently emerging latent defects.
[3]   See also CHAPTER 19.
[4]   See Halliday 37-06 to 37-11.

18.10 To take a simple example, suppose that in 1977 Whippy Developments sold a house to Frank Smith. After that the following transactions have taken place:

1983	Disposition by Frank Smith to Philip Marlowe
1988	Disposition by Philip Marlowe to Philo Vance
1995	Disposition by Philo Vance to Sam Spade
1998	Disposition by Sam Spade to Miles Archer
2001	Disposition by the Executor of Miles Archer to Steve Carella (the seller)

In this example the foundation writ (assuming the sale took place in 2004) would be the 1988 disposition by Marlowe to Vance, and the progress of title would include that deed, all the subsequent dispositions and the confirmation of Miles Archer's executor.

18.11 In practice the only check on the capacity of the parties to grant the deeds in the progress of title is through the searches in the Personal Register which are contained in the Form 10 and Form 11 reports examined by the purchaser's solicitor. These searches are discussed below, but for the moment it is worth noting that checking the searches alone is not a perfect check as these will not reveal some forms of incapacity, for example, mental disorder affecting capacity to contract.

18.12 The final element in establishing a prescriptive title is, of course, possession. In practice it is normally assumed that the property has been possessed consecutively by those appearing to be its owners over the period of the prescriptive progress. The reason for simply assuming this is that 'demanding evidence of possession would be a real menace for everyday conveyancing'[1]. In virtually every case the assumption will be justified.

[1]   G Gretton 'Searches' 1989 JLSS 85 at p 85; see also McDonald 32.15.

ABSENCE OF OBJECTIONABLE BURDENS

18.13 The seller has an obligation to provide a title free from unusual or unduly burdensome real burdens. In the past the following have all been held to be breaches of this obligation entitling the purchaser to rescind: the existence of a servitude right of access preventing redevelopment along the entire frontage of a property[1]; a prohibition on building[2]; a right of access and prohibition on rear windows on the second floor of a two storey building[3]; a servitude right of way through a small garden[4]; and a prohibition on selling alcohol[5]. It is only fair to say, however, that the law in this area is not entirely clear with some of the older cases, when deciding in favour of the purchaser, failing to distinguish clearly between conditions which are commonplace and those which are restrictive. One example is *Smith v Soeder*[6]. In this case a condition that only dwelling houses should be built on the land and a condition requiring a passage to be left for access by the superior were both regarded, on appeal, as being objectionable. Conditions such as the former are, however, commonplace in dispositions of land for building. In this case, also, the Lord Ordinary had taken the view that the conditions were unobjectionable.

1   *Armia Ltd v Daejan Developments Ltd* 1979 SLT 147.
2   *Louttit's Trustees v Highland Railway Company* (1892) 19 R 791.
3   *Smith v Soeder* (1895) 23 R 60, although this decision seemed to turn, at least in part, on the fact that the purchaser was foreign and did not have legal assistance in the early stages of the transaction.
4   *Welsh v Russell* (1894) 21 R 769. Where there was doubt as to whether a servitude right running across the site of a kitchen extension had been discharged the title was not marketable: *McLennan v Warner* 1996 SLT 1349.
5   *Umar v Murtaza* 1983 SLT (Sh Ct) 79, although this decision has been criticised: see K Reid 'Good and Marketable Title' (1988) 33 JLSS 162 at p 163.
6   (1895) 23 R 60.

18.14   In cases where the purchaser has actual knowledge of the restriction or such knowledge can be imputed to him then, at common law, he will be barred from resiling from the contract[1].

1   *Rofts v Stewart's Trustees* 1926 SLT 577; *Mossend Theatre Co v Livingstone* 1930 SC 90, eg per Lord Anderson at 103.

18.15   In view of the lack of clarity of the law and the lack of modern precedent it is advisable that where a use of the property (eg sale of alcohol) is contemplated which might fall foul of a title restriction this should be specifically dealt with in the missives. Any such specific term will add to the seller's common law obligation[1].

1   *Armia Ltd v Daejan Developments Ltd* 1979 SLT 147 at 161.

18.16   In order to discover what burdens and conditions affect the property the purchaser's solicitor will have to examine any deeds outwith the progress of title which impose burdens or conditions. It will also be necessary to consider the effect of the Abolition of Feudal Tenure (Scotland) Act 2000 and Title Conditions (Scotland) Act 2003. Although the former abolishes feudal burdens enforceable by the superior, this does not mean that burdens which originally took this form will cease to exist. In the first place, the former superior can retain the right to enforce such burdens by registering a notice in the Land Register[1], so the purchaser's solicitor will need to see if this has happened or not. Secondly, if such a notice has not been registered third party rights of enforcement derived from these burdens may exist without notice[2]. This will mean that in most cases there will be uncertainty as to the continued existence of any onerous condition, and in those circumstances the title would not be marketable.

1   See CHAPTER 14.
2   Title Conditions (Scotland) Act 2003, ss 52 & 53.

DEALING IN REGISTERED PROPERTY[1]

18.17   Where a property is already registered there should be no problem about the marketability of the seller's title because of the state indemnity given by the Keeper of the Registers of Scotland. The documentation that the seller will have to produce is his Land Certificate with no exclusion of indemnity, and any deeds relating to subsequent dealings in the property. The existence of any adverse real conditions can be easily ascertained from the certificate. The only relevance of prescription here is that possession for ten years on a registered title involving an exclusion of indemnity cures that defect[2].

1   See McDonald, 32.101-32.102.
2   Prescription and Limitation (Scotland) Act 1973, s 1(1)(b)(ii).

OCCUPANCY RIGHTS

18.18   Where the seller's title is in the name of an individual (rather than joint names of husband and wife) it is possible that there may be a non-entitled spouse having occupancy rights to the property. In order to protect the purchaser against the claim of a non-entitled spouse having such rights it is necessary, first of all, to see all the relevant documentation (ie form of consent, renunciation, affidavit or decree dispensing with consent[1]) for the current transaction. Secondly, since occupancy rights last for five years from the date of last occupation by the non-entitled spouse[2] it is necessary also to see this documentation for any transaction within the last five years in which a question of occupancy rights may arise – basically those where the seller had sole title to the property. In the case of dealings in registered land this second check may be unnecessary as the Keeper of the Registers of Scotland may have certified on the title sheet (copied on the Land Certificate) that no occupancy rights exist in respect of prior proprietors[3].

1   See CHAPTER 14.
2   Matrimonial Homes (Family Protection) (Scotland) Act 1981, s 6(3)(f).
3   See *Registration of Title Practice Book* 5.23; 6.28.

Clear searches

18.19   The obligation of the seller is to deliver or exhibit clear searches[1]. The searches required in any transaction will depend on whether the transaction will result in the purchaser's title being recorded in the Register of Sasines or registered in the Land Register, and in the latter case, whether the title is already registered or will be registered for the first time. The main forms of search will be discussed below, with separate consideration of transactions involving companies.

1   See Halliday 36-78 to 36-93; McDonald 32.17–32.34; G Gretton 'Searches' (1989) 34 JLSS 50 and 85; Gretton & Reid ch 9.

FORM 10 REPORT

18.20   This is used in first registration transactions and comprises three parts. The first of these is a search in the Register of Sasines which will cover: the foundation deed for the prescriptive progress of title and subsequent deeds in that progress; undischarged securities for 40 years prior to the date of the search, including any dealings with older securities within that period; a list of discharges granted within the past five years; and any other deed, excluding deeds of transfer, affecting the property. An example of this last category would be a deed creating burdens affecting the property.

18.21   The second section is a report on the Land Register and will show whether any part of the land has been registered in that register.

18.22   The final section is a search in the Register of Inhibitions and Adjudications[1]. Certain types of notice which in practice prevent an individual from dealing with his property must be registered in this register if they are to be effective. The main types of notice are notices of litigiosity, inhibitions, awards of sequestration and notice of a trust deed for creditors.

1   See G Gretton *The Law of Inhibition and Adjudication* (2nd edn) ch 12.

18.23   A notice of litigiosity is a notice that an action affecting land has been started. This may take the form of an action of adjudication, an action for reduction of the deed conferring the right to the land or an action for rectification of a deed affecting the land under the terms of the Law Reform (Miscellaneous Provisions) (Scotland) Act 1985.

18.24   An inhibition is available as a form of diligence in execution of a court decree; on the dependence of a court action, to preserve the defender's property pending the outcome of the action; or, very unusually, as a remedy for a creditor proceeding on a document of debt. For these purposes a document of debt has been defined as 'any probative document whereby a debtor binds himself to pay'[1].

1   G Maher & D Cusine *The Law and Practice of Diligence* 9.10; see generally 9.01–9.36 on inhibitions.

18.25   Finally an award of sequestration against a bankrupt must be forwarded by the clerk of court for registration in this register[1] and a trust deed granted for creditors may be so registered.

1   Bankruptcy (Scotland) Act 1985, s 14.

18.26   The effect of a notice of litigiosity is that the title of any person acquiring the property after this has been registered can be set aside. Inhibitions and notices of award of sequestration have similar consequences. They both operate to prevent future voluntary transactions relating to the property of the debtor or bankrupt, with the result that any such transaction can be set aside. The important qualification is that *future voluntary* transactions are struck at. This means that if missives are concluded before an inhibition is registered against the seller, that inhibition will not prevent the effective transfer of the property to the purchaser. Such a transfer is not a *voluntary* act by the seller as the purchaser can go to court and secure an order for implement requiring the seller to fulfil his obligations undertaken in the missives. Registration of an inhibition in such circumstance will, however, as noted below, mean that the seller cannot exhibit a clear search.

18.27   Notices of litigiosity prescribe in five years or six months after final decree in the court action, whichever is earlier[1]; inhibitions prescribe in five years[2]; and notices of award of sequestration last for three years, but may be renewed for further three-year periods[3]. It was suggested in the first edition of this text that there should normally be a search against everyone having an interest in the property within the ten-year prescriptive period for a period of five years immediately prior to their disposal of the property. However, the application for a Form 10 Report refers only to the period of five years prior to the date of the search certificate[4].

1   Conveyancing (Scotland) Act 1924, s 44(3)(a).
2   Conveyancing (Scotland) Act 1924, s 44(3)(a).

3   Bankruptcy (Scotland) Act 1985, s 14(4).
4   For various views on what the correct period should be see Gretton & Reid 9.20; G Gretton *The Law of Inhibition and Adjudication* (2nd edn) 185–188; McDonald 32.31; and Halliday 36-88 to 36-89.

FORM 11 REPORT

18.28   The recommended practice is to instruct a Form 10 Report when the property is put on the market for sale and have it brought up to date by a Form 11 Report nearer the date of entry[1].

1   *Registration of Title Practice Book*, 3.4.

FORM P16 REPORT

18.29   This is also relevant in first registration, and takes the form of a request to the Keeper of the Registers of Scotland to compare the boundaries of the property as disclosed by the title deeds with those appearing on the Ordnance Survey plan which forms the basis of the register. The importance of this is that a serious discrepancy between the two will require remedial action or may result in indemnity being excluded or partially excluded by the Keeper[1].

1   See *Registration of Title Practice Book* 4.10.

FORM 12 AND 13 REPORTS

18.30   These reports are appropriate in dealing with a registered interest. The Form 12 Report contains a report from the Land Register and a report from the Register of Inhibitions and Adjudications. The Form 13 Report is simply an update of the Form 12[1].

1   See McDonald ch 35; Halliday 21-87; Gretton 'Searches' 1989 JLSS 50; Gretton & Reid 28.09–28.10.

TRANSACTIONS WITH COMPANIES

18.31   Transactions with companies are, of course, quite common, as a result of the growth in home ownership and the number of new private dwellings sold by housebuilding companies. Where the seller of property is a company additional searches are necessary. This is so for two reasons.

In the first place the company may have granted floating charges affecting the whole of their property, including their heritable property[1]. Such charges, even though they affect heritage, need not be recorded in the Register of Sasines or registered in the Land Register, and so will not be disclosed by a search there. A floating charge may contain conditions prohibiting the sale of property without the consent of the creditor, or it may have crystallised as a result of the appointment of a receiver or the commencement of liquidation. On crystallisation the floating charge becomes a fixed charge over the company's property which effectively prevents its sale.

[1]   See PARAS **15.69–15.74**.

18.32   Secondly, even if the company has not granted floating charges which might affect the sale the company may have gone into administration (a process designed to rescue ailing companies)[1] or liquidation. The significance of the appointment of a liquidator or administrator is that he/ she becomes the only person entitled to enter into transactions on behalf of the company, and in the case of a liquidator can disclaim contracts entered into before his appointment.

[1]   Insolvency Act 1986, Pt 2.

18.33   In order to check for the existence of floating charges or the appointment of a receiver, administrator or liquidator a search must be made at Companies House[1]. In addition, further steps are usually taken to protect the purchaser against crystallisation of a floating charge or liquidation or administration. These include obtaining a personal undertaking from directors of the company that it is not insolvent and either a deed of release from the creditor in a floating charge releasing the property being sold from the charge or a certificate of non-crystallisation[2].

[1]   This can be done via www.direct.companieshouse.gov.uk.
[2]   McDonald 34.18, Gretton 'Searches' (1989) 34 JLSS 50 at p 52.

RIGHTS TO BUY

18.34   In the case of land in a rural area it may be necessary to check for a notice registering a community interest or a consent to an application under the crofting community right to buy. In addition where property being sold is subject to an agricultural tenancy it will be necessary to check if a notice registering interest has been registered by the agricultural tenants [1].

[1]   See CHAPTER 17.

WHAT IS A CLEAR SEARCH?

18.35   A clear search is one which indicates that the seller has a marketable title; in other words there is nothing on the face of the search, apart from entries which the operation of statute renders ineffective, which would appear to prevent or limit the granting of a good title to the purchaser. Examples of entries which are rendered ineffective by the operation of statute are inhibitions more than five years old which have prescribed in terms of the Conveyancing (Scotland) Act 1924, s 44, and inhibitions lodged against a debtor in a standard security after the grant of the security where the property is being sold by the creditor in exercise of his right of sale[1]. An example of an entry which would prevent a clear search, though not prevent the granting of a good title, is an inhibition lodged after the conclusion of missives. In this case, as noted above, the granting of a disposition is not a future voluntary act which is struck at by the inhibition as it can be compelled by court action. The search is, nonetheless, not clear, as to establish that this is the case would involve reference to material extrinsic to the search, in this instance, the missives[2].

[1]   *Newcastle Building Society v White* 1987 SLT (Sh Ct) 81 referring to the Conveyancing and Feudal Reform (Scotland) Act 1970 s 26(1).
[2]   See *Henderson v Dawson* (1895) 22 R 895 at 902, per Lord McLaren.

18.36   There is one type of entry commonly found on a search which means that, in law, the search is not clear. This is the grant of a security over the property to a bank or building society to secure the loan used for its purchase. In practice this is not usually a problem as the loan will be repaid on sale of the property and a discharge of the security will be handed over to the purchaser's solicitor at settlement of the transaction or will be included in the letter of obligation.

LETTER OF OBLIGATION[1]

18.37   It is not possible for the seller to deliver or exhibit a clear search at the time when the price is paid and the transaction settled. The reason for this is that any search report will have been applied for before the settlement date and will reflect the position (normally a few days) before settlement, the search can obviously not also ensure that nothing will be registered before the purchaser's title which might have an adverse effect on that title. In order to get over this problem the seller's solicitor grants a letter of obligation, which in effect is his/her personal guarantee[2]. The guarantee takes the form of an undertaking to clear the registers of any entry which would lead to exclusion of indemnity, provided that such an entry is registered between the date of the Form 10 or 11(or, in a dealing with land already registered, Form 12 or 13) Report and a second date, usually 14 days after settlement[3].

[1]   See Halliday 38-09 to 38-10 and 38-21 to 38-24; McDonald 32.35- 32.43; Sinclair 8.17–8.22; D J Cusine 'Letters of Obligation' (1991) 36 JLSS 349.
[2]   *Johnston v Little* 1960 SLT 129.
[3]   *Registration of Title Practice Book*, 8.14, 8.43.

18.38   As well as this basic requirement, letters of obligation will normally contain a responsibility to deliver a duly recorded discharge of a loan. A letter of obligation containing these terms is referred to as a classic letter of obligation. It is common for other obligations to be added to these, for example, delivery of a completion certificate for improvement works. There are dangers in doing this, particularly in respect of items which are not within the control of the seller or his solicitor[1]. It has been suggested by the Conveyancing Committee of the Law Society of Scotland that letters of obligation should never contain an obligation regarding a matter which is not within the solicitor's control[2].

[1]   McDonald 32.42, Sinclair 8.22, Gretton & Reid 9.26.
[2]   'Clarifying the classic Letter of Obligation' (2003) 48 JLSS Apr/26.

Delivery of valid conveyance

18.39   This involves the seller in delivering a conveyance of the property which meets the contractual requirements and is adequate to convey the interest in land being purchased.

Possession

18.40   The obligation of the seller at common law is only to give possession of the subjects of sale within a reasonable time of the date of entry. What is a reasonable time will depend on the circumstances of the particular case. It is usual, however, as noted at PARA **17.21**, to specify in the missives for actual vacant possession of the property to be given on the date of entry. The effect of this is that if the seller does not give entry on the due date the purchaser can resile.

Other terms of the contract

18.41   Missives of sale can contain a variety of provisions which are not covered by the obligations examined above. Examples would be the exhibition of a completion certificate for work undertaken on the property, or a warranty relating to central heating. The final obligation of the seller, then, is to comply with any terms of the missives not covered above.

Obligations of the purchaser

18.42   The principal obligation of the purchaser is to pay the purchase price and as a matter of general law that is the only obligation which is incumbent on him. It should be recalled that unless there is express provision to the contrary in the missives the purchaser's obligation is to pay within a reasonable time.

18.43   It is, of course, possible that the purchaser will undertake other obligations in the missives, eg to pay interest on late payment of the price or to apply for planning permission, and if this is done the purchaser must fulfil these additional obligations.

The purchaser's title following examination of title

18.44   Although examination of title involving scrutiny of the relevant deeds relating to the property and searches will disclose some of the possible defects in the seller's title, not all defects will be brought to light by this process. Thus, for example, naturally occurring incapacities affecting the seller (or one of the owners in the prescriptive progress), such as insanity or incapacity due to age, servitude rights over the property, latent defects in prior title and occupancy rights under the Matrimonial Homes (Family Protection) (Scotland) Act 1981 will not necessarily be disclosed by examination of title.

18.45 Clearly, to establish a complete absence of any such defects in title would require an extremely long and exhaustive investigation. In practice, then, armed with searches or reports, having closely examined the titles to the property and ancillary documents, having placed suitable protective conditions in the missives (eg relating to occupancy rights) and having received a Letter of Obligation, an assumption will be made by the purchaser's solicitor that, if all of these are satisfactory, it is safe to accept the title as one not affected by any incapacity of the seller or subject to any defect[1]. The result will be that the purchaser, on registration of his/her title, will get a good unchallengeable title to the property purchased[2].

1   Further protection for the purchaser being offered by warrandice; see CHAPTER **19**.
2   Providing, of course, that the Keeper shares the solicitor's view.

18.46 There is one exception to this that should be noted. Where a purchaser knows of a prior sale to another person who has not completed title his/her right to the property may be successfully challenged by that third party[1]. This happened in *Rodger (Builders) Ltd v Fawdry*[2]. In this case the defenders entered into missives to sell property to the pursuers. There was a delay in the payment of the price and the sellers purported to withdraw from the contract and subsequently sold the same property to a Mr Bell who completed title to it. The pursuers raised an action against the sellers arguing that their purported withdrawal had been unlawful and asking for Bell's title to be reduced. The court accepted that the withdrawal was ineffective and granted the reduction sought. The reason for this was that Bell knew of the sale to the pursuers and of all the circumstances surrounding the sellers' withdrawal. He was therefore not acting in good faith in relying on the sellers' assurances that the previous agreement was at an end and in failing to make proper enquiries of his own to establish that this was indeed the case. This rule, often referred to as the 'offside goal' rule, has recently undergone a possible change as controversial as recent changes to its namesake. In *Alex Brewster & Sons v Caughey* it was suggested that, as well applying in cases where the purchaser acquired knowledge of the prior right before conclusion of missives[3]:

'... the opinions in *Rodger (Builders)* are clear authority for the proposition that bad faith constituted by the acquisition of knowledge between the completion of a personal contractual obligation [ie conclusion of missives] and the completion of the real right by the registration of the conveyance is sufficient to justify reduction of that conveyance.'

1   Or the existence of any other personal right which was capable of being made real in respect of the property.
2   1950 SLT 345; see also *Trade Development Bank v Warriner & Mason (Scotland) Ltd* 1980 SLT 223; *Higgins v North Lanarkshire Council* 2001 SLT (Lands Tr) 2.
3   (2 May 2002, unreported), OH, per Lord Eassie at [73]. For a critical assessment of this extension see S Wortley, 'Double Sales and the Offside Trap' 2002 JR 291.

18.47   Where a purchaser has completed title by recording in the Register of Sasines the effect of reduction on this ground is to take title away from him/her. As we will see below the position is more complex where the purchaser has registered his title in the Land Register. As an alternative to reduction it may be possible to obtain an order of implement against a bad faith purchaser requiring them to implement the seller's obligation[1]. For example, in the *Rodger* scenario the pursuers could have sought an order requiring Bell to implement the defender's contractual obligation to sell to them.

1   *Davidson v Zani* 1992 SCLR 1001, in which case an order was granted requiring the bad faith purchaser to implement an option to buy granted in favour of a tenant by the seller.

Breach of obligations[1]

18.48   Where one of the parties is in breach of any of their obligations prior to settlement of the transaction the normal remedies are rescission or an action for implement of the obligation not complied with. In the case of rescission it may be necessary to issue an ultimatum to the party in default requiring compliance by a certain date before rescission takes place. The reason for this is that many of the obligations involved need only be fulfilled within a reasonable time unless clear provision is made in the missives that time is of the essence. Examples include the obligation to exhibit a good title and the obligation to pay the price. Any time limit fixed must be reasonable and what is reasonable will depend on the circumstances of each case[2].

1   McDonald 28.71-2879; Cusine & Rennie ch 8.
2   *Rodger (Builders) Ltd v Fawdry* 1950 SLT 345 at 350.

18.49   After settlement, provided that *restitutio in integrum* (ie restoration of the parties to their pre-contract positions) is still possible the appropriate remedy is rescission. Where *restitutio* is no longer possible the remedy is either action for specific implement or damages[1]. In cases of rescission, either before or after settlement, the party withdrawing is entitled to claim damages for any loss resulting from the breach.

1   Contract (Scotland) Act 1997, s 3.

CONVEYANCE OF THE PROPERTY

18.50   Missives merely constitute a binding contract to transfer heritage at some future date in exchange for payment of the price or other consideration. The actual transfer of the property is effected by a further document, referred to generally as a conveyance. At this stage, as we have already noted, the purchaser still has only a personal right in the property.

18.51   The fundamental requirement for such a deed is that it must be in writing[1], in particular it will normally take the form of a self-proving deed, with the signature of the granter being witnessed by one witness[2].

1   Requirements of Writing (Scotland) Act 1995, s 1(2).
2   Requirements of Writing (Scotland) Act 1995, s 3.

18.52   The same requirements as to contractual capacity apply to conveyances as apply to missives, with the additional requirement that the granter of the conveyance must have title to the land being transferred. That is, the granter's interest in the property must be extensive enough to allow him to sell it so that, for example, a tenant could not grant a valid conveyance of the property he leases.

18.53   The particular form of the conveyance will depend on the precise nature of the transaction. The two main types are:

1   *Disposition.* This is sometimes referred to as a special disposition as it conveys a particular piece of the seller's property, as opposed to a will, for example, which operates as a general disposition of all of a person's property[1].

2   *Contract of excambion.* This will be appropriate where the consideration for the purchase of a piece of land comprises in whole or in part another piece of heritage. The contract of excambion takes

the form of a document signed by both parties which has the effect of a reciprocal transfer of the pieces of land involved so that only one document is needed rather than two separate dispositions. The various clauses of these deeds and their effect will be discussed in CHAPTER 19.

¹   Previously under the feudal system of tenure a feu disposition or feu contract would be used to create a new relationship of superior and vassal; see CHAPTER 1.

EFFECT OF DELIVERY OF DEED OF CONVEYANCE

18.54   Until recently the general consensus was that even after a signed deed of conveyance had been delivered to the purchaser (or more usually the purchaser's solicitor) the purchaser still only had a personal right in respect of the property. In other words, even at this stage, the purchaser would have no rights against any other individual who obtained title to the property through the seller. Thus, for example it is quite possible for a seller to sell the same piece of property twice, with the person who completes title to the property first acquiring a good right against everyone else, including the other purchaser from the fraudulent seller¹. The first suggestion that this might not be the case came in *Gibson v Hunter Home Design*². There it was suggested that on delivery of a disposition some part of the right of property was parted with by the seller. The issue arose again in *Sharp v Thomson*³. In that case, the defenders had purchased a flat in Aberdeen from a building company. They paid the price of the property and took entry. However, it was not until approximately a year later that the purchaser's solicitors received an executed disposition of the property from the sellers. The purchaser's solicitors then went ahead and completed title to the property, but before they did this a floating charge held by a bank over the property of the builders of the flat crystallised. The effect of this was that all property and undertakings of the company at the date of crystallisation vested in the company liquidator, in this case Sharp. The question that arose for decision was whether at the time of crystallisation, the flat was part of the property and undertaking of the building company. Both the Outer⁴ and Inner Houses⁵ of the Court of Session took the view that it was. They adopted the view which was set out earlier, that the right of the purchaser at this stage was merely a personal right, that all property had to have an owner, and that since it was not the purchaser it had to be the seller. The case then went to an appeal to the House of Lords. The opinions in the House of Lords suggested that the matter could have been resolved simply on a question of statutory interpretation, in other words what did the word 'property' mean for the purposes of the precise statutory provision in the company's legislation which provided for transfer of property on crystallisation of a floating charge. Instead, however, Lords Clyde and Jauncey offered an analysis of the process of transfer of ownership of heritable property in Scots law. On the analogy of case law concerned with trusts and with establishing jurisdiction they took the view that once the disposition was delivered the sellers had divested themselves of the beneficial interest in the property, and could therefore no longer be described as the owners of the property. This suggests that at the time of delivery of the disposition this beneficial interest vests in some way in the purchaser. The difficulty with this analysis is that it was not clearly restricted to the precise circumstances of the case, and that the nature of this beneficial interest, and the time at which is it transferred is problematic. For example, one of the reasons for saying that the beneficial interest was transferred at the stage of delivery of the disposition was that after that stage the seller could no longer transact with the property except fraudulently. However, it can be argued that this same situation is reached as soon as missives are concluded; once that is done, if the seller purports to sell again, he or she does this in fraud of the intending purchaser.

[1]   Assuming they were not penalised for being in an 'offside' position.
[2]   1976 SC 23.
[3]   1997 SLT 636.
[4]   1994 SLT 1068.
[5]   1995 SLT 837.

18.55   In *Burnett's Trustees v Grainger*[1] the House of Lords reasserted the view expressed at the beginning of this section and treated *Sharp v Thomson* as being concerned solely with the interpretation of the legislation governing company insolvency. The result of this is that once a disposition is delivered the purchaser still has a personal right but the personal right is now based on the deed of conveyance. At this point the purchaser is then in a position to complete title at his own hand, without relying on a third party to do anything.

[1]   2004 SLT 513.

18.56   *Burnett's Trustees* involved a disposition by Burnett in favour of the Graingers. The disposition was delivered when the Graingers took entry. The disposition was not registered until 14 months later. In the meantime, Burnett was sequestrated and the trustee appointed in her bankruptcy registered a notice of title, despite knowing of the disposition in favour of the Graingers, which had the effect of conferring ownership on the trustee. In holding that the trustee had acquired ownership the House of Lords noted that delivery of a disposition does not transfer any real right in property and that there is no intermediate right in Scots law between a real right and a personal right. Reference was also made to the position of an adjudger in Scots law, since the effect of the bankruptcy legislation is to put the trustee in the position of an adjudger. On the basis of an analysis of the law relating to adjudgers it was held that the offside goal rule did not apply to adjudgers, and therefore could not apply against the trustee. Reference was also made to the problems caused for the reliability of the registers if someone could challenge a trustee's title on the basis of an unregistered transfer. If that was the case anyone buying from the trustee would have no way of knowing if there was someone holding such a right who might be able to challenge their rights in the property[1].

[1]   For a discussion of this problem and associated possibilities of fraud see SLC Discussion Paper 114, *Sharp v Thomson*, 2.13–2.14, Part 2 has a general discussion of the issues.

18.57   The Scottish Law Commission proposed reversing the decision in *Sharp v Thomson* in a discussion paper issued in 2001 as well as some associated reforms[1]. No report on this issue was published pending the House of Lords' decision in *Burnett's Trustees*.

[1]   Discussion Paper 114, *Sharp v Thomson*.

COMPLETION OF TITLE–REGISTRATION

18.58   The registers in which title is recorded or registered, as well as the Register of Inhibitions and Adjudications[1], the Books of Council and Session and some other registers[2], are maintained by a state official known as the Keeper of the Registers of Scotland, whose headquarters are situated at Meadowbank House in Edinburgh.

[1]   See PARA **18.22**.
[2]   For example the Register of Community Interests in Land. A full list can be found at www.ros.gov.uk.

18.59 Registering a legal document in the appropriate register can achieve several purposes. It can save the deed from being lost by preserving the original. As we have see in relation to property transactions, registration provides a formality whereby real rights in property are created.

18.60 Arguably, the most significant feature of the Scottish registers is that they are open to the public. This right of public access to the registers is of great importance. First of all, it safeguards the position of the person acquiring rights under the document in question by making these rights a matter of public record. As a real right is one that can be defended against anyone in the world, it is appropriate that anyone in the world has the right to check its existence, and this brings us to the second great advantage of public access. Not only does it protect the owner of legal rights, but it helps safeguard the position of a third party having legal dealings with that person. As we have seen, an intending purchaser of heritable property, before committing themselves legally, can find out what deeds (including security deeds) appear on the relevant register. They can also find out from the Register of Inhibitions and Adjudications whether there is any legal impediment against the seller that would prevent him from transferring his title.

Books of Council and Session

18.61 This register has two quite different functions: registration for preservation and registration for execution:

1   *Registration for preservation.* As the name suggests, the purpose of registration for preservation is to secure valuable legal documents against being lost or destroyed. The deed concerned may be any type of legal document, including deeds relating to heritable property. Registration may take place immediately after the document has been signed, or at any time thereafter. For a fee, the Keeper of the Registers in Scotland will keep the document in the safety of his vaults and issue in its place an official photocopy (called an 'extract') This extract is legally equivalent to the original deed and can be used in court or for any other legal purpose as if it were the original[1]. Also, provided that the requisite fee is paid, any number of extracts may be obtained, which can often be very useful.

2   *Registration for execution.* Preservation of documents is the principal function of the Books of Council and Session. However, if the document contains a consent to registration for execution, this process

can be carried out at the same time as registration for preservation. The Keeper holds on to the document in the usual way and issues an extract, but in this case he adds to the extract a warrant for all necessary action to enforce any sums payable (or any other obligation) under the deed, ie to proceed with diligence. Such an extract for execution has the force and effect of a decree of the Court of Session.

This process is known as *summary diligence*, ie it allows a person owed a legal obligation, usually a creditor, to bypass the usual process of first having their right established in court before proceeding with diligence. The reason is that the obligant has consented to the process in advance by signing a deed containing a consent to registration for execution. A clause containing such a consent is standard in many deeds, including leases and standard securities, where it can provide a valuable method of recovering rent or mortgage arrears.

1   Writs Execution (Scotland) Act 1877, s 5.

Register of Sasines

18.62   Prior to 1 April 2003 the process of completing title following sale of a property, in at least some areas of Scotland, required registration in the Register of Sasines. The Register of Sasines is a register of deeds which was first created in 1617. Until 1981 (when it was gradually replaced by the Land Register) the document of transfer of the property was sent through to the register, the deed was checked for any obvious errors and omissions, a photocopy of the deed was taken and retained in the register and the original returned to the purchaser's solicitor together with details of the date of registration, and the volume of the register in which a copy of the deed can be found. The register is divided up into 33 divisions, each corresponding to a (historical) county as these existed prior to the reorganisation of local government in Scotland in 1973. The copy deed is entered in the register for the appropriate county.

18.63   The consequences of recording are considered at PARAS **18.72ff**.

Land registration

18.64   The system of land registration was introduced into Scotland by the Land Registration (Scotland) Act 1979. Starting in 1981, the Land

Register was gradually introduced until it covered the whole of Scotland. What this means is that an operational date was fixed for particular counties, all transfers of land in that area after that date then had to be registered in the Land Register rather than being recorded in the Register of Sasines. The process of introduction was completed in April 2003.

18.65 The essential difference between the Land Register and Register of Sasines is that the Land Register is a register of title. In other words rather than simply containing a copy of a deed transferring land, the Land Register indicates who is the legal owner of the property and the act of registration is what gives rise to this ownership[1]:

'The scheme of the Act is that once the Keeper has given effect to a disposition or other deed by registration without exclusion of indemnity, the real right of the registered proprietor derives by force of statute from the fact of registration in the Land Register.'

[1] Per Lord President Hope in *Short's Trustees v Keeper of the Registers* 1994 SCLR 135 at 142A.

18.66 This statement of ownership is accompanied by a state guarantee or indemnity, which essentially guarantees that the person named in the Land Register as owner of the land is the legal and unchallengeable owner of the property. The consequence of this is that the interest of the owner cannot be affected, except in certain exceptional circumstances which will be considered below. A further corollary is that the Keeper of the Registers in Scotland has to be satisfied as to the validity of the purchaser's title before his or her name will be registered as owner of the property.

18.67 The procedure for Land Registration depends on whether the application for registration is the first application relating to the piece of land or the land is already registered.

First registration

18.68 On first registration the document of transfer is sent to the Keeper of the Registers in Scotland together with a completed application form, a prescriptive progress of title, any deeds containing real burdens or conditions affecting the property and any other relevant documentation. From this documentation are extracted: a description of the property which is transferred onto a title plan taken from Ordnance Survey maps, the owner(s) of the property and the price paid, details of any securities or other charges affecting the property and any real burdens and conditions affecting the property. These details are transferred to the Land Register and used to create a Title Sheet. In brief a Title Sheet contains the following elements:

– An Ordnance Survey plan showing the location of the property and the property boundary. This replaces the often imprecise verbal descriptions of properties which are found under the Register of Sasines.

– A property section describing the property and the interest being registered. As well as ownership interest; it is possible to register security interests, and also interests under a lease which is for a period in excess of 20 years.

– Details of the owners of the property in an ownership section.

– Details of any securities affecting the property.

– Details of any real burdens, servitudes etc affecting the property. The Keeper may excise some burdens which are contained in the deeds relating to property in compiling this section, on the understanding that some of the burdens and conditions will be obsolete[1].

Once the title sheet has been created, a copy of that sheet in the form of a Land Certificate is issued to the owner of the property.

---

[1]   Though see *M R S Hamilton Ltd v Keeper of the Registers of Scotland (No 4)* 2000 SLT 352 for some of the difficulties which may arise if burdens are excised in this way.

Transactions subsequent to first registration

18.69   Here all that is really required is the document of transfer of the interest concerned and an application form, as all the details of the property will be stored in the Land Register. In addition any documents or deeds which affect the land and have come into being since the register was last updated, eg a deed creating a servitude right affecting the property, must be forwarded so that the register can be altered to reflect the actual situation relating to the land. Aside from such alterations all that is involved is the substitution on the register of the new proprietor(s) in place of the seller(s). Once the registration process is completed a Land Certificate will be issued to the applicant.

18.70   In certain circumstances the Keeper of the Land Register may exclude indemnity; this means that ownership of the whole, or more commonly a part of the property[1] is not guaranteed, and therefore may be open to challenge.

[1]   For example, a small area of riverbed in *Safeway Stores plc v Tesco Stores Ltd* 2004 SLT 701.

Automated registration of title

18.71   A system of automated registration of title has been piloted in Scotland. Once introduced there will be no further need for paper deeds or hard copies of other documents, the whole process will be conducted online. There is a suggestion that this process might be introduced in 2006[1].

[1]   I Davies, 'Automated Registration of Title' (2003) 13 C & L 13 'Waste Paper' (2004) 49(5) JLSS May /54.

COMPLETION OF TITLE – CONSEQUENCES

18.72   The precise consequences of completion of title depend on whether an individual's title is recorded in the Register of Sasines or registered in the Land Register.

Register of Sasines

18.73   The fact that the purchaser acquires a real right on recording in the Register of Sasines does not mean that the title recorded there is beyond challenge. This is because, as noted above, the Register of Sasines is not a register of title and does not set out to conclusively determine who owns a particular piece of property. The mechanism for challenging a title recorded in the Register of Sasines, is to seek reduction of the deed purportedly effecting the transfer of the property. This can be done in certain circumstances created by a statute, for example gratuitous alienations in the case of bankruptcy, and also under the common law 'offside goal' rule[1]. Once the court decree of reduction is recorded in the register the title deriving from the reduced deed of transfer is nullified, along with any title deriving from it[2].

[1]   See PARAS **18.46–18.47**.
[2]   See also the discussion of redemption and pre-emption in CHAPTER **19**.

18.74   A further feature of recording in the Register of Sasines, is that if a title of the person who has done this is challenged, it is not sufficient to simply produce the recorded title; instead the person whose title is challenged must be able to produce a prescriptive progress of title to rebuff any complaints[1].

1   See PARAS **18.8–18.12**.

Land Register

18.75   Once a title is registered that title is guaranteed. This does not mean, however, that the register is necessarily entirely accurate. Inaccuracies might arise because of mistake in the description of the boundaries of a registered property so that it includes land actually owned by someone else[1], errors in generated in the register itself[2] or because the purchaser has scored an offside goal in registering his title. This illustrates what the Scottish Law Commission describes as the bijural nature of the system of land registration. The register identifies one person as the owner of the property, whilst underlying property law identifies someone else[3]. The obvious solution to this difficulty would be to allow changes to the register to reflect the underlying legal position, but doing this would undermine the stability and reliability of the register, so the current system restricts the scope of possible correction (referred to as rectification) and prioritises the registered owner (provided he or she is in possession) over the 'true' owner[4]. In the absence of rectification, a person who is disadvantaged may be eligible for compensation by way of indemnity, and such compensation may also be payable to someone who has suffered loss as a result of rectification. It will be possible to seek rectification for 20 years following the date of registration. This has the consequence that in some ways a registered title with no exclusion of indemnity takes longer to secure than a Sasines title or a title registered with exclusion of indemnity. In the last two cases any defects are remedied by ten years' possession[5].

1   See *Higgins v North Lanarkshire Council* 2001 SLT (Lands Tr) 2.
2   For example the mysterious technical fault in *Safeway Stores plc v Tesco Stores Ltd* 2004 SLT 701.
3   See Scottish Law Commission Discussion Paper 125, *Land Registration: Void and Voidable Titles* (2004).
4   The position and its possible disadvantages is discussed at paras 4.1–4.10 of *Land Registration: Void and Voidable Titles*, above.
5   D Johnston, *Prescription and Limitation*, 15.63; see also CHAPTER **3**.

RECTIFICATION

18.76 The Keeper of the Registers in Scotland is empowered to correct inaccuracies in the Land Register to reflect the true underlying position by rectifying entries in the register. Where rectification would result in detriment to the proprietor in possession, for example, by depriving them of some of their land, the register can only be rectified in the following circumstances[1]:

1   To note an overriding interest or correct an entry relating to such an interest. Overriding interests are interests such as servitude rights affecting the property or occupancy rights under the Matrimonial Homes (Family Protection) (Scotland) Act 1981.

2   If the proprietor in possession agrees to the rectification. The term proprietor means someone who owns the land or has a similar interest in it, for example the tenant under a long lease, but not the holder of a security over the land unless they have entered into possession of the land in exercise of their powers on default[2]. A person can become a proprietor even without applying to be entered in the register as such, as when a computer error extended the boundaries of the land acquired by the purchaser beyond those stated in the disposition transferring ownership[3].

The requirement for possession involves actual possession of the land rather than simply possession of a right over land, such as a security right. The nature of possession required has been distinguished from that required for prescriptive possession, and it has been suggested by implication that possession might arise where any rectification would disrupt the activities or enjoyment of the registered proprietor. The nature of the activities required to establish possession will be different depending on the type of property concerned. It has been suggested that possession[4]:

'… imports some significant element of physical control, combined with the relevant intent; it suggests actual use or enjoyment, to a more than minimal extent, of the subjects in question as one's own.'

In the case from which this extract is taken making plans for the land and making enquiries of the local planning authority were not regarded as sufficient to establish possession. Finally, the answer to the question 'when must the proprietor be in possession?' is not clear. In *Safeway Stores plc v Tesco Stores Ltd*[5] the suggestion was that consideration would have to be given to an (indeterminate) tract of time preceding any application for rectification[6].

3   If the error in the register was caused by fraud or carelessness on the part of the proprietor in possession. The fraud or carelessness referred to here is fraud or carelessness in the process of registration of title and will cover actions on behalf of the proprietor by his solicitor[7]. An example of this would be carelessness in answering the questions on the form required to secure registration of a title[8]. There will be no fraud or carelessness if the process of registration does not involve any careless or fraudulent statements even though the underlying transaction was secured by fraud. Where it is claimed that the proprietor has been careless it will be necessary to spell out the nature of this carelessness, the appropriate standard of care and the ways in which the proprietor or his solicitors have fallen below this standard[9]. It will also be necessary to identify some act or omission on behalf of the applicant which was reasonably foreseeably likely to result in the inaccuracy and it must have been possible for the applicant to take steps to avoid the inaccuracy arising[10]. It is not carelessness or fraud to rely on a description of a property in the register which an applicant knows to be mistaken and which confers a wider right than that conferred in the documentation which underlies the registration. In *Dougbar Properties Ltd v Keeper of the Registers of Scotland*[11] the assignee of a lease was aware that the registered title conferred rights over an area of land let to another tenant which were not conferred by the actual lease as amended by a Minute of Agreement. It was held that this knowledge did not mean that the proprietor had been fraudulent or careless[12].

4   If the rectification is made in respect of a title or part of a title from which the indemnity has been excluded.

1   Land Registration (Scotland) Act 1979, s 9(3).
2   *Kaur v Singh* 1998 SCLR 849.
3   *Safeway Stores plc v Tesco Stores Ltd* 2004 SLT 701.
4   *Safeway Stores plc v Tesco Stores Ltd* 2004 SLT 701 at 720, Lord Hamilton.
5   2004 SLT 701.
6   For possible further complications arising from prioritising possession see Professor Gretton's commentary following the report of *Kaur v Singh* 1998 SCLR 849.
7   Scottish Law Commission Discussion Paper 125, *Land Registration: Void and Voidable Titles* (2004), para 3.37.
8   *Stevenson-Hamilton's Exrs v McStay (No 2)* 2001 SLT 694.

9 *Wilson v Keeper of the Registers of Scotland* 2000 SLT 267; though it is not clear that this was done in *Stevenson-Hamilton'd Exrs v McStay (No 2)* 2001 SLT 694.
10 *Dougbar Properties Ltd v Keeper of the Registers of Scotland* 1999 SCLR 458.
11 1999 SCLR 458.
12 Though note that this was a case involving a claim for indemnity. The register had been rectified to reflect the true position as, at the time of rectification, there was therefore no proprietor in possession.

18.77 If the register is rectified, the rectification will take effect from the date of rectification and will not be retrospective[1]. This would mean, for example, that if an area of land was returned to someone as a result of rectification, they could not claim for damage done to the land by the then registered proprietor before the date of rectification.

1 *Stevenson-Hamilton's Exrs v McStay* 1999 SLT 1175; *Keeper of the Registers of Scotland v M R S Hamilton* 2000 SLT 352.

18.78 If an inaccuracy is brought to the attention of the Keeper there are two possibilities. The first is that the register is rectified (eg if there is no proprietor in possession); the second that there is no rectification because there is a proprietor in possession. Both possibilities involve loss being caused to someone. In the first case it is the registered proprietor who has lost all or part of a title guaranteed by the register; in the second it is the person refused rectification whose legal rights to the property have been denied by the process of registration of title. Both are entitled to claim compensation by way of indemnity for the loss.

18.79 Indemnity is payable, subject a long list of exceptions, where somebody suffers a loss as a result of [1]:
1 Rectification of the register.
2 A refusal or omission by the Keeper to make rectification. Although this wording might suggest that indemnity is payable only where the Keeper has power to rectify but refuses to do so, it is now clear that it can also be claimed where the Keeper has no power to rectify, for example because of the existence of a proprietor in possession[2].
3 Loss or destruction of a document while lodged with the Keeper.
4 An error or omission in a Land or Charge Certificate or in certain other types of information given by the Keeper. This provision would apply where, for example, as a result of error a Land Certificate did not reflect the true position in the underlying title sheet[3].

1 Land Registration (Scotland) Act 1979, s 12.

2   *Short's Trustee v Keeper of Registers of Scotland* 1996 SLT 166.
3   *Keeper of the Registers of Scotland v M R S Hamilton* 2000 SLT 352.

18.80   The exceptions to entitlement to indemnity include:

1   A title which has been reduced, particularly under certain statutory provisions, including the Bankruptcy (Scotland) Act 1985[1].
2   Loss resulting from an inability to enforce a servitude or real burden entered on the register.
3   Loss arising from an error or omission in noting an overriding interest.
4   Cases where the claimant has caused the loss by his own fraudulent or careless act[2]. In *Dougbar Properties Ltd v Keeper of the Registers of Scotland*, discussed above, the registered proprietors having, as noted, not been guilty of either of these were entitled to indemnity even though their rectified title actually reflected what they knew to be the true position, benefiting from an error in the register which wrongly gave them more than they were entitled to[3].

1   Land Registration (Scotland) Act 1979, s 12(3)(b); though see the comments on the apparent pointlessness of his provision in *Short's Trustee v Keeper of Registers of Scotland* 1996 SLT 166.
2   See the discussion above at PARA **18.76**.
3   Scottish Law Commission Discussion Paper 125, *Land Registration: Void and Voidable Titles* (2004), paras 7.5–7.6 discusses whether this position is satisfactory.

18.81   Finally, in the context of land registration, it is still possible for an aggrieved party to have a transfer of property in favour of another set aside. For example a trustee in bankruptcy may have a disposition by the bankrupt which was effectively a gratuitous alienation set aside, similarly an aggrieved party may make use of the 'offside goal' rule to have a disposition set aside. However, the effect of this in the system of land registration is quite different from what would normally happen in the system of recording in the Register of Sasines. In land registration, the aggrieved party cannot have their name substituted as owner unless their case falls within one of the specific circumstances in which rectification of the register is permissible. Instead, what is likely to happen, is that the aggrieved party will be entitled to compensation payable by the Keeper of the Land Register[1]. However, this is not the only remedy available to the aggrieved party. He may also be able to require the person who is the registered proprietor to reconvey the property to him. This is certainly the case where a trustee in bankruptcy is concerned[2] and may also be available in other cases[3]. The consequence of this is, of course, that the aggrieved party can then enter the register as registered proprietor and the previously registered proprietor has no claim for indemnity as their loss of title was not the result of rectification or any other act where this can be claimed. The result, therefore, is similar to that which applies where a title is recorded in the Register of Sasines.

1   *Short's Trustee v Keeper of Registers of Scotland* 1996 SLT 166.
2   *Short's Trustee v Chung (No 2)* 1999 SLT 751.
3   See Scottish Law Commission Discussion Paper 125, *Land Registration: Void and Voidable Titles* (2004), para 6.16; *Stair Memorial Encyclopaedia*, vol 18, 700; *Davidson v Zani* 1992 SCLR 1001, discussed above at PARA **18.47**.

CHAPTER 19

Clauses in deeds

19.1 As indicated in CHAPTER 18 a large part of examination of title consists in the examination of prior deeds affecting the property. Although this process will become less important over time it will still be necessary for the foreseeable future in cases where land is to be registered in the Land Register for the first time. This chapter, then, will consider the structure of the main types of deeds.

DISPOSITIONS AND FEUDAL GRANTS

19.2 Dispositions and feudal grants of property have a large number of common clauses; the additional clauses found in a feu grant will be considered at the end of this section. Although no new feudal grants can be made after 28 November 2004 the titles to properties being registered for the first time may contain such deeds.

Narrative clause[1]

19.3 The narrative clause is the introductory clause in the deed and will contain details of the grantor, the consideration and the grantee. The grantor must be described in such a way as to identify him clearly. In most cases all this involves is his name and address, though where the grantor has moved since the transfer in his favour was granted, the new address will be given and the grantor linked to the previous deed by the phrase 'previously residing at'. Similarly, if the grantor's name has changed, for example on marriage, the new name will be linked to the old. If the grantor is acting in any special capacity (eg as a trustee) this will also be mentioned here.

1 McDonald 7.2–7.5; Sinclair 9.3–9.4.

19.4 In the case of feu grants the grantor had to have a title either recorded in the Register of Sasines or registered in the Land Register; in the case of a disposition this is not essential and the grantor without such a recorded or registered title can deduce title[1] from a previous owner who had such a title by a deduction of title clause[2]. This clause will normally appear after the clause of entry, and involves linking the title of the proprietor without a recorded or registered title back to the last proprietor with such a title by reference to any intermediate document or documents which transfer ownership but for one reason or another (perhaps because it is not appropriate) have not themselves been recorded. Examples would be where an executor who has not recorded title in his own name links title back to the deceased via the confirmation, or the holder of an unrecorded disposition uses this as a link back to the grantor of that deed who had a recorded title. Deduction of title is not necessary where the transfer involves a title which has already been registered in the Land Register[3]. A deduction of title clause is still necessary where a disposition will result in first registration of a title, but if the clause is missing or defective it can be made good by producing the links in title to the Keeper of the Registers of Scotland[4].

1 Conveyancing (Scotland) Act 1924, s 3.
2 Conveyancing (Scotland) Act 1924, Sch A, Form 1, see Halliday 37-06 to 37-11; Sinclair 9.7.
3 Land Registration (Scotland) Act 1979, s 15.
4 *Registration of Title Practice Book*, 5.75.

19.5 The consideration involved will, in most cases, be the payment of money, though it may involve some other consideration or, indeed, no consideration at all. In this last case it may be expressed to be for 'love, favour and affection'. In the case of feu grants the usual consideration used to be payment of a feuduty. After 1 September 1974 it has no longer been possible to create new feuduties, although other conditions could still be imposed on the vassal[1]. The abolition of the feudal system means, of course, that there will be no new feudal grants.

1 Land Tenure Reform (Scotland) Act 1974, s 1; see also CHAPTER 14.

19.6   If there is an agreement in the missives to apportion the price between heritage and moveables the consideration appearing in the disposition or feu grant will be the amount apportioned to heritage.

19.7   Finally, the narrative clause will identify the grantee of the deed. Normally this will be done in the same way as identification of the grantor.

Dispositive clause[1]

19.8   The dispositive clause is often described as the ruling clause in any grant or disposition. The reason for this is that this clause is the one which determines the nature and extent of the rights in property transferred by the deed. This clause must therefore contain a description of the property, details of any reservations in favour of the grantor and any real burdens affecting the property. Restrictions on the use of the property, or any other statement affecting the interest transferred found elsewhere in the deed will be ineffective. There are four main elements found in the dispositive clause:
(a)   words of conveyance;
(b)   designation of the grantee;
(c)   description of the property:
(d)   qualifications of the grant or transfer.

[1]   Gretton & Reid, 11.2-11.16; Sinclair 9.5-9.6.

Words of conveyance

19.9   No special word or form of words is necessary as long as what is said indicates a clear present intention on the part of the grantor to transfer the property to the grantee[1]. The precise form of words will depend on the nature of the deed. In dispositions the word 'dispone' is normally used, though not legally required, whereas 'in feu farm dispone' was common in feu grants.

[1]   Conveyancing (Scotland) Act 1874, s 27.

The grantee

19.10 The grantee will already have been identified in the narrative clause. This section of the dispositive clause will, however, contain additional details relating to the grantee and the rights in property he/she is obtaining. It will indicate whether the property is being transferred to the grantee acting in any special capacity, eg as a trustee. It will also usually contain a destination to the 'executors and assignees' of the grantee, though this is unnecessary as it would be implied by law in any event. A destination is essentially a mechanism to determine what will happen to the property on the death of the grantee. Where a disposition is granted in favour of a husband and wife (though also in other cases) it is common to find a survivorship destination. This is usually in the form of a conveyance to: 'A and B equally between them and to the survivor of them.' The effect of this is that if A dies before B then A's share of the property will go to B. A survivorship destination does not prevent A or B selling their share of the common property during their lifetime, though their ability to avoid the destination by a provision in a will or other testamentary document is limited[1].

[1]   See H Hiram, *The Scots Law of Succession*, 6.49–6.57 for a detailed discussion.

Description of the property[1]

19.11 As the dispositive clause is conclusive as to the extent of the property obtained by the grantee, it is clearly of great importance that the description of the property is accurate and that it reflects the prior agreement between the grantor and grantee. There are a variety of ways of describing property, though it should be noted that whichever of these is used it will normally be preceded by the address of the property, and, in the case of flats, the position of the flat. The classification below is derived from Halliday[2].

[1]   Halliday ch 33; McDonald ch 8; Gretton & Reid ch 12.
[2]   Halliday ch 33, judicially approved in *Beneficial Bank plc v McConnachie* 1996 SLT 413 at 416, per Lord President Hope.

GENERAL DESCRIPTION

19.12   A general description may refer to the general name by which a property is or was known. The problem with this type of description, which is often found in older deeds, can be that as time passes it becomes increasingly difficult to establish precisely the area of land, and especially the boundaries, which the general name includes. For example, it may now be very difficult, if not impossible, to define accurately the boundaries of a piece of land described by a general name in the Eighteenth century. A description of a property by reference to its postal address would also normally be classified as a general description[1].

[1]   Lord President Hope notes the possibility that a postal description of a flat may be a particular description: *Beneficial Bank plc v McConnachie* 1996 SLT 413.

PARTICULAR DESCRIPTION

19.13   This consists of a precise description of the property by reference to its boundaries and for this reason it is sometimes referred to as a bounding title. There are a number of elements which can be found in particular descriptions. These include:

(a)   Reference to any physical feature forming part or all of the boundaries to the property, for instance, a road or a fence. Measurements for the boundaries may or may not be given, and if they are will usually be expressed in such a way as to leave a little leeway (generally by the addition of the words 'or thereby' after each measurement)[1].

(b)   The area of the property may be referred to. As this is of little use on its own it will usually be combined with one of the other elements.

(c)   The clause may refer to a plan annexed to the deed which shows the boundaries. Historically there was a problem in identifying property in this way. Until 1934 no record of plans annexed to deeds was kept in the Register of Sasines so that if the principal deed was lost, and this was the only form of description used, problems could arise. From 1924 this problem could be overcome by lodging a duplicate plan in the Register[2].

[1]   Such measurements must now be metric: see *Registration of Title Practice Book*, 4.49 ff.
[2]   Conveyancing (Scotland) Act 1924, s 48.

19.14   In practice it is common in framing a particular description to use more than one of these elements, and, in some cases, all three. This, in turn, can give rise to problems if there are inconsistencies between different elements of the description. For example there may be inconsistency between the boundaries and measurements stated in the deed and the attached plan, or a boundary may be expressed to run for a certain distance along a feature, but the actual distance differs from that in the deed. Where such disagreements arise the courts will attempt to give effect to the intentions of the parties. There are some general rules used in cases of conflict[1], and applying these to the examples above would suggest that the measurements stated in the deed would be preferred in the first example[2] and the actual physical boundary in the second. Difficulties can also arise as to interpretation where a physical feature is stated to be a boundary. For example, if the boundary is stated to be a road, does the property end at the near side of the road, the middle of the road or the far side of the road? Again, the courts have developed a series of presumptions[3], and these would mean that the road was excluded from the property unless it was a public road, in which case the boundary would be the middle of the road.

1   Halliday 33-13; McDonald 8.18.
2   *Anderson v Harrold* 1991 SCLR 135.
3   Gordon, ch 4.

19.15   Because of these problems great care is necessary in framing particular descriptions. Even the use of a measured boundary referring to physical features, statement of area and reference to a plan may still leave room for doubt over the precise location of a boundary[1].

1   *Suttie v Baird* 1992 SLT 133.

DESCRIPTION BY REFERENCE AT COMMON LAW

19.16   At common law it is possible to describe subjects by simply referring to an earlier deed in which they are fully described. The precise requirements for this are unclear[1], though the basic requirement seems to be that the deed referred to for the full description is sufficiently identified. In one case this was held to be achieved by inclusion of the family name of the grantor, the full name of the grantee and the date of recording[2].

1   Halliday 33-14; McDonald 8.20.
2   *Matheson v Gemmell* (1903) 5F 448 at 451, per Lord McLaren. In this case the description of the prior deed was considered adequate even though the wife of the grantor was described, in error, as being the grantor.

DESCRIPTION BY REFERENCE TO A GENERAL NAME

19.17   There is a statutory provision[1] which allows a general name to be created for a particular piece of land. Once this is done the property is in future referred to simply by the general name. In practice this type of description is uncommon.

[1]   Titles to Land Consolidation (Scotland) Act 1868, s 13.

STATUTORY DESCRIPTION BY REFERENCE

19.18   This is the type of description which is most commonly encountered in practice, and consists of a reference to an earlier deed which contains a particular description of the property. As this is a procedure regulated by statute[1], the requirements set out there must be fulfilled to have a valid statutory description by reference. It should be noted that even if the precise terms of the statutory provisions are not met the description given may be adequate as a description by reference at common law or as a general description (eg for the purposes of the latter, the address of the property may be sufficient).

[1]   Conveyancing (Scotland) Act 1874, s 61; Conveyancing (Scotland) Act 1924, s 8 and Sch D.

19.19   The principal requirements for a statutory description by reference are, firstly, a statement of the county, or if appropriate, the burgh and county in which the property is situated. This refers to the county in which the property is situated for the purposes of registration, reflecting historical local authority boundaries. The second requirement is reference to a deed containing a full particular description of the property. It is not adequate to refer to another deed which contains only a description by reference. The deed must be clearly identified and this will involve stating the type of deed, the parties, the date of recording, the division of the Register of Sasines in which it is recorded and, if necessary to avoid possible confusion, the volume in which the deed is recorded and the folio number. This last would be necessary if there were two deeds of the same type involving the same parties recorded on the same date, although failure to include it would not vitiate the description by reference provided that the rest of the information given was sufficient to identify the prior deed[1].

[1]   Conveyancing (Scotland) Act 1924, s 8(3).

DESCRIPTION IN REGISTRATION OF TITLE

19.20 In transactions inducing first registration the property will usually be described in the same way as it would be in a sasines transaction, ie in most cases simply by reference to a previous deed, or, in new houses, with a particular description or plan. However, in applying for registration the applicant must provide the Keeper of the Registers of Scotland with sufficient information to allow the property to be identified by reference to the Ordnance Survey map[1]. This information need not be contained wholly in the disposition in favour of the applicant, and deficiencies may be made good from other sources. In transactions involving property which is already registered all that is necessary to describe the property is a reference to the number of the title sheet for that property[2], though the postal address should also be included[3].

1   Land Registration (Scotland) Act 1979, s 4(2)(a).
2   Land Registration (Scotland) Act 1979, s 15(1).
3   *Registration of Title Practice Book*, 5.28.

CONCLUSION

19.21 However it is done, the description of the property should include the whole rights of property which are being transferred. This is true not only of the description in the disposition in favour of a purchaser, but also of the description in any prior titles affecting the property, particularly those in the progress of title. This means that if the transfer is to include any interests in land which need to be specifically mentioned to effect a transfer (for example) salmon fishings, the description should expressly include these. It should also be borne in mind that if a tenement flat is being purchased and the understanding is that there will be a right of common property in the roof, *solum*, walls etc, this should also be expressly provided for, otherwise the law of the tenement will apply[1].

1   See CHAPTER 11.

Qualifications of the grant or transfer

19.22 Qualifications of the grant or transfer can take a variety of forms. The main examples are reservations of rights in favour of the grantor; real burdens; and conditions and servitudes. These can all be created both in feu grants and in dispositions. Only the first two are considered here; servitudes, which of course do not have to be created by a formal deed, are considered in CHAPTER 13.

RESERVATIONS

Reservation of minerals[1]

19.23   Minerals lying under land are a separate tenement in land and are therefore capable of separate ownership. It is common to find that ownership of the surface and ownership of the underlying minerals has been split. This is usually achieved by way of a reservation of minerals inserted into a disposition or feu grant. The effect of this is to reserve ownership of the minerals to the grantor of the deed, usually the superior since most reservations are found in feu grants, though he may then transfer them to a third party. If there is no express reservation of the minerals the person owning the surface will also, subject to statutory provisions mentioned below, own the minerals.

[1]   Halliday 34-01 to 34-03; McDonald ch 9; see also PARA **9.19FF**.

19.24   The nature of the right reserved will depend on the precise terms of the reservation. Normally this will reserve a right of property in the minerals and a right to work them, though the latter is implied in the former. Where a right to work the minerals is reserved this implies a right only to work them underground; a right to enter onto the property to work and/or transport the minerals over it must be specifically created. Rights of support and to compensation for damage caused by underground workings together with the answer to the question: 'What is a mineral?' are considered in CHAPTER 9.

Right of pre-emption[1]

19.25   A right of pre-emption is a form of real burden which requires the owner of the property, before selling it, first to offer it to the person in whose favour the right is reserved. This would normally be a superior. Rights of pre-emption in favour of a superior survive the abolition of the feudal system if, before 28 November 2004, the superior registered a notice either realloting the right (which is in the nature of a real burden on the land) to land which the superior still owned[2] or, if the superior did not own land, continuing it as a personal real burden[3]. Rights of pre-emption can also be created in non-feudal transfers. The terms of the right, as with other real burdens, must be clear enough to allow the land owner to know exactly what the burden is, for example the price to be paid by the holder of the right[4].

[1]   McDonald 18.30 and 18.52.
[2]   Abolition of Feudal Tenure (Scotland) Act 2000, s 18.
[3]   Abolition of Feudal Tenure (Scotland) Act 2000, s 18A.
[4]   *Grampian Joint Police Board v Pearson* 2001 SLT 734.

19.26   There are two options for someone who wishes to sell land burdened by a right of pre-emption. The first of these is to obtain an undertaking from the person entitled to exercise the right not to do so for a fixed period of time. If the land is transferred and the transferee registers title within that period the pre-emption right is extinguished unless it is in the form of a rural housing burden[1]. The alternative requires that an offer is made to sell the land to the person entitled to the pre-emption right. If they do not accept within 21 days then the right is extinguished unless it is in the form of a rural housing burden[2]. It is the corollary of these provisions that failure to comply with them means that, as well as the possible consequences noted below, the right of pre-emption will continue in existence. Note that these provisions only apply where the right of pre-emption was a feudal right and has been continued as explained above or where it was created in a non-feudal transfer of land after 1 September 1974. Non-feudal rights created before that date require an offer to sell to be made to the person holding the right if the property is being sold, but the right is not extinguished if the offer is not accepted.

[1]   Title Conditions (Scotland) Act 2003, s 83; see PARA **14.19**.
[2]   Title Conditions (Scotland) Act 2003, s 84.

19.27   Where land is being sold to a tenant exercising their right to buy the existence of a right of pre-emption is no impediment to this exercise[1]. Rights of pre-emption will not affect the exercise of the community right to buy or the crofting community right to buy. In both cases the right is suspended during the purchase process and revives once this is completed or the community body fails to complete the purchase[2].

[1]   *Ross and Cromarty District Council v Patience* 1997 SLT 463.
[2]   Land Reform (Scotland) Act 2003, ss 65 & 84.

19.28   Except as noted in the previous paragraph, failure to offer the property to someone having a right of pre-emption before completing a sale means that any disposition granted by the seller can be reduced at the instance of the person holding the right[1]. Following such reduction the person holding the right of pre-emption will not be entitled to buy the land affected unless the clause creating the right provides for this[2]. A right of pre-emption is a title condition in terms of the Title Conditions (Scotland) Act 2003, and so application may be made to the Lands Tribunal for discharge[3].

[1]   *Matheson v Tinney* 1989 SLT 535; see also the discussion of rectification of the Land Register in PARAS **18.76–18.80**.
[2]   *Roebuck v Edmunds* 1992 SLT 1055.
[3]   See, for example, *Banff and Buchan DC v Earl of Seafield's Estate* 1988 SLT (Lands Tr) 21; see also CHAPTER **14**.

Right of redemption[1]

19.29   A right of redemption is a right on the part of the person to whom it is reserved (again probably the superior) to reacquire the property, either on the happening of a specified event or at his own discretion. The reservation of the right will also normally specify the price (if any) to be paid, or a formula for ascertaining the price, eg by arbitration. Rights of redemption created before 1 September 1974 exist in perpetuity; rights created after that date which are exercisable either on the happening of an event which is bound to happen or at the option of the holder prescribe in 20 years[2]. Rights of redemption are also title conditions which may be varied by the Lands Tribunal. Rights of redemption created in favour of a superior can be continued after the demise of the feudal system by the means explained above in connection with the right of pre-emption. Though rights of redemption are rare, they are serious for the potential purchaser, who should ensure that any such right will be waived prior to his/her purchase.

[1]   McDonald 15.10.
[2]   Land Tenure Reform (Scotland) Act 1974, s 12.

REAL BURDENS

19.30   Most of the material relating to these will be found in CHAPTER **14**. While the system of completing title by recording in the Register of Sasines continued, the position was that once real burdens had been created they had to be repeated or referred to in subsequent deeds relating to the property. Statutory intervention meant that it was not necessary to repeat them at length in a deed of transfer; instead there could be a reference to a recorded deed which did describe them at length, and this was achieved in the same way as in a statutory description by reference. The need for repetition or reference will continue for deeds which will trigger first registration. Once the property has been registered in the Land Register a reference in a deed to the title number, as well as sufficing to describe the property, is sufficient to incorporate real burdens and conditions noted on the title sheet[1].

[1]   Land Registration (Scotland) Act 1979, s 15(2).

Clause of entry

19.31   This clause simply states the date when the grantee obtains entry to the property. If no clause of entry is stated in the deed, entry will be at the first term of Whitsunday (28 May) or Martinmas (28 November) following the date or last date of the conveyance, unless there is a clear contrary intention in the deed[1].

[1]   Conveyancing (Scotland) Act 1874, s28; Term and Quarter Days (Scotland) Act 1990, s 1(1)(a).

Assignation of writs

19.32   The assignation of writs clause made explicit the right of the grantee to call upon the grantor or his predecessors for production of any deeds necessary to defend his interest in the property. Production of such deeds might, of course, be necessary to enable the grantee to demonstrate a prescriptive and unchallengeable right to the property, for example in the event of sale or challenge to his title by a third party. It is no longer necessary to include a clause of assignation of writs as there is now a statutory obligation on anyone in possession of deeds relating to any land to make these available to anyone who has, or is entitled to acquire, a real right in the land[1].

[1]   Abolition of Feudal Tenure (Scotland) Act 2000, s 66.

Assignation of rents

19.33   The effect of this clause was to transfer the right to receive any rents payable on the property to the grantee. Such a clause is no longer necessary as a result of s 16(3)(a) of the Land Registration (Scotland) Act 1979, which imports an implied term into the deed.

Obligation of relief

19.34   The effect of the obligation of relief was to relieve the grantee of all feuduties and local and public burdens (eg council tax or rates) payable in respect of the land prior to the date of entry. This effect is now achieved by s 16(3)(b) of the Land Registration (Scotland) Act 1979 and a specific clause is no longer necessary (and, of course, feuduties came to an end on 28 November 2004).

Warrandice[1]

19.35   Warrandice is a personal guarantee on the part of the grantor of the deed to the effect that:

1   The grantee will not be evicted from the whole or any part of the subjects conveyed because of any defect in title. In this context mere lack of title is insufficient to found a claim based on warrandice; there must also be eviction in the form of a court decree against the grantee, or a court action to which the grantee has no defence[2]. It is not enough that there is a possibility of a challenge to the grantee's title, there must be an actual challenge, though the action for breach of warrandice can be raised without actual removal from the property[3].

2   There exist no real rights affecting the subjects conveyed which are adverse to the interests of the grantee and of which the grantee was unaware at the date of delivery of the deed in his favour. Such a situation might arise, for example, where a right of way which substantially interfered with the grantee's use or enjoyment of the property was discovered[4].

---

[1]   Halliday 4-31 to 4-40; McDonald 10.8-10.20; K Reid 'Warrandice in the Sale of Land' in D Cusine (ed) *A Scots Conveyancing Miscellany* 152; Reid & Gretton 18.05–18.13.

[2]   Reid *(above)* p 157; *Watson v Swift & Co's JF* 1986 SLT 217 at 220H.

[3]   *Clark v Lindale Homes Ltd* 1994 SLT 1053; *Mutch v MavisbankProperties Ltd* 2002 SLT (Sh Ct) 91.

19.36   The effect of the guarantee is that the grantor is bound to indemnify the grantee if either of these situations arises. The practical value of warrandice therefore depends on the ability of the grantor to pay compensation, and, perhaps more fundamentally, the ability of the grantee to find the grantor at the time when the claim arises. The grantee's position will be strengthened if the defect is something which should have been discovered by his solicitor, in which case a claim may lie against him for professional negligence. How far and in what circumstances the grantee is protected by warrandice depends on the degree of warrandice involved. There are three degrees of warrandice: absolute, fact and deed and simple.

19.37   Absolute warrandice is an absolute guarantee that nothing will happen to interfere with the grantee's property rights. Therefore, if any interference does take place, whether or not arising from a cause under the control of the grantor, the grantee will be entitled to compensation. This form of warrandice is implied in all transfers of land for valuable consideration (and, therefore, all sales), and is the form of warrandice implied by statute to be conferred by the normal warrandice clause found in deeds which takes the form 'I/We grant warrandice'[1].

1   Titles to Land Consolidation (Scotland) Act 1868, s 8 and Sch B1.

19.38   Warrandice from fact and deed is a guarantee against any loss caused by or arising out of any action by the grantor, whether the action is past present or future. This is the form of warrandice usually granted by trustees.

19.39   Simple warrandice provides the lowest form of protection for the grantee. It merely guarantees that the grantee will not suffer loss as a result of a future voluntary act by the grantor. Simple warrandice would be appropriate in a gratuitous transaction.

19.40   Where no warrandice is provided for in the deed the appropriate degree will be implied. So in a sale absolute warrandice would be implied. On the other hand an express statement of a certain degree of warrandice supersedes any implied degree, so that a provision for simple warrandice in a sale would supersede absolute warrandice.

19.41   It is worth noting that as well as relying on the warrandice contained in the transfer of property, the purchaser will also be able to rely on the seller's obligations undertaken in the missives, at least to the extent these have not been terminated[1]. In order for a purchaser to sue, for example for breach of the seller's obligation to provide a good title, it is, of course, not necessary that they are first evicted from their property.

1   A Steven, 'Eviction Evicted? Warrandice after the Contract (Scotland) Act 1997', 1998 SLT (News) 283; see PARA **17.42**.

Certificate of value

19.42   This certificate is included for the purpose of assessment of stamp duty land tax. Stamp duty land tax is currently payable at three different rates in three bands above the threshold value of £60,000 for residential properties and £150,000 for non-residential properties[1]. The duty is payable on the whole consideration, for example if the consideration is £61,000, stamp duty land tax is paid not just on the excess over the threshold figure, ie £1,000, but on the whole £61,000.

1   The £150,000 limit also applies to residential properties in disadvantaged areas: Finance Act 2001, s 99; Stamp Duty (Disadvantaged Areas) Regulations 2001 (SI 2001/3747).

Testing clause

19.43   Although all that is required for a valid disposition is that it is signed on the last page by the grantor it is common for the signature to take place in the presence of a witness. This makes the document self proving, avoiding any question as to whether it was in fact signed by the grantor[1]. The testing clause simply records details of the execution of a self proving deed, in this case a disposition. Thus it contains details of the place and date of signature by the grantor(s) and details sufficient to identify the witnesses to these signatures.

1   Requirements of Writing (Scotland) Act 1995, s 3; the previous requirement was for two witnesses.

19.44   A natural individual (as opposed to a corporate body), even if acting in a special capacity such as trustee, will normally simply sign the deed himself in the presence of the witness, who will then also sign the deed, adding the word 'witness' after his signature. It is not essential that the witness actually sees the signing, as long as the person signing acknowledges the signature before the witness signs. Certain categories of people cannot act as witnesses; these include the blind, corporate bodies and children under 16. It is in general no objection to a witness's competence that he/she is a beneficiary in terms of the deed witnessed.

19.45 Dispositions are now commonly made by companies and local authorities and there are special provisions regarding the execution of deeds by these bodies. As far as companies are concerned there is now a number of ways in which they may execute a deed. These are signature by two directors, signature by one director and the company secretary, signature by two persons authorised by the company, and witnessed signature of either a director, the company secretary or an authorised individual[1].

1   Requirements of Writing (Scotland) Act 1995, s 3 and Sch 2, para 3. See Gretton & Reid, 14.16 for a tabulation of the changing rules for company execution.

19.46 Local authorities execute deeds by having them signed by a responsible officer; if in addition either the signature is witnessed by one witness or the deed is sealed with the seal of the local authority the document will be self proving[1].

1   Requirements of Writing (Scotland) Act 1995, s 3 and Sch 2, para 4.

19.47 Normally the testing clause will specify the number of pages in the deed, the place(s) of execution, the date(s) of execution, the name(s) of those signing, the names and designations of the witnesses and contain details of any obvious alterations made to the deed prior to execution.

Warrant for registration

19.48 This was only necessary where the deed was going to be recorded in the Register of Sasines. It took the form of a warrant endorsed on the deed, usually signed by the grantee's solicitor, instructing the Keeper of the Registers of Scotland to record the deed in the appropriate division of the Register.

Tenendas and reddendo clauses

19.49 These are peculiar to feu grants. The *tenendas* clause sets out the feudal nature of the holding, and the *reddendo* clause sets out the return in exchange for the vassal's holding. Once the creation of new feuduties had been prohibited the latter clause was normally omitted from feu grants.

DEEDS OF CONDITIONS

19.50   A deed of conditions provides a means whereby real burdens affecting a number of properties can be created in a single document[1]. They are commonly used where a number of properties are to be sold off, eg in a block of flats or even in a complete housing estate. Where a new deed of conditions is registered against both the burdened and the benefited property it will normally create burdens from the date of registration, though the coming into effect of the burdens can be delayed[2]. Deeds of conditions recorded or registered before 28 November 2004 will still need to be referred to in dispositions triggering first registration and will be an important source of implied enforcement rights and community burdens[3].

[1]   See also PARAS **14.5–14.9** for the requirements for creating new real burdens.
[2]   Title Conditions (Scotland) Act 2003, s 4.
[3]   See PARAS **14.28–14.39**.

RECTIFICATION OF DEEDS

19.51   There is provision for application to court for the correction or rectification of deeds under the Law Reform (Miscellaneous Provisions) (Scotland) Act 1985, s 8(1). This allows rectification where either a deed intended to give effect to an earlier agreement fails to reflect the intention of the parties as expressed in that agreement or, in the case of other types of deed, fails to express the intention of the grantor. An example of the former category would be a disposition which did not reflect the agreement reached in the preceding missives. It has been suggested that before the court can order rectification in this type of case six matters must be established:

1   that there is a document to be rectified;
2   that the document was intended to express or give effect to an already existing agreement arrived at between two (or more) parties;
3   that there was, when the document was executed such a pre-existing agreement – whether or not enforceable;

4   that the agreement itself embodied and was an expression of one or
more intentions common to (that is, shared by) the parties;
5   that the intentions were actual (not deemed) intentions;
6   that the agreement itself must have been reached at a definite point in
time[1].

Cases where this provision has been invoked have involved the erroneous
inclusion of an additional piece of land in a disposition[2], an error in
numbering a unit in an industrial estate in a disposition of that unit[3], and
omissions in filling in a pro forma security document[4]. If there is no prior
agreement then there can be no rectification. It has been commented that
rectification is not available to 'recast an initial agreement in the terms
which might have been used had the parties been alert to some particular
overlooked factual circumstance'[5].

1   *Oliver v Gaughan* 1990 GWD 22-1247.
2   *Shaw v William Grant (Minerals) Ltd* 1989 SLT 121 at 121; see *Renyana-Stahl
Anstalt v MacGregor* 2001 SLT 1247 at 1256 for an alternative listing.
3   *MAC Electrical and Heating Engineers Ltd v Calscot Electrical (Distributors)
Ltd* 1989 SCLR 498.
4   *Bank of Scotland v Graham* 1991 SLT 879.
5   *Co-operative Wholesale Society Ltd v Ravenseft Properties Ltd* 2003 SCLR 509
at 523B.

Index